AGING MYTHS

Books by Siegfried Kra

Is Surgery Necessary?
Examine Your Doctor
Aging Myths

AGING MYTHS

Reversible Causes of Mind and Memory Loss

SIEGFRIED KRA, M.D.

McGraw-Hill Book Company

New York • St. Louis • San Francisco
Toronto • Hamburg • Mexico

This book is not intended to replace the services of a physician. Any application of the recommendations set forth in the following pages is at the reader's discretion and sole risk.

ISBN 0-07-035229-1

LIBRARY OF CONGRESS CATALOGING-IN-PUBLICATION DATA

Kra, Siegfried J.
    Aging myths.
    Includes index.
    1. Senile dementia—Etiology.   2. Senile
dementia—Prevention.   3. Memory, Disorders of—
Etiology.   4. Memory, Disorders of—Prevention.
5. Diseases—Complications and sequelae.
6. Aging.   I. Title.
    [DNLM: 1. Aging—popular works.   2. Brain
Diseases—etiology—popular works.   3. Brain
Diseases—in old age—popular works.
4. Memory—drug effects—popular works.
5. Memory Disorders—etiology—popular works.
6. Memory Disorders—in old age—popular works.
WT   150   K89a]
RC524.K73 1985 618.97'68983   85–18053
ISBN 0–07–035229–1

Book design by Roberta Rezk

Acknowledgments

I wish to acknowledge the excellent help I received from Dr. Alan Sholomskas, Assistant Clinical Professor of Psychiatry, Yale University School of Medicine, as well as Dr. Lewis Levy, Clinical Professor of Neurology, Yale University School of Medicine; Dr. George Kraus, Director of Health, City of Milford, Connecticut, Lecturer in Public Health, and Assistant Clinical Professor, Yale University School of Medicine; and Dr. Leonard Kent, Professor of English, Quinnipiac College.

Contents

Introduction

Old age has a great sense of calm and freedom. When the passions relax their hold you have escaped not from one master but from many.

PLATO

"You are old, Father William," the young man said,
"And your hair has become very white;
And yet you incessantly stand on your head—
Do you think, at your age, it is right?"

"In my youth," Father William replied to his son,
"I feared it might injure the brain;
But now that I'm perfectly sure I have none,
Why I do it again and again."

LEWIS CARROLL

At a recent dinner party, some of my colleagues and I discussed what we all feared most—cancer, heart disease, blindness, a plane crash, poverty, and confinement in a snakepit, to name a few. Although each of us has special personal fears, we all agreed that the one thing that would make life unbearable would be mental impairment—with ignorance of who and where you are and complete dependence on family or society.

"But if you don't know any longer what's going on, what's the difference? You won't be suffering," said one colleague.

"Not so," I disagreed. "Losing your memory can cause great and continued pain. I remember one of my patients who was completely demented from Alzheimer's disease. He lost his wife after fifty years of marriage. At the funeral, he kept asking for his wife.

His son said, 'Papa, Mother is being buried now.' And when they arrived home, he had forgotten that he had been at his wife's funeral and again asked for his wife. Repeatedly he was told that his wife had died and each time he had to go through the torment and trauma of learning of her death as if it were for the first time. This went on for almost two years, until he finally died."

Senility is itself a connotatively nasty term and should no longer be generally used because it strongly implies an irreversible condition of mental deterioration. Most people still think that senility is part of aging, which is not necessarily true. So often, patients tell me: "I can see my parents failing, especially my father, and there is nothing anyone can do." This sense of hopelessness and inevitability stems from, and itself creates and perpetuates, a pessimism which is often unwarranted.

Until recently, many physicians felt that dementia (brain degeneration) is a permanent and irreversible condition, despite evidence to the contrary. A recent article in *The Journal of the American Medical Association* (August 1982) reported that 60 percent of cases "referred with a tentative diagnosis of dementia" may have reversible causes. The consensus at the present time is that only 30 percent of cases may have a reversible cause. In another survey, it was discovered that 50 to 70 percent of residents of nursing homes were intellectually impaired. How many of these have reversible illness is unknown.

Confusion, depression, hallucination, and memory loss are not part of the aging process. Eighty percent of people who live to old age do not suffer any memory impairment. Creativity, likewise, does not have to end with the aging process. We merely have to look at the efforts of people such as Margaret Mead, Arturo Toscanini, Pablo Picasso, George Bernard Shaw, and Arthur Rubinstein—and the list goes on and on. These people maintained their intellectual abilities well into their nineties, remaining creative and productive until death.

Dr. B. F. Skinner, the renowned psychologist and scholar, once said, "the decaying rot of old age that society should be working harder to ward off is not an inexorable biological process, but a change in the physical and social environment."

It often happens that elderly patients who are admitted into the hospital with all their faculties intact become disoriented and suffer memory loss after a few days. The change of environment and their poor tolerance of medications (especially tranquilizers and sleeping pills) are many times responsible.

The signs of early brain impairment are so elusive and nonspecific that it would be unreasonable and hazardous to simply assume that brain degeneration is the cause of forgetfulness. There are many reasons for memory lapses which are not due to brain degeneration. The brain is such a sensitive collection of cells that even a minor insult—physical or psychological—can cause a temporary loss of memory. Depression, anxiety, preoccupation, excessive alcohol, and medication are some causes.

Unfortunately, a hasty diagnosis of brain degeneration is too often made before a thorough investigation is undertaken. For example, when an elderly patient is in the hospital, it is common practice for the house officers to post certain questions in order to determine if the patient is "with it" or not. Some of the questions may go like this:

"What is your name?" Most people will be able to answer this question unless there is a serious malfunctioning of the brain.

"How old are you?" Older people often forget their age, but this does not imply that they are suffering from brain damage.

"What day is today?" Many patients will not be able to tell what day of the week it is because every day seems the same to them in the hospital.

"What's the date?" Most of us would find this question quite difficult to answer if we did not have a calendar or newspaper handy, especially if we are asked on the spur of the moment, in a hospital setting.

"Who is the President of the United States?" Some elderly people can't read the newspapers or watch television and may have no idea who the President is.

"Where are you?" The patient will know that he or she is in the hospital, unless there is brain disease.

"What is the name of the hospital?" It is not uncommon that the patient does not know the name of the hospital, which, to be sure, does not imply brain damage.

Any person confined to the hospital, with his or her brain dulled with tranquilizers and other medications, is almost certainly in some emotional stress because of the hospitalization (which is why the tranquilizers are given) and might have trouble answering most of these questions.

The definite diagnosis of brain damage is often difficult, if not impossible. Psychological tests are difficult to interpret and are fraught with error. There are no clinical tests or x-ray examinations that make the diagnosis of brain damage. Too many older patients are being diagnosed as senile when, in fact, they may be suffering from a treatable illness.

It is the responsibility of the family not to passively accept brain degeneration as a natural consequence of aging. A thorough examination must be performed, a nutritional program should be outlined and both must be coupled with a psychiatric evaluation. At the same time, every effort must be made to provide a stimulating environment for the elderly person. In some families, all responsibilities and chores are taken away from the elderly patient. He or she no longer has to make decisions or be concerned about planning a meal. This can happen in a home environment and to a greater extent in a nursing home. When one is shut into a silent world surrounded by people of the same generation and having no outside stimuli, there is no necessity to use one's memory or the imaginative or constructive instinct of earlier years.

Forgetting where you put your glasses is not considered abnormal, but forgetting that you wear glasses in the first place signals brain impairment.

Two hundred years ago, the great British wit, author, and scholar, Dr. Samuel Johnson, noted that, "If a young man or a middle-aged man, when leaving a company, does not recollect where he laid his hat, it is nothing. But if the same inattention is discovered in an old man, people shrug their shoulders and say his memory is going."

When my wife, who is a member of Phi Beta Kappa and an archaeologist, recently could not remember the first name of someone we had met at a cocktail party, she became perturbed and wondered whether this was not the beginning of a course downhill.

Undoubtedly, some people have always had poor memories. A renowned psychiatrist-lawyer was speaking of the best restaurants in Paris but was unable to recall the restaurant atop the Eiffel Tower that cost him almost $300 for dinner. He said "I can't remember the name, but, for that matter, I've always had trouble with names." So many of us do; indeed, many have had trouble with names even in our youth.

In nursing homes this problem is worse; 78 to 80 percent are intellectually impaired. Currently, there are 1.3 million people living in nursing homes, and, by the twenty-first century, this will increase to about 4 million people. It is now commonly held that 10 percent of persons over age sixty-five have significant intellectual impairment.

Recently, in my own practice, a 74-year-old woman consulted me as follows because she was afraid that her brain was degenerating:

"I can't remember anybody's name, Doctor. I'm afraid I'm losing my mind. I forget where I put my glasses. I don't remember where I put anything down, and, sometimes, when I go into a room, I don't remember the reason. My friends think I'm becoming a recluse because I don't call them back but, the truth of the matter is that I forget to call them back. When somebody tells me a story, a half-hour later I've forgotten what they've told me. Isn't there a vitamin that you can give me that can help restore my memory? I always had an excellent memory until just a year or two ago."

In years back, doctors would have probably attributed this poor woman's problems to aging. Today, it's another matter, or it *should* be.

I asked her the following questions: "Do you recall what has happened to you in the past two years? Can you remember anything that has changed?"

As soon as I put those questions to her, tears came to her eyes and she informed me that her husband had died and that she now lived alone.

"Do you have trouble sleeping?"

"I fall asleep early in the evening," she stated, "because I'm so bored and have nothing else to do, and then I'm awake several hours later for the rest of the night."

"Are you able to concentrate?"

"That is another thing, Doctor. I don't like to read papers or watch television anymore."

"How is your appetite?"

"Generally, poor. I've lost some weight because I don't feel like eating."

"Do you feel unhappy?" I asked her.

"A little," she said, "but, most of all, I feel lonely. My best friend has been taken away from me. I have no reason to continue living. My children are grown, my grandchildren are of high-school age, and there is no need for me. I don't want to be a burden to them."

The woman was dressed in shabby, old, dark clothing, and she looked pale, gaunt, and chronically ill. After a thorough physical examination and blood tests, there were no abnormalities which I could detect, except that she was suffering from a serious depression. She was started on antidepressant medication, and, three weeks later, she returned to the office. She wore a bright-colored dress, her hair was well-groomed, and there was a smile on her face. Her interests had returned, her memory for names had improved, and she no longer considered herself a useless individual. Her memory was "magically" restored. However, undiagnosed and untreated, this patient would have continued to deteriorate and would have become another tenant diagnosed as senile in a nursing home.

There are indeed inevitable changes in the body as it ages. Elderly patients, for example, do not have the same metabolism as younger persons. The kidneys do not work as efficiently, the circulation is slowed, and the intestinal tract is sluggish. Sloppy monitoring of medications, always a serious problem, is most critical when dealing with older patients. Such carelessness can, in fact, cause serious mental impairment. A list of common medications will be cited in Chap. 11 that should be used with great caution with the elderly patient. *Too many* of the elderly are getting *too much* medication and in inappropriate dosages. For example, if a medication was prescribed ten years ago, it does not mean it has to be automatically continued. However, it is often the case that once a patient is transferred to a convalescent home or back to the care of the family, prescriptions are endlessly refilled, even though the pill may no longer be needed, or, unfortunately, may even be harmful.

A physician has the obligation before prescribing any medication to an older person to know whether the patient's kidneys, heart, and liver can tolerate the medication and whether the brain function is adequate. Giving a person who has some mental impairment an incorrectly prescribed drug can convert that patient into a demented individual.

Let me illustrate this point. An 82-year-old woman who had no heart disease complained of headaches. She was brought to her family physician who found a high blood pressure reading. The general examination of this woman was normal, and there was no evidence of any disease of her heart, lungs, brain, or kidneys. A low-salt diet was prescribed, along with a diuretic. The physician was cautious to include potassium along with her medications. One week later, when the patient was seen again, the blood pressure was normal. The headaches had disappeared, and the patient was scheduled for another office visit in a month.

Now, however, her family noticed that she had begun to "slow down." She no longer complained of headaches, but now she was constantly drowsy. She became very forgetful and, at times, disoriented. At the end of the month, when the family brought their mother into the office, the physician was suspicious that the diuretic was responsible for the change in her entire personality. She recorded the blood pressure while the patient was sitting; it read normal. Then she asked the patient to stand; the blood pressure dropped to an abnormally low reading. *Some* drop in blood pressure is common in older people when they are standing, especially if they receive blood pressure pills, but, if this dramatic change in blood pressure had not been discovered, this woman might have continued her deterioration and could have sustained a stroke. The story had a happy ending. The patient no longer received a diuretic in the given dosage, and so her mental impairment was reversed.

The vascular system in an older patient is extremely sensitive to changes in the water and salt content of the body. Diuretics reduce the salt and water levels in the body, but, when the dosage is too high, these drugs can lower the blood pressure to such a degree as to weaken the elderly patient. In a middle-aged person, a drop of blood pressure to a figure somewhat below normal may not affect him or her, but in an older person the brain is especially dependent on a strong supply of blood, and, if the flow is reduced, the sensitive brain cells are affected, causing brain impairment, or a stroke.

A well-known judge lived next door to us, and, in the evenings, he enjoyed visiting, drinking tea, and telling stories. He was a marvelous storyteller and delighted us with whimsical tales of Warsaw and of the famous people he knew. My parents first noticed a change in his behavior when they played bridge together one day. The judge was unable to recall the cards and then became angry. Never once in the fifteen years we had known him did we recall an occasion when he had raised his voice.

He continued to come for tea and tell us his stories, but now he had some difficulty with his words. Sometimes he started to cry and at other times he would burst out laughing at inappropriate moments. He became abusive, insulting, and demanding. He asked that his tea be served in a special glass; its color and temperature had to be just right.

At that time, we lived on Riverside Drive in New York City, and the judge would park his car in a different spot each day. One morning, I saw him wandering through the streets looking frantically for his car, which he had parked the previous night. He was about to call the police to report that his car was stolen when I spotted it at the end of the street. He felt embarrassed and humiliated because he realized that his memory was failing.

The court ceased to assign him cases, and he was arrested twice for lewd behavior. After seeing several psychiatrists, his "sentence" was passed—"brain degeneration"—and apparently there was nothing further that could be done. However, his wife refused to accept this diagnosis and began to seek out the advice of different physicians. She found a psychiatrist who agreed with her and who referred the judge to a diagnostician.

After a thorough examination, the doctor suspected that the blood flow through the arteries to the brain was blocked. To confirm his diagnosis, he ordered a variety of tests which confirmed the diagnosis, and, during a short hospitalization, surgically reamed the arteries that were clogged with cholesterol plaques. Six weeks later the judge had regained almost 80 percent of his previous intellectual abilities; he is still alive and very much an active person, still telling those wonderful stories.

Abnormalities of the heart can, thus, cause severe brain impairment since not enough blood is being pumped to the brain. The following case also illustrates this condition:

A 62-year-old businessperson, after returning from vacation, complained of enormous fatigue, especially in the early afternoon. His concentration markedly diminished, he became forgetful, and he had difficulty in making decisions. His secretary found him on numerous occasions sitting alone with a blank expression on his face. Once or twice she saw him staggering as he walked from one end of his office to the other. His eyes, once glittering with intelligence and excitement, now had a dull expression. Even the lines of his face had changed. His doctors diagnosed him as "burned-out" and depressed, and they advised his retirement. He retired from his corporation, but his condition worsened in spite of anti-depressant medications and psychotherapy.

One morning, he collapsed at home, and, when examined in the emergency room, was found to have an extremely low pulse. A pacemaker was subsequently implanted to make his heart beat faster; thereafter, his mental deterioration became reversed, his fatigue disappeared, and his memory returned.

These cases serve to illustrate how different medical conditions can cause symptoms of brain degeneration. Once the particular illness is cured, the brain function returns to the level maintained before the illness.

Unfortunately, there are other times when there is no cause found for the brain degeneration, and the diagnosis of Alzheimer's disease is made. A disease known for centuries, once rarely discussed, it has now become tragically common. Families, friends, and the patients themselves need guides for management of this tragic predicament which is now the fourth leading cause of death in the western world (following heart disease, stroke, and cancer).

Some physicians have named this catastrophe of brain damage the "silent epidemic" because families are often ashamed to admit that one of their members has fallen prey to this illness. Brain degeneration does not start in the nursing home but may begin years before the final stage of life. Symptoms may begin in an insidious fashion, progressing slowly at first, and then accelerating to total disability.

Brain failure may be a preventable event in some patients. This book is written to serve as a guide for those who think they are losing their memory and becoming senile, for others who have already been labeled as senile by their family and doctors, and, of course, for all other parties involved. If the brain chemistry of these patients is put back in order, there will be a remarkable and gratifying return of brain function. As an editorial that appeared in *The New York Times* on February 21, 1984 stated: "New research rebuts the idea of inevitable decline amongst the elderly." Most of the decline in intelligence and memory among elderly patients *can* be prevented and reversed with proper prevention and treatment, and it is to this end that this book is dedicated.

Why do most people who live to a "ripe old age" maintain excellent memories and intellectual vitality, while others, suffer from mild senility or dementia (some 10 percent of the 2.5 million people over the age of sixty-five) or from severe mental impairment (5 percent of the total aging population)? The answer may lie in abnormal chemistry of the brain.

For generations, patients' physicians held the dreadful, hopeless misconception that senility is part of the aging process—and cannot be prevented or treated.

After questioning thousands of patients in the age range of 70 to 95, whose brains are still sharp as tacks, I found that they all have a similar brain chemistry, which is the subject of this book.

Much too often, older people are expected to suffer a decline in intelligence and mental capacity. Standardized IQ tests, stressing speed rather than experience and discretion, almost invariably present a depressed, distorted, and misleading picture of an older person's intelligence. Richard M. Torack, in his impressive 1981 book, *Your Brain Is Younger Than You Think*, makes the case that *all* IQ scores, especially those from subjects older than age sixty, who have just taken the exams, should be approached with extreme suspicion. Indeed, I would argue that such testing can be worse than useless in dealing with the older population. Isn't it interesting to observe, for example, how dramatically the scores almost always improve when these tests are given at a leisurely pace in an unstressful environment? Older people *do* function differently from younger people, but this is certainly no reason to extract simply the noxious conclusion that they are, ipso facto, less intelligent.

Of persons over age 65 who are suffering from mild brain failure, many of these patients may suffer from causes whose conditions may be reversed. The chemicals of the brain can be altered by numerous causes, to be addressed in subsequent chapters, from poor nutrition (many older people are malnourished), medications they are receiving, and dozens of illnesses, some of which are not recognized, others which are not treated vigorously.

CHAPTER 1

The Fingerprints of Aging

Old age isn't so bad when you consider the alternative.

MAURICE CHEVALIER

*　　*　　*

The Summer of Her 96th Year

Did you ask where I am?
I'm in a very comfortable place, a hotel.
No, I don't know where it is
   but they are very nice to you here
   you can do whatever you like, it's very nice.

What day is it you say? Oh, it's a summer day,
   warm, I like it warm, it reminds me of my father,
   he would smile when I sang.
It was so long ago, you know,
   so many summer days.

The year? I always had trouble with numbers.
I remember the year my brother was born,
   I was seven and I made believe he was my baby.
I wish my mother was here. Are you here momma?
Are you my mother? Oh, I thought for a moment . . .

Did you say you are a doctor?
I've always admired the medical profession.
I knew many doctors years ago,
   most of them were kind.
Does the light fade early in the summer?

13

No, I can't eat anything. I'm not hungry.
I'm afraid of this food.
I'm sorry I can't hear, did you say
    I hurt my hip and had an operation?
Well, for heavens' sake, I didn't know that.

Hospital? No, this is a hotel, it's warm here.
God bless you doctor,
I'm glad we met but don't let me keep you,
    you must have patients to take care of
    and I'm all right.

JOHN MANN ASTRACHAN, M.D., NEW YORK

Scientists have known that the length of human life is fixed, even though our life expectancy is increasing. If all major causes of death were eliminated, the life span would still be approximately between the ages of 100 and 110. Death in later years is due to the body's increased vulnerability to developing disease, infections, accidents, and the inexorable decline in function.

Alexis Carrel, a French surgeon and 1912 Nobel Prize laureate, was able to keep certain cells (fibroblasts) alive for thirty years. In 1960 Dr. Leonard Hayflick of Stanford University disproved the hypothesis that cells can live indefinitely if properly cultured. Carrel had continually added new cells to his media, which kept the population of cells in the culture alive.

Cells are constantly dying and are replaced by new cells (except nerve cells). These new cells do not make the organism younger. If certain kinds of body cells, called fibroblasts, are grown in a laboratory, they will divide many times, stop dividing, and then finally die. The ability for a cell to maintain itself is coded in the "magical" DNA of the cell nuclei. The DNA can repair itself as it wears down for a limited number of times but, eventually, it fails. The DNA has a genetic clock which has already, at the time of birth, set the time limit of the cell's survival.

Changes of the aging cell have now been clearly studied. The cell, with its major tenant called the nuclei, and its bedfellow of chemicals, is found to shrink and to fragment, and is then replaced by inactive substances. Blood vessels become more rigid. Some organs may increase in size (as does the prostate gland in the male), and some may decrease (as does the brain). The muscle mass diminishes beginning in the third decade in males, and in the fourth decade in females. Microscopically, there is shrinkage of muscle fibers and an increase of fat (much of this change can be delayed with exercise). The liver shrinks, the kidneys become smaller, and the lungs become lighter in weight.

There is evidence that our immune system becomes markedly weakened. Cells, called T and B, which the body manufactures, protect the individual from illness and perhaps even cancer. Alas, age suppresses the activities of these cells, especially the T cells, and makes older people more prone to infections and the development of certain diseases. The loss of these T-cell functions has recently been found to occur in people who change their sexual partners frequently, especially in some homosexuals, and is found in the Acquired Immune Deficiency Syndrome (AIDS).

Some of the changes that occur in elderly adults thought at one time to be attributable to the process of aging, may have a medical cause. Not long ago, we thought that atherosclerosis was a consequence of aging. It is now commonly accepted by scientists that atherosclerosis is related to hereditary and dietary causes and may be reversible. Many of the changes occurring as the results of aging can be slowed down with physical activity.

The effects of aging on the cardiovascular system consist of the heart's not pumping out as much blood, the decline of the pulse, and the diminishing of the various phases of heart muscle contraction. Blood pressure increases. There is also a shift of body fluids. For example, the total body water level falls from 62 percent at the age of twenty-five to 50 percent at the age of seventy-five. The volume of the blood decreases, and the number of red blood cells diminishes. The fluid compartments contract. Fat content in the blood increases, especially that of cholesterol and triglycerides. This is more evident in individuals who are not physically active.

Calcium is lost, and the mineral content of bone diminishes at the same time that there is thickening of the bone substance. These findings occur in people who are inactive physically, regardless of age. The less the organ is used the sooner it atrophies. Physicians,

at least since the time of ancient Babylonia, have been advocating
activity and exercise as sources of vitality. Take a young person,
put him or her in a cast for six weeks, and the injured leg is going
to be much smaller than the one that has been active.

The metabolism of the body also changes with aging. Certain
chemicals are decreased in the brain—chemicals such as norepinephrine and dopamine which I will discuss in a later chapter.
Other detrimental chemicals, called tyrosine, are increased. Certain hormones as the thyroid and adrenal hormones, undergo change
which regulates the general metabolism of the body.

Decreased sexual activity with age is most likely due to decreased interest and stimulation. Male hormone levels actually
remain unchanged. The declines in sexual and mental activities
may very well parallel each other and are not related to aging.
Sexually active men in their seventies who are in the mainstream
of life have less memory loss, and their brains function better!

The pattern of sleep changes in the elderly. Insomnia is a common problem in all age groups, but particularly so in older people.
A brief review of the normal sleep pattern will demonstrate the
change that occurs. Normal sleep has regular cycles and stages.
There are two stages called the rapid eye movement stage, or
REMs, and the nonrapid eye movement stage, or non-REM. The
controlling center in our brain for the non-REM stage is speculated
to be in a part of the brain called the hypothalamus, while the
REM sleep is contained in another portion of the brain. Chemicals
in the brain regulate sleep patterns, one of which is called serotonin
(to be discussed later in some detail). Older patients have a marked
reduction of their sleep, and the number of times they are awakened increases with aging. Individuals older than the age of seventy
spend more time in bed but less time actually sleeping. Even
healthy elderly people are more sleepy during the day. Nighttime
sleep is fragmental, decreasing daytime alertness. The duration of
sleep can normally vary from 5.5 to 9.5 hours per day.

The older patient should desist asking the physician for a sleeping pill, for the pill will only make the sleep irregularities worse.
It is important that the doctor take a careful history of the patient's
sleep pattern to ascertain the cause for poor sleep—sleep patterns
of the elderly can be worsened by too much caffeine, alcohol, worry
and tensions, and sometimes certain medications and medical dis-

orders. Restless-legs syndrome, a common disturbance in the elderly, can disturb sleep. This is a disagreeable sensation in the legs that prompts many of the elderly to continuously move their legs and leave their beds. The cause has not been found. Specific ventilatory problems, called sleep apnea, can result in insomnia. The sleeping pill can not only worsen the sleep of the elderly patient but can also actually cause marked mental impairment, consisting of memory loss, disorientation, hallucinations, and depression.

The abuse of sleep medication is astounding! It has been estimated that over fifty million Americans are taking some form of sleeping pill, or six hundred tons of sleeping pills a year. Forty percent of the eight million prescriptions written per year for sleeping pills were for people over the age of sixty. Another two million people are taking sleeping pills beyond the prescribed time because the pharmacists keep renewing their prescriptions. The elderly individual should understand that it is normal to wake several times during the night, that it is not a crime to take catnaps during the day, and that one does not need eight hours of uninterrupted sleep. Lack of adequate sleep in any person eventually leads to lack of concentration, inattentiveness, memory loss, and decreased performance. "My grandmother does nothing but sleep all day. Can you please give her something to sleep at night, Doctor?" is the constant lament of many families. The doctor obliges, and soon the loved one is worse off than before.

All patients, especially elderly patients, should be encouraged not to take sleeping pills, except under strict supervision, because they interfere with the normal sleep pattern discussed before and can actually accentuate insomnia. However, short-acting benzodiazepines can be safely used in selected patients. Memory loss, depression, and a generally poor feeling during the day are common aftereffects of sleeping pills. Patients can develop dependence and become devious in obtaining prescriptions from different physicians. For example, the weekend call to a covering physician, "I've lost my prescription. Could you please give me 3 or 4 pills to carry me over the weekend?" is a favorite method of obtaining pills. Another is to change physicians frequently in order to get new prescriptions. (These same methods, of course, are also used to obtain painkillers and other pills.)

Here are some suggestions for the elderly patient to use for going to sleep, instead of running to the physician or to the drug-store for over-the-counter medication. Remember, almost every medication can affect the function of the brain:

1. Warm milk before bedtime is recommended. Some "old wives' tales" have been proven to have scientific value. Warm milk is an example. Milk contains a compound called tryptophan, a substance needed to make a chemical called serotonin, which, as previously noted, is important for the regulation of sleep. Tryptophan found in milk is a natural sleeping pill. Tryptophan, given twenty minutes before going to sleep, often produces the type of natural cyclical sleep I discussed under the normal sleep patterns. Dr. Ernest Hartman of Boston State Hospital is credited for these findings.

   The brain wave test, or EEG, registers certain patterns during sleep. People who receive sleeping potions develop an abnormal brain pattern, while those who receive tryptophan have a pattern similar to normal sleep. Some scientists are disputing the benefits of warm milk, which they label as a placebo. I advise my patients to drink warm milk before bedtime. It often works. Not only does milk contain the much needed calcium for bones and nerve function, but it is safe, cheaper than a sleeping pill, and you don't need a doctor to prescribe it. If you have an allergy to milk, the amino acid tryptophan can be substituted for milk. The tryptophan contained in milk can be purchased in a drugstore without a prescription. It is taken at bedtime.

2. A warm bath is a traditional remedy, and it works. Warm temperature increases the blood flow to the skin and makes people sleepy.

3. A glass of wine, not more than six ounces, can be very helpful, provided it does not interfere with medicines.

4. Sexual intercourse is an excellent promoter of sleep, not only from the point of view of unwinding, but also because it decreases muscle tensions and anxiety.

5. Reading, if possible, is helpful. Some material especially lends itself to falling asleep. (I hope this does *not* include the book you are now reading!)

Some psychologists recommend eyeshades, earplugs, electrical blankets, or soft music in the background. Dr. Richard R. Bottzin of Northwestern University has instituted a reeducation program for sleeping. He advises patients to lie down only when they are tired, and, if they don't fall asleep within ten minutes, they are instructed to leave the bedroom and to do something else. If the urge to sleep returns, they should return to the bedroom. If, once again, there is failure to fall asleep within ten minutes, one should again get out of bed, and so forth. The purpose of this program is to have the person associate the bedroom with sleep. It is a form of retraining. Techniques of biofeedback have been proven to be relaxing. Self-hypnosis works very well for me. It consists of lying on the bed, raising one's eyes toward the ceiling, closing them, taking a deep breath, and pretending that one's body is suspended in the air. I repeat to myself that I am slowly slowly falling asleep and in this manner I release all the thoughts from my mind.

The brain undergoes structural changes with aging. There is no loss of intelligence with advanced age, but there *is* some loss of memory and a decrease in taste sensitivity, along with a diminished sense of smell. One of the tests that physicians and psychologists use to measure brain activity is the EEG, as previously mentioned. Older people are found to have a consistently slower pattern on the EEG, which can result from decreased activity of the brain. Medical students who were experimentally placed at bed rest with no stimuli for prolonged periods of time had similar EEG findings. These students, not involved in any physical or mental activity developed all the other physiological changes found in the elderly, including the sleep pattern! These findings were interpreted as resulting from a prolonged period of not having any kind of sensory or physical stimulation. The sleep pattern I have described in older people has also been found in people who have been at bedrest for a long period of time.

The aging brain gets smaller and the number of brain cells or neurons decreases. In one calculation, by the age of ninety, 60 percent of the brain cells are gone. To study this phenomenon, scientists have gone through the painstaking procedure of slicing up the brain and counting the number of cells. This may sound like bad news to the reader, because it would appear that if you ultimately lost 60 to 70 percent of the brain cells, you may live long enough so that there wouldn't be any left. But this does not happen. The loss of brain cells does not correlate with the loss of intelligence. The brain cells which are lost may not be from areas concerned with memory, and there are enough brain cells left to maintain excellent brain function. Some parts of the brain, interestingly, do not experience this destruction of neurons. The hindbrain, the cerebellum, loses no cells. The hippocampus, the seat of memory, loses 40 percent of its cells by the time the individual reaches the age of ninety. In the normal aging individual, this is of little consequence.

The brain cell demonstrates certain changes. In the cell, there is a "manufacturing plant" called a lysosome, which manufactures and releases enzymes in order to clean up the waste products formed by the cells. By the enzymes' actions, unwanted material is destroyed and carted away by the white blood cells. As aging occurs, these sanitation factories slow down and the waste products accumulate, further slowing the work energy of the cell. Finally, the factory stops working and it closes down for good, no matter what efforts are made by the body to keep the mills running.

One of these waste products is a pigment, the same kind of pigment that illustrates the outstanding fingerprint of aging—the brown spots on the hands and face. This pigment is called lipofuscin (brown spots found on the brain). Lipofuscin consists of a variety of chemicals and waste products from the destroyed cells. It is possible that the pigment *does* slow down the work of the neuron, and this accumulation occurs because the "factory's sanitation plant," the lysosome, is not working properly. As this pigment accumulates, the lysosome begins to fatten up and explodes. Some illnesses which have to do with the lysosome abnormalities are inborn inherited diseases, such as Tay-Sachs disease found predominantly among Jews. These abnormal storage diseases cause death in a few years. Scientists, such as J. Nande of Boston University, who are experts in the study of lipofuscin, cannot agree whether these lipofuscin pigments are good or bad for you, or whether they do interfere with memory. Just as brown spots on your body have no detrimental effect, these pigments are merely the marks of wear and tear. These pigments start to accumulate in young brains.

Lipofuscin pigments are already found at birth, and nobody has proven that that material is poisonous.

Scientists also describe a development called senile plaques in the nerve of the brain. This is actually a scar, a mark resulting from brain degeneration, rather than a cause of it. Senile plaques are multiple small islands of dead material containing specific compounds. Their origin is unknown. These plaques consist of a substance called amyloid which is found in certain chronic illnesses, as in chronic infection. It has been estimated that 80 percent of patients over age sixty-five have senile plaques. They are not distinct from dental plaques that cause loss of teeth and the arteriosclerotic plaques (to be described in Chap. 8) found in arthrosclerosis.

Another change that pathologists describe consists of an abnormality called neurofibrillary tangles in the nerve cells. A normal nerve cell looks like a small plant with branches, stem, and many roots. As aging occurs, the roots, which are called the dendrites, begin to shorten and lose some of their structure. Eventually, the ends of the roots of these dendrites begin to accumulate into a sort of halo that resembles a small starfish. These findings are more numerous in the portion of the brain called the hippocampus, the seat of memory.

All the changes of aging that occur in the brain should not interfere with everyday living, as there is ample organ function left to go on to a "ripe old age" as long as there is no disease to accelerate the aging process. We lose some brain cells as we age, but there are millions of healthy ones left for our intellectual endeavors.

CHAPTER 2

The Substance of Memory

Old age must be resisted and its deficiencies supplied by taking pain. We must fight it as we do disease.

CICERO

All of us can recall how some of our classmates had extraordinary memories and never needed to spend dreary hours of studying to get "straight A's." Forgetfulness is not considered abnormal, and, in some circles, is considered chic or even cute. The "absent-minded professor" is forgiven for not remembering the day, the time, or the name of a student since he or she remains preoccupied with "profound" thoughts. When my 19-year-old daughter has difficulty in remembering a name, she says "I'm so stupid: I can't remember anything"; yet, she is an "A" student. Others say, "I never forget a face, but I can't remember a name." This is all considered "normal."

But, in 1984, if a 65-year-old man cannot remember the name of a movie or the name of a hotel, others begin to wonder if this isn't the beginning of senility. One of my friends, a renowned computer specialist, teaches calculus at a university. Before departing on a trip, he decided to hide all of his wife's jewelry in different parts of the house. He was very proud of himself for thinking of all the hiding places, but it took him *six months* to find the jewelry once he returned.

Memory loss is not a sign of decay. As we get older, there is some mild impairment in our recollection of recent events. This may become evident in the most ridiculous manner—as in going into a room and totally forgetting the reason, or in misplacing a pair of glasses (though my daughter, who is nineteen, does this all the time, too). Severe memory loss, however, is a sign of brain disease and not of aging. The ability to retain and to recall varies with the individual. For some, it is an inherited trait. The substance of memory is related to mental development, motivation, interests, family background, and social environment and is just beginning to be understood by scientists.

Most of the information that arrives at our brain will be selected for recall according to importance and then stored. The selection will depend on the individual's environment, interests, personality, and intelligence. The more material that is stored in the brain, the more likely it is that new information will be selected. Information that we find unuseful or unappealing we reject.

Attention is the ability of the person to apply the mind to an object of sense or thought without being distracted. This is *not* to be confused with alertness, which is the ability to respond to an outside stimulus. A person can be alert but inattentive. Alert persons will respond to movement and sounds occurring around them. You can be alert but not attentive, but attention requires alertness. Vigilance or concentration is the ability to focus your attention over an extended period of time; in the learning process, memorization requires both. If you are interested in this book and your attention is focused on what I have said thus far, you will have probably retained most of what you have read. Later on, we will see that the ability to concentrate is necessary in order to do well on memory tests. Intellectual jobs require concentration. Some workers, for example, air traffic controllers, assembly line inspectors, astronauts, and surgeons, are required to maintain unusually long periods of concentration. Impaired ability to concentrate can result from depression, overstimulation, or diseased states of the brain.

The storage of memory has been defined as "the ability to recall," so-called memory retrieval. It is based upon the length of time it takes between the moment something is first memorized and then recalled. The memory time span is differentiated between long-term and short-term memory. Short-term memory may be converted into long-term memory. Short-term memory has a limited time span. Long-term memory lasts a lifetime.

As we get older, concentration and attention may decrease for numerous reasons other than biological ones. Loneliness, lack of outside stimulation, and other psychological factors accelerate the aging of minds. It is almost a universal expectation that the older population show evidence of memory and intellectual impairment.

The process of memorization is highly complicated. Some of the steps which have been outlined by physiologists are as follows:

The brain, through our senses, recognizes new information, some of which is considered significant and weeded out for retention. This is called registration. Information is presented to the brain at every waking moment and what we retain requires attention. Lack of attention is tied to how much interest we have in a subject. (I recall during my teenage years that one of my friends did poorly in school, but was able to give us the names of all baseball players, their batting averages, ages, and hundreds of other facts about players of previous years. My friend was much more interested in baseball than he was in American history. He lacked interest, and, therefore, attention—but *not* memory!)

The brain is capable of registering only one event at a time, even at the most attentive times. If two things are occurring at the same time—for example, if one is reading and listening to music— one hour later, it may be difficult to recall what the musical composition was, but there should be little trouble in recalling the story being read if interest was focused on reading. Information needs to be deemed worthy of storage in the brain by each individual.

Any individual who has received electroconvulsive therapy knows that this form of shock therapy wipes out short-term memories but leaves the long-term ones safely intact. Vestiges of memories that are short-term remain in an electrical form in the brain. Short-term memory, for example, is the ability to recall some numbers immediately after hearing them. It is a way of categorizing events which may occur from day to day—for example, the individual remembers what was eaten for breakfast, news events, and so on. Memory begins with an electrical event. The nerve cells, or the neurons, have projections called dendrites that receive the electrical pulses. These are spinelike projections that connect to the next neuron to form a circuit. It is these spines which are perhaps the backbone of memory, as Dr. James Francis Cralk speculates. As we try to remember seven digits, such as a phone number, the electrical impulse reaches the neuron and compresses the spines:

this is how short-term memory is retained. As these long spines reshape, the memory disappears. Short-term memory may be converted into long-term memory. In order to keep unimportant stimuli, events, or conversation from cluttering up our brain, there are structures in the brain that act as clearinghouses which help the neurons to sense what is worth remembering. Neurons undergo change in response to memorization. Dr. Eric Kendall, of Columbia University, states that ". . .memory is written into chemicals." Long-term memory is contained in millions of neurons in a closely linked network; for example, hearing a few notes of a song can bring back one's entire memory of an event. Some chemicals (for example, vasopressin, which acts as an antidiuretic) actually help to increase memory power.

Another chemical substance known as noradrenalin helps to improve memory. For example, when a person is attacked by a mugger, adrenalin flows through his or her body; it will be hard for the victim to forget the color of the attacker's shirt. People who have experienced the most terrifying near-death experiences, such as plane crashes, can recall every detail of what happened.

Recent short-term memory loss can occur after a night of too much drinking. The actor in this role may have total loss of recall of the preceding night. Excessive alcohol affects the hippocampus, the "seat of memory" in a part of the brain that looks like a sea horse ("hippocampus" is derived from the Greek word for "sea horse" or "sea monster").

The memory loss of aging is generally short-term, as, for example, in the inability to recall a name, an appointment, a telephone number, a movie, or reasons for entering a room. As Cicero put it, "I never heard of an old man forgetting where he had hidden his money," but Cicero may have been referring to money in a long-time hiding place. Most people who have short-term memory loss have no problem with long-term retrieval. Many older persons will brag that they can recall the details of what happened on December 14, 1902, and they will not be in the least troubled that their recent retrieval mechanism is defective.

Short-term memory loss may, however, be the earliest sign of a more catastrophic event occurring in the brain, especially if forgetfulness is severe and progressive. In the genuinely senile individual, as will be discussed later, there is a serious progressive defect of short- and long-term memory. The cells of the "sea horse," or hippocampus, are destroyed, which interferes with the process of recall.

Long-term and short-term memory loss, although a symptom of dementia and senility, may also be the outstanding symptoms of numerous medical conditions, as well as side effects of medications and depression. Memory loss may not be a signal of brain disease, just as a pain in the chest does not necessarily designate a heart attack, or losing weight does not always mean cancer. Physicians have been trained to recognize that similar symptoms can arise from different illnesses. Bizarre behavior, memory loss, and disorientation are not always products of aging.

There seems to be a different mechanism in the brain for short-term memory versus long-term memory. Most memory depends on repetition. Short-term memory can be converted into long-term memory by repetition and, unless you are blessed with a photographic memory, you depend on repetition for long-term storage. Some short-term events, although brief in time, can have such a profound impact that the storage is permanent. It would be impossible to review everything that we have ever learned in order to maintain a long-term memory. Doctors and nurses, for example, are urged to take refresher courses in order to strengthen their long-term storage of important information learned throughout the course of their medical training and of new information which emerges each year. The ability to store material seems to be unaffected by age.

It is believed that the long-term storage memory is the result of chemical processes, genetic materials, and the actual fingerprinting of information. The memory center of the brain, the hippocampus, is located underneath the two lobes of the major part of the brain, the cerebral cortex. It was accidentally discovered that the hippocampus is the "seat of memory" when the surgeon W. P. Scoville treated epilepsy by the removal of one of the two hippocampuses. After the surgery, the patient completely lost the ability to remember.

Nerve cells, once destroyed, will not regenerate, as do skin cells, for example. Thus, nerve cells cannot be replaced. The estimated number of cells in the brain cortex is approximately two to fifteen billion. From the age of twenty-five onward, we tend to lose brain cells. In patients with severe memory impairment resulting from illness, such as Alzheimer's disease, there is a dramatic decline in the number of brain cells. The normal person also loses brain cells diffusely from different parts of the brain, in contrast to people who have brain degeneration, in which case brain cells are lost from the hippocampus. Although it has been estimated that by the age of ninety, approximately 60 percent of cells will be gone, it is the location of these nerve cells which is important. Areas involved with memory and intelligence may have minimal loss of nerve cells.

A study performed by Dr. Marian Diamond, a neuroanatomist at UCLA, showed that rats deprived of exercise and sensory stimulation have an increased rate of death of nerve extensions. Similarly, when the rats are exposed to numerous stimuli and allowed to exercise, their brain weight increases and the branches of the nerve cell widen. This situation resembles the roots of a tree which are spreading out instead of retracting. Similar retraction of the nerves results from infections, head injuries, and a condition called anoxia, which means that not enough oxygen arrives to the brain during such periods when the individual is deprived of oxygen—in a fire, when drowning, or when subject to carbon monoxide intoxication.

Adults submerged under water for five minutes or so do not survive, but very young children (age 3 to 8 years) who are submerged in cold water and not rescued for much longer have survived with no brain damage. This was another fortuitous discovery that occurred several years ago in an emergency room.

An eight-year-old boy was brought to the emergency room after a drowning accident. He was not breathing. The intern immediately started CPR, and the victim was resuscitated. Unknown to the intern, the boy had been submerged for five hours in cold water. Scientists have discovered that some very young children, as is the case with marine life, possibly can suspend all their metabolic activity to near standstill in cold water and then regain their function. Brain cells, under these circumstances, suffer no damage. Hibernating animals during the winter can suspend all their metabolic activities to almost a standstill—the groundhog's pulse drops to five beats per hour. On the other hand, in the adult, oxygen deprivation for a few minutes causes brain cells to die.

After patients sustain cardiac arrest, immediate resuscitation is necessary in order to supply precious oxygen to the nerve cells; otherwise, the brain cells will die. Sometimes, enough brain cells survive so that there is no mental change.

One of my colleagues had a cardiac arrest, and, by the time the ambulance arrived and resuscitation efforts were started, five minutes had elapsed—the critical period for brain survival without oxygen. He did survive, and, once he was fully conscious, talking, and alert, he became aware of what happened. To test himself if he suffered any brain damage, he asked his wife to bring his daughter's algebra book to the coronary care unit. At first, he had some difficulty solving the algebra equations, but, by the third day, he ran through them like an expert. Fortunately, he did have an abundance of brain cells remaining that were not destroyed, and his intellectual abilities were not impaired.

The nerve cells depend on a good supply of blood, and research at the Sandoz Institute in Basel, Switzerland has found that the size of these tiny vessels becomes larger and wider as we get older. Blood flow does decline in the brain with age, despite physical fitness, and the new blood vessels actually compensate for the reduced blood flow by enlarging, according to the metabolic activity of the brain.

The brain has another cell, called the glia cell ("glia" means "glue" in Greek), which tends to grow in size to compensate when damage occurs from infection, injury, or toxic substances. These cells are much smaller than the neuron. As they increase in size, the blood vessels do so as well. The growth of these cells is called gliosis, and the glia are suppliers of blood vessels for the larger neurons. However, in the aging brain, the glia cells may do the opposite. As they tend to grow at an accelerated rate in the aging brain, they contribute to further brain damage by crowding out and gluing the normal neurons. Dr. H. Hydren, at the University of Goteborg in Sweden, found that the number of these cells is increased in many of the brain disorders such as Parkinson's disease; we see that a system that compensates us when we are younger does the opposite in the older brain.

But don't lose heart. Loss of nerve cells, gliosis, lipofuscin, and senile plaques (which all add up to making the brain look like Swiss cheese) still do not seem to be related to significant memory loss or brain degeneration. The autopsy findings on Winston Churchill, who lived well into his nineties, showed his brain to be filled with all the findings that I have described, and to a severe degree, yet his intellectual capacity and functioning were superb, right to the day of his death.

Researchers have learned about the brain through the use of electrical probes and the observation of the body's responses to them. The size of the brain is not linked to intelligence or to the ability to remember. The size of the brain depends on physical stature and gender. A woman's brain is about nine-tenths of the size of the average male's brain, but this does not indicate the number of active brain cells nor the level of intelligence. (Brain weights are determined at the time of autopsy.) As soon as the brain is removed from the skull, it is placed on a scale. The older the person, the smaller is his or her brain. For example, the brain of a 24-year-old may weigh from three to four pounds, a weight which will reduce with age. The larger the brain, the more weight it tends to lose. The most shrinkage seems to occur in the cerebral cortex, the area of intelligence. Shrinkage of the brain does not, however, parallel loss of intelligence. Reduction of the brain can be determined by special x-rays, called CAT scans, which will demonstrate a space between the skull and the brain. The radiologist will diagnose this space as mild or serious brain atrophy, depending on the size of the space. In demented individuals, brain atrophy is severe.

However, the CAT scan alone cannot diagnose dementia. Most older patients will display some insignificant brain atrophy on the CAT scan. Some of the most brilliant and alert elderly individuals can show evidence of the changes I have described, with *no* noticeable alteration in brain function or behavior.

Summary. Despite huge advances in knowledge of the way in which memory works and in medical technology, there is no quick single test that can determine whether memory impairment's cause is an organic or reversible problem. It is important for the patient to have a complete and thorough physical, including a check for factors such as depression, medications, and even, as we shall see in Chap. 3, malnutrition.

The Chemistry of the Brain

The following description is a brief, simplified version of the complicated chemistry of the brain.

Electrical impulses are generated from the roots of the brain nerves, and chemicals called neurotransmitters transport messages from one nerve to the other. Each nerve cell is connected to its neighbor by a constant stream of chemicals. The more connections and the greater the transmission of messages, the higher is the ability to remember, to perceive, to formulate ideas, and to have the power of association. Most of this chemistry is inherited and genetically coded. Transmission of these chemicals across bridges is instigated by the cells. A triggering enzyme called a precursor pushes and releases the neurotransmitter across the nerve. One of these transmitter chemicals is called acetylcholine, which is necessary for the steps in memorization mentioned earlier.

Scientists call this the cholinergic system; the trigger enzyme called choline acetyltransferese is needed to push the chemical across the nerve cells. The amount of chemical acetylcholine declines in the aging brain. Other important chemical transmitters are in the group called the catecholamines, consisting of dopamine and adrenaline; the latter chemical causes our hearts to beat faster, makes us sweat, and makes the hair on animals rise. It is the chemical that increases blood pressure for us to respond during "fear and flight." These substances are also essential for the memory process and tend to decline in the aging brain and with inactivity. (Decreased dopamine levels in the brain are found in Parkinson's disease.)

Serotonin, another compound produced by these nerves, controls sleep, mood, and appetite. Serotonin depends on the availability of a protein called tryptophan, found in fish and meat. Experiments have shown that feeding animals large amounts of tryptophan will increase the concentration of the serotonin level which results in an increase in appetite and sleep. Tryptophan is an amino acid, the basic building block of proteins. Do you remember our glass of warm milk helping us to fall asleep (Chap. 1)?

The production of acetylcholine depends on a protein called choline. This substance is found in eggs, meat, and milk. The more choline there is in the brain, the more acetylcholine is made available, and there is increased transmission across the nerve tissue. The production of catecholamines also depends on tyrosine, an amino acid found in our diet.

In the hippocampus of the brain, the area of brain storage, the majority of neurons, entitled cholinergic neurons, manufacture acetylcholine. We can block the formation of acetylcholine in the brain by the administration of drugs like scopolamine, which was once used for gastrointestinal diseases. We do this to try to reproduce the pathological state of diseases like Alzheimer's disease. Young people who have received scopolamine have temporary memory impairment, similar to that found in older people. (We shall later see how we can increase the acetylcholine in the brain to improve memory.) Some brain chemicals do *not* decline in number; the so-called monoamine oxidase (MAO) actually increases with age. (MAO has been linked with depression in older patients.)

A new body of chemicals called endorphins has been identified in the brain, which is ten times more powerful than morphine; in addition the number of endorphins is increased in the elderly. Endorphins help to dull pain. Some scientists believe that when people are confronted with an episode of severe physical pain the endorphins are secreted in large amounts, helping to dull the pain, and older people seem to produce the endorphins more effectively than do younger people. Some patients with terminal cancer may at times have no pain at all, which is probably the result of the brain's ability to mobilize endorphins to combat severe pain. Today, we are using medications to indirectly increase our neurotransmitters. For example, the level of dopamine is low in Parkinson's disease and can be increased by the administration of dopamine. Pharmaceutical companies are trying to produce endorphins in their laboratories, and neurophysiologists are experimenting on animals to find a way to release these chemicals. When acupuncture is effective, it is probably because it stimulates nerve endings to produce endorphins.

It was once believed that brain manipulation could change emotions, influence personality, and improve memory. Franz Josef Gall, an eighteenth-century neuroscientist and the first to associate the mind with the cerebral cortex, formulated this theory in 1810. He developed the idea that mental faculties could be improved as the number of bumps in the skull increased. He believed that he could evaluate a patient's mental capacity by feeling the bumps on his or her head, and that by hand-manipulating these bumps—the so-called bump massage—he could manipulate the patient's mind. This view is the basis for the circus side shows of phrenology, still practiced today.

Summary.   The aging brain produces fewer chemicals, such as choline, dopamine, and norepinephrine. But intellectual impairment is not an inevitable consequence of this change in physiology.

CHAPTER 3

Food for Thought: Nutrition for Brain Function

Age appears to be best in four things—old wood best to burn, old wine to drink, old friends to trust, and old authors to read.

FRANCIS BACON

Nutrition has long been a neglected discipline in the education of medical students and physicians. Patients who are in a coma, even for brief periods, suffer brain starvation. Doctors in clinical practice have given ample oxygen to these patients and supplied them with enough fluids, vitamins, and medicines, but it is only recently that we have begun to realize how critical it is to supply calories to these unfortunate individuals—calories by intravenous feeding or through a tube into the stomach. Protein supplements are given to provide calories that patients need to survive even though they are lying unconscious.

Nutritional requirements of the elderly is another area that has also been long neglected. The actual body mass declines in both males and females, and this decline accelerates after age seventy. As we lose our body mass, some of us actually get smaller in size. However, our total weight may be unchanged because there is an increase in fat. Tissues and organs respond differently to this weight loss. Some organs, such as the prostate, become larger; others, like the brain, become smaller because of tissue change. For example, by the time a person reaches the age of seventy, the kidneys and lungs have lost 10 percent of their weight; the liver, 18 percent;

muscle, at least 18 percent; and skeletal muscle, 40 percent. The major loss in body mass is due to muscle loss.

Does change in body weight affect survival? The answer to this question still remains to be determined. However, there are certain interesting facts that we do know. People who are obese and people who are underweight tend to have shorter life spans. There are desirable levels of weight, but the familiar weight charts, such as the Metropolitan Life Insurance chart, have been incorrectly assessed, and the desired conventional weights should be 10 percent greater than those which the charts have so long advocated. This will make most people happy, including me! Just as criteria have been changed for intelligence tests, the criteria for the weight chart test have also recently been changed, after almost forty years. Some of us have needlessly felt that we were overweight all our lives.

Other changes occur in the aging body, the most obvious being the loss of bone strength, which is called osteoporosis. This occurs more frequently in women. The consequence of osteoporosis, or loss of calcium from the body, is believed to be linked to estrogens. It has the detrimental effect of increasing the tendency for fractures after the age of forty, especially in women. It has been estimated that the daily calcium intake in Americans is about 800 mg., but we need 1200 mg. or even more, which is approximately equivalent to a quart of milk. Vitamin D is necessary for the strengthening of bone.

Numerous studies, including the U.S. Department of Health, Education, and Welfare Survey (1968–1970), found that the elderly were taking inadequate amounts of vitamin C in their diet. It was found that the level of vitamin C in elderly patients is about one-half of that in younger adults. The rate of metabolism tends to diminish with age, as does the rebuilding of proteins. When sugar is given to older people, it is metabolized much more slowly, and that is why older people tend to have higher blood sugars, a situation which sometimes leads to diabetes.

A question that the reader might rightfully ask is: "Does nutrition in any way affect survival and prevent mental deterioration?" To look for some of the answers to this question, we have to examine experimental work done with the rat population. From such studies we have learned that nutritional requirements change as we age, and these modify the length of life. Fifty years ago, Dr. Clyde McKay of Cornell University showed that if the amount of food given to rats is restricted they live longer than do those who are allowed to eat as much as they wish, the longevity rate being in direct proportion to the amount of food given. McKay reported his findings in the *Journal of Nutrition* in 1939. These experiments were performed on young animals, and there is as yet not enough data to show that if we restrict food during maturity we may increase survival; however a recent review of rat population studies has concluded that if food is restricted, the life span is increased because of the decrease in the rate of aging.

Certain kinds of food will influence the occurrence of certain illnesses. If you restrict food in rats, it delays the onset of kidney disease and tumors. Let the rats eat what they wish, however, and they will develop premature diseases.

Older people use less energy and, consequently, need fewer calories. It is also well documented that the amount of certain specific nutrients decreases in older people, and that consequently they are more vulnerable to developing deficiencies. For example, they show a tendency to have difficulties in absorbing food. Food contains iron, a lack of which results in anemia which is a common finding in older patients. In one study, conducted by Dr. Richard Torack in 1978 in England and reported in a text, "Your Brain is Younger than You Think," poor nutrition was found among patients confined to nursing homes. Studies have disclosed that the most common deficiencies are those of iron, and vitamins B_1, B_2, B_9, C, and D. In addition, the intake of potassium is markedly reduced, resulting primarily from poor eating habits.

Recently, a study, reported in the *New England Journal of Medicine*, 1984, was performed on patients who were admitted to the hospital with cardiac arrest and then subsequently resuscitated. The study disclosed that many of these patients had low potassium in their blood—low potassium, in many cases, is implicated in causing the sudden, irregular heart rhythm which leads to cardiac arrest. The finding in young adults of low potassium in the blood is usually caused by diuretics, but in elderly patients can be attributable to decreased potassium intake. In the elderly, deficiency of thiamin, coupled with an onset of fever, can cause confusion.

Different neurological abnormalities of the nerves in elderly patients who develop even a minor infection have been associated with niacin deficiency, a vitamin important for nerve function. Poverty is an obvious and important cause of malnutrition in the elderly (even as it is in the younger poor). Older people may not have the stamina or transportation necessary to shop for food, and it is difficult for them to obtain a balanced diet.

There is a strong theory held by some researchers, in particular by Dr. Richard Wurtman, of the Massachusetts Institute of Technology, regarding foods or nutrients that may modify the function of the brain. His theory is that nutrients can act as drugs—that nutrients such as choline and tryptophan can influence brain function, especially in the diseased brain. (Tryptophan is an amino acid; choline, a protein component of egg yolks, liver, and soy beans.)

In Chap. 2, I discussed the role of neurotransmitters, substances which are fired from a neuron and that help to carry the nerve impulse from one neuron to another. Tryptophan is converted in the center of the neurons into the important transmitter, serotonin, and choline is changed into acetylcholine, which is also another chemical neurotransmitter. Tyrosine is changed into the catecholamines dopamine, norepinephine, and epinephrine. As these substances—tryptophan, tyrosine, and choline—are increased, they increase the activity of the neurotransmitters, which means that there are more signals between neurons. These substances may act indirectly as therapeutic agents for the treatment of depression, Parkinson's disease, and memory problems.

There are daily variations in the metabolism of these amino acids, depending on the kinds of foods that are eaten. Most people eat their meals on a regular schedule and the level of amino acids in the blood will show definite daily rhythms. For example, the amino acids may be twice as high between 3 P.M. and 3 A.M. (as compared to the remainder of the day) in somebody who eats a normal protein diet. In people who eat little protein, the amino acids in the blood may fall to half the amount during these hours. These variations in amino acids in the blood have been known for a decade.

The amino acid tryptophan is converted to serotonin. Serotonin affects sleep, mood, and appetite. The amount of serotonin in the brain of an animal can be increased with large doses of pure tryptophan. It is found that increasing the amount of choline in animals also increases the amount of acetylcholine released.

Certain neurological illnesses are characterized by small amounts of choline in the brain and by low levels of acetylcholine at the nerve ending. To further prove that choline is essential for the transmission of nerves, a chemical called physostigmine was administered to rats. The chemical caused enhancement of function of the respiratory tract and stomach and increased cognitive brain function. This medication inhibited the effect of choline and the transmission across the nerve, but, when the animals were given lecithin which contains choline, these effects did not occur.

The aging brain shows not only a decrease in nerves and neurons, especially at the level of the hippocampus as described before, but is also associated with a decreased number of choline neurons, called cholinergic neurons. As we shall see later, the nutrient choline, which increases this transmission, may be effective not only in the treatment of memory disorders but perhaps also in their prevention.

Tyrosine, another nutrient found in our diet, lowers blood pressure in animals. There is speculation that large doses of this nutrient may someday be used to treat hypertension in human beings. It is too early at this time, however, to recommend pure tyrosine as a form of treatment for hypertension.

The implication of all these studies is that the diets of older people should be enriched with such nutrients as tryptophan, choline, and tyrosine. It is interesting to speculate that poor nutrition in elderly persons who have low levels of tyrosine, lecithin, choline, tryptophan, and other nutrients may account for some memory loss and confusion.

Protein and amino acid requirements can be met by the intake of lean meat, fish, or poultry at least once a day. Older patients, however, may not have the ability to absorb the food. Scientists are now just beginning to study the nutritional requirements of the elderly. Nutritional requirements have been outlined for adults between the ages of 20 and 60, but they have not been outlined for people who are between ages 80 and 90. My older patients lose weight primarily because it is too much trouble to cook and to shop. They will skip meals and substitute pure starch for proteins. In nursing homes, patients may have to be fed, which sometimes is not possible. The food becomes cold and unappetizing, and eating thus becomes a chore. However, most patients look forward to meals if they are capable of going to the dining room.

The recommended dietary allowance (RDA) for older adults has been estimated from younger adult standards. Dietary needs may be altered by individual differences in the rate of aging and in the level of physical activity. There is almost no information on the nutritional status of people who are over age seventy-five. Numerous dietary surveys have shown that the intake among the elderly, especially women, falls below the RDA. More than 10 percent of elderly adults ingest less than two-thirds of the RDA for calcium, iron, vitamin A, the B vitamins, and vitamin C. Patients over age 75 also ingest less than two-thirds of the RDA intake for protein. It has been estimated that six to eight percent of elderly patients are malnourished—with inadequate intake of proteins, carbohydrates, and fats, and, above all, vitamins.

The older person has less caloric needs because of decreased activity; the changes in his or her body metabolism require less energy. Although less calories are needed, vitamins, minerals, and proteins are as important as in the younger person. Older persons have to be more careful in order to get the same amount of nutrients in a decreased amount of food.

There are general rules which I recommend to my older patients which are based on a balanced diet, as recommended by the Council on Foods and Nutrition of the American Medical Association. I advise my patients to maintain a low-salt diet and to avoid excessive fatty foods or sweets. I caution them against "junk foods" or snacks as their primary form of nourishment. I encourage smaller regularly spaced meals and advise them *not* to skip meals. Having the major caloric intake at noontime is sensible and relaxing, especially for the retired person. Going to bed overfed has no salutary effects. Eat less, as you need less calories!

A balanced diet consists of the following:

1. Two or more glasses of milk per day (can be substituted with cottage cheese or even a little ice cream or yogurt.)
2. Two or more servings of meat, fish, poultry, eggs, cheese, dried beans, peas, or milk.

3. Four or more servings of vegetables and fruits, including dark green or yellow vegetables, citrus fruits, or tomatoes.
4. Four or more servings of enriched or whole grained breads and cereals.

Older persons experience a decrease in digestion and absorption of substances, such as calcium, minerals, vitamins, and proteins.

Calcium is essential in the diet, especially in women for the prevention of softening of the bones or osteoporosis. One gram of calcium per day, equivalent approximately to a quart of milk is recommended. Iron is necessary and is found in fortified cereals and red meats.

Vitamin B deficiencies can cause mental confusion. A balanced diet rich in whole grain low-fat dairy products can supplement vitamin B.

Diets which are low in fat and high in soft foods, such as buns, cereals, and baby foods, can result in deficiency of fat soluble vitamins A, D, and E. I recommend that ample amounts of fluid be taken during a twenty-four hour period, predominantly in the form of juices and that carbonated soft drinks should be avoided because of their high acid content. One cup of coffee is allowable, but the caffeine-free brands are preferred, since coffee makes the heart beat faster, raises the blood pressure, and causes sleep disturbances. I discourage artificial foods and flavorings and encourage fresh vegetables whenever possible. Fish is an excellent supplement of the proteins which the elderly need and is relatively inexpensive. It is easily digestible, and, with a little imagination, can be prepared for a gourmet's delight. For example, a fillet of sole with a brown meat sauce can be delicious.

Foods which contain high salt should be avoided, such as canned soups, soy sauce, canned vegetables, tomato juice, and dill pickles. I also ask my patients to include a one-a-day multivitamin along with their balanced diet. I discourage older patients from eating at late hours or eating foods which are too rich in sauces and condiments. Ideally, an atmosphere of good dining should be practiced each day.

Another important general rule for the older patient is to keep the urine flowing and the bowels moving. Adequate fluid intake will help the flow of urine to continue and will help to prevent infection. Regular bowel habits are necessary. Older patients have a tendency to hold their stools, as it is too much trouble sometimes to march to the other side of the house to the bathroom. Simple substances, such as Metamucil, are very effective in maintaining regular bowel habits, if there is a tendency toward constipation.

Obviously, the nutritional needs of patients who have chronic illnesses will require a great deal more modification and will depend on each individual. TV dinners should be used only in emergency situations when proper eating is not otherwise possible.

As I will demonstrate in later chapters, malnutrition can be an important cause of brain loss in the elderly.

The following list delineates the vitamins (and their sources) essential for healthy vision, metabolism, formation of red blood cells, and maintenance of teeth, blood vessels, body functions, and brain tissue. Do not take excessive vitamins, however, as they can actually *cause* health problems if abused!

Vitamin A: Milk, butter, margarine, liver, leafy green vegetables, and yellow vegetables.

Vitamin B_1 (thiamin): Enriched bread, fish, lean meat, liver, pork, and poultry.

Vitamin B_2 (riboflavin): Eggs, leafy green vegetables, lean meats, liver, and milk.

Vitamin B_3 (niacin): Lean meats, liver, dried yeast, enriched breads, and eggs.

Vitamin B_6: Vegetables, meat, and whole grained cereals.

Vitamin B_9 (folic acid): Leafy green vegetables and liver.

Vitamin B_{12}: Fish, oysters, lean meat, and kidney.

Pantothenic Acid: Eggs, nuts, liver, kidney, and leafy green vegetables.

Vitamin C: Citrus fruits, berries, tomatoes, cantalopes, potatoes, and leafy green vegetables.

Vitamin D: Fortified milk, cod liver oil, salmon, tuna, and egg yolk.

Vitamin E: Vegetable oils, whole grained cereal, and lettuce.

Vitamin H (biotin): Liver, kidney, eggs, and fresh vegetables.

Vitamin K: Leafy vegetables.

Poor Nutrition as a Cause of Memory Loss

Chronic illnesses, prolonged hospitalization, limited income, and a change of social environment are all factors contributing to malnutrition in the elderly. Diagnostic work-ups, when elderly patients are deprived of food for long periods of time, can swiftly cause them to become malnourished and result in their confusion. Prolonged hospital stays for a six-week course of antibiotic therapy or severe heart failure can place the patient in a negative nutritional balance.

Protein deficiency is a particular problem beyond the age of seventy. As a rule, a dietary history is not obtainable if the patients live by themselves and it is not known whether they are taking in adequate food. As often is the case, the patients refuse or are unwilling to cook for themselves. One patient I had recently seen in consultation subsisted on only bread and butter, with no vegetables or any types of nutrients because it was too much trouble to cook. The patient did not appear malnourished but was actually starving and showed signs of a vitamin deficiency, accompanying hair loss, and brain deterioration. Protein caloric malnutrition presents frequently with a history of confusion or an alteration in the mental status.

Malnutrition (or subnutrition) is probably one of the most common illnesses seen in the elderly but is not always identified as such because of the overriding signs of their other illnesses. A thorough clinical examination including a history of the weight loss and a mental status examination is important. The appearance of the patient can provide a clue. Is the skin dry? Does he look wasted? Does she look emaciated and haggard?

Below are a group of symptoms which can signal malnutrition. Some of these may not be considered abnormal findings but should raise the suspicion of vitamin, protein, and amino acid deficiencies.

Any person who is suffering from memory loss, confusion, and disorientation should be carefully observed for the following:

HAIR AND NAILS: Is hair sparse and dull? Are nails spoon-shaped or brittle-ridged? These could reflect chronic iron deficiency and protein deficiency.

SKIN: Are there blue spots? Purple spots? Increased pigmentation? Thickening or loss of fat? These could reflect both deficiencies of vitamins C, B_3, and A, and a lack of caloric intake.

EYES: Are they dry, with infections and crusting? Dull red dry conjuctiva could reflect vitamin A and B complex (especially thiamin) deficiencies.

AREAS AROUND THE MOUTH: Rashes? Fissures? These reflect vitamin B complex (especially B_2 and B_6), riboflavin, and protein deficiencies.

MOUTH: Are the gums bleeding? Swollen? Swollen Tongue? These could reflect deficiencies of zinc, iron, and vitamins B_2, B_3, B_6, B_9, B_{12}, and C.

PAROTID GLANDS (the glands underneath the ear): Are they enlarged? This reflects protein deficiency. Is the thyroid enlarged? This is the result of iodine deficiency.

CARDIOVASCULAR SYSTEM: Is the heart enlarged with a fast heartbeat? Thiamin deficiency or too much alcohol can be the causes.

LIVER: Is the liver enlarged? Protein deficiency, heart failure, or cancer or other diseases may be the causes.

MUSCULAR EXTREMITIES: Wasting between the thumb and index finger? Calf muscle wasting? Pain in calves? Weak thighs? Swelling? These could reflect protein deficiency.

BONES AND JOINTS: These could reflect vitamin D, calcium, and vitamin C deficiencies or cancer.

Neurological diseases, in addition to the mental changes of confabulations, disorientation, weakness and numbness, could reflect multiple amino-acid, vitamin B_1, B_6 and B_{12}, and pantothenic acid deficiencies.

One of the most important measurements in the assessment of nutritional status of an individual is the albumin measurement in the blood. Decreased albumin levels are invariably present in patients who are poorly nourished.

Elderly patients also have a marked decrease in their immune mechanisms, especially in certain types of lymphocytes called T cells which make the elderly patient more susceptible to infection. An unexplained anemia may have an underlying poor nutritional cause, besides other causes.

Unfortunately, elderly patients who are partially demented cannot recall what they have eaten or give a daily dietary history. Loss of appetite is a common feature in any ill patient, and this becomes particularly important in the older person.

There are groups of medications which can interfere with and jeopardize the nutritional status of patients. I list the medications and their effect below—and the list is far from complete:

Drug Interferences with Nutritional Status

Drugs	*Effects*
Antiinfectives	
Aminoglycosides	Reduced carbohydrate metabolism
Chloramphenicol	Protein-binding inhibition
Isoniazid	Pyridoxine deficiency
Neomycin	Reduced vitamin B_{12}, carotene, iron, sugar, triglyceride absorption
Trimethoprim	Folate deficiency
Antihypertensives	
Ganglionic blockers	Generalized malabsorption
Gastrointestinal drugs	
Aluminum hydroxide	Reduced phosphate absorption
Antacids	Thiamine deficiency
Anticholinergics	Generalized malabsorption
Cathartics	Calcium and phosphorus loss
Cholestyramine	Vitamin A, D, E, and K deficiencies
Clofibrate	Reduced carbohydrate absorption, weight loss, reduced vitamin B_6, carotene, iron, sugar, triglyceride absorption
Antineoplastics	
Aminopterin	Reduced vitamin B_{12}, carotene, cholesterol, lactose, D-Xylose absorption; megaloblastic anemia, steatorrhea
Methotrexate	Same as above; decreased folic acid synthesis
Antirheumatoids	
Colchicine	Same as above
Central nervous system drugs	
Amphetamines	Weight loss
Benzodiazepines	Weight gain

Drug Interferences with Nutritional Status *(continued)*

Drugs	*Effects*
Central nervous system drugs *(continued)*	
Levodopa	Reduced phenylalanine and tyrosine absorption
Phenobarbital	Vitamin D deficiency
Phenothiazines	Weight gain
Phenytoin	Osteomalacia
Tricyclic antidepressants	Weight gain

Anemia as a Cause of the Symptoms of Dementia (Senility)

The aged brain is extraordinarily fragile and the brain chemistry must be always kept in balance. We saw what happens when the brain is either overloaded with sugar or depleted of sugar, calcium, and sodium, causing a variety of brain syndromes and mental retardation. Proper nourishment is also needed for brain function and an ample supply of oxygen. The younger brain can function with a low red blood count longer than the older brain can. The red blood cells and the hemoglobin concentration, are the carriers of oxygen. The oxygen binds to the hemoglobin, and, as it passes to the brain, it unloads its oxygen supply, nourishing the sensitive cells.

Anemia means that there is a deficiency of either red blood cells or hemoglobin, or both, or a total loss of volume of blood. Red blood cells are manufactured by the bone marrow and need important nutrients, such as iron, and certain vitamins, such as B_9 and B_{12}. Anemia can result in deficiencies of these substances or can be caused by an actual loss of blood from the body, as in bleeding inside or outside the body.

If there is a mild anemia, there may be minimal symptoms, except for some slight fatigue. Other times, as the anemia becomes moderately important, there may be in addition to exhaustion and fatigue symptoms arising from specific deficiencies of vitamins B_{12} and B_9. In the older patient who may already have a partially compromised brain deficiency, further insult can be added by the presence of anemia, passing the patient from a state of mild dementia to a severe state of confusion, with alteration of consciousness or awareness, and with the other symptoms that I will describe as occurring in the failing brain.

There is a great deal of controversy as to whether there is such a state as anemia of senescence after the age of sixty. There is a fall of 1 to 2 g. in the hemoglobin of the older person, explained by decreased body weight, a reduced oxygen requirement, and possibly a reduction in red cell manufacturing. The amounts of bone marrow, as well as the length of time the red blood cell lives and produces, are all diminished. Although there is a fall in the hemoglobin concentration, few studies have ever demonstrated an actual decrease resulting from aging alone, unless there is an associated disease.

Iron Deficiency Anemia

The average male possesses about 3500 mg. of iron at the age of sixty, and the average woman about 2500 mg. Older men tend to lose about 10 percent and older women about 15 percent of their iron stores. Ten percent of dietary iron is absorbed from what we eat. The recommended dietary allowance of iron is 10 mg. per day. Nutritional iron deficiency is rare. It can occur in cases of malabsorption, as already described. In order for iron to be absorbed, there must be acid in the stomach in the presence of vitamin C. Older patients tend to have less acid, and some have no acid at all (a state called achlorhydria), which may interfere with the absorption of iron and other substances, such as vitamin B_{12} from the food that we eat. The body has a great many iron stores in the bone marrow which are needed to make red blood cells. Prolonged deficiency or iron first depletes the iron in the blood. Eventually, the stores are also depleted, and then anemia results. Some older people have adequate iron stores in their bone marrow, but the iron is unable to be incorporated into the making of red blood cells. The sluggish aged blood system can cause a chronic anemia.

In addition to the symptoms of weakness and pallor, elderly patients may exhibit signs of confusion, hallucinations, and the mixing up of words and names. Anemia of the brain can be superimposed on some brain degeneration which is occurring, completing the picture of senility.

The most common cause of iron loss in any person is secondary to blood loss from the gastrointestinal (GI) tract. There may be a subtle oozing of blood either from a benign or a malignant process.

Any elderly patient who exhibits signs of dementia must have a blood count included in his or her work-up. The hemoglobin examination is swift and inexpensive. If anemia is found, the type of anemia has to be determined. If it is secondary to an iron-deficiency anemia, a stool examination for blood is mandatory, along with a gastrointestinal survey, looking for a cause of the bleeding (a commercial product boasting of iron supplements, however, should not be taken). Some elderly patients ingest aspirin or aspirinlike products for a number of years for joint pains and headaches. Unfortunately, one of the complications of aspirin is bleeding from the GI tract, which may be insidious, resulting in a slow fall in the blood count until the patient becomes weaker and the brain suffers.

A 72-year-old retired banker who had rheumatoid arthritis for many years was taking aspirin and ibuprofen for his arthritis. He became progressively weaker and more disabled, which was attributed to his arthritis, and there were prolonged periods of depression, difficulty in identifying objects, and mixing up of words. He smoked a pipe, and, one day, said to his wife, "Would you bring my chair to me, and I have the salt in my closet."

It was at that point that his wife sought medical attention for her husband, and it was found that he was critically anemic. His wife remembered that over a period of several months he had become more confused and lethargic and had already informed the family that Dad was deteriorating rapidly, but, when Dad received several pints of blood, he perked up like a revivified flower. His red blood cells began to circulate through the brain, unloading precious oxygen. His confusion disappeared, along with his verbal absurdities.

A low serum iron in an elderly patient is corrected by administering iron tablets along with a suitable vitamin C to enhance the absorption. When taking iron replacement, the patient often complains of black stool, which come from the iron, and chronic constipation. The addition of a mild laxative or bulk along with the iron prescription can make constipation less of a problem.

It is not sufficient to just give iron and vitamin C and then assume that the blood correction will automatically occur. A follow-up blood count is needed at the end of two months, along with a review of the nutritional status of the patient.

Pernicious Anemia (Vitamin B_{12} Deficiency)

There are dozens of reasons why anemia occurs. For example, it may be the result of a chronic inflamation, infection, or malignancies, kidney failure, liver disease, and so forth. One of the common anemias, called pernicious anemia or vitamin B_{12} deficiency, is a disease of those aged sixty or older, is frequently seen in people of northern European descent, and is less common in blacks and Asians. In this condition, there is no acid formed in the stomach and so the lining of the stomach is destroyed, so that vitamin B_{12} is not absorbed. The deficiency is also found after stomach operations, in the malabsorption states previously described, and in chronic inflamation of the pancreas. Pernicious anemia is often associated with iron-deficiency anemia. The diagnosis is simply done by measuring the level of vitamin B_{12} in the blood.

There are some medications which can actually cause pernicious anemia, or vitamin B_{12} deficiency, such as neomycin, sometimes used for intestinal disorders; and para-aminosalicyclic acid, used for the treatment of tuberculosis.

In 1925, a diagnosis of pernicious anemia was an automatic death sentence. In spite of the treatment of gorging patients with liver and liverlike products, the anemia did not improve and the afflicted patients deteriorated to the complete picture of pernicious anemia. Marked general weakness, coupled with neurological manifestations such as numbness, the inability to walk, weakness of arms and legs, loss of reflexes, inability to hold objects, diminished sensations and vibration of arms and legs, with unsteadiness and a waddling gait which can look like a stroke, was apparent. Severe memory loss can occur, as well as moodiness, confusion, confabulations, and disorientations. Some patients eventually became frankly psychotic.

It was through the efforts of Drs. George R. Minnow and William Murphy that intramuscular injection of vitamin B_{12} became a reality in the treatment of pernicious anemia. Minnow would have never discovered the cure for pernicious anemia if it were not for his friend and colleague, Dr. Fred Banting. Minnow, a Harvard University Medical Professor, was suffering from diabetes, which had the appearance of cancer, and was slowly dying. His friend, Banting, who had just discovered the curative properties of insulin, realized that Minnow was indeed suffering from diabetes and was able to save his life by insulin administrations, making it possible for Minnow to discover the cause of pernicious anemia.

The administration of vitamin B_{12} used to be a cherished, fashionable form of treatment by the old-time physicians for persons complaining of weakness or numbness, depression, anxiety, or memory loss. Many other doctors made fun of this vitamin B_{12} injection and called it a pure placebo effect. Even to this day, I see patients asking for monthly B_{12} shots: "It perks me up and makes me feel great until the next time."

Undoubtedly, there are many patients who feel better after B_{12} injections, for no demonstrable medical reasons other than placebo. I do not recommend the use of B_{12} injections, unless it is proven that there is a B_{12} insufficiency.

Folic Acid (Vitamin B_9) Deficiency

Another common deficiency found in nutritional failure and chronic illness is folic acid (B_9) deficiency. Folic acid deficiency is probably even more common that vitamin B_{12} deficiency, since it can result from malnutrition and malabsorption. (Folic acid is particularly rich in vegetables, liver, yeast, and fruits.) It is commonly found in alcoholics as well. It can also result from taking certain medications, such as isoniazid (INH) for the treatment of tuberculosis, neomycin, and certain drugs used for the treatment of cancer, such as methotrexate. Dilantin, used for the treatment of seizures, can cause folic acid deficiencies. Today, to lower cholesterol in blood, we are using an excellent medication called cholestyramine, a natural bile salt. It binds the cholesterol but can, on occasion, also cause folic acid deficiency.

The diagnosis of folic acid deficiency can be made by measuring the serum folate in the blood. This test is also performed on any elderly patient who is anemic.

My Aunt Jo, for as long as I can remember, had a scrawny appearance. She was a remarkable character right out of an Edith Wharton story. After several marriages with writers and poets, multiple children, and extracurricular activities such as mountain climbing, she marched for women's rights in the 1920s as part of the entourage of Stefan Zweig. Her mind was as sharp as a tack at the age of eighty-five. She subsisted predominantly on vegetables and fresh fruits, and, for the past few years, had not eaten beef, chicken, or veal, having read somewhere that meat was contaminated with carcinogens.

Periodically, I would visit her at her apartment on West End Avenue in New York and invariably found her doing yoga, painting, or writing letters to friends all over the world. I began to notice that she had started to become rather listless. Her agility disappeared and she developed a peculiar coloration, which made her look sallow and greenish from the reflections of her Tiffany lamps.

It was on a Friday afternoon that I realized that she was critically ill. She was sitting comfortably in a chair when I walked into her apartment. Her knitting was lying on the floor, and it became clear that she had not washed in days.

"Your Uncle Morris called yesterday," she said, "and he is going to be returning back from Africa shortly."

Uncle Morris had been her second husband and had died twenty years before. She called me "Joseph," the name of another of her husbands, and I said, "Aunt Jo, I'm your nephew. Don't you recognize me?"

"But *of course* I recognize you. What do you think, I'm losing my mind?" And then she proceeded to again discuss her conversation with her late husband.

When I asked her to get up from the chair, it was apparent that she was unable to do so and that she had been sitting there for days. My aunt never cared much for the medical profession, or for anything that came in bottles, especially medications. All in all, being vigorous to the age of eighty-five without receiving medical care wasn't a bad record at all.

An ambulance brought her to a local hospital in New York City where the doctors swiftly discoverd that she had a severe anemia and that she was starving. Her proteins were abnormally low, and her ankles were slightly swollen. Her heart was enlarged, and her brain-wave test and other examinations disclosed a diffuse abnormal function.

The hospital staff, much to her reluctance, began to feed her with fresh meats and vegetables, and, within several days, she began to perk up. Her blood tests returned and disclosed an abnormally low folic acid and vitamin B_{12} level. With replacement of the folic acid and vitamin B_{12}, my aunt returned to her old, healthy cantankerous self again in a period of two weeks. We could not dissuade her from abandoning her vegetarian diet, but she did consent to have injections of B_{12} on a monthly basis and of folic acid to supplement her diet. She is now age eighty-nine and is living in an apartment in the Marais section of Paris.

This is a classic example of nutritional failure, with B_{12} deficiency, a common occurrence in patients who are true vegetarians without supplementary vitamin preparations.

As we have seen, poor nutrition and diet can have a devastating effect on mind chemistry and behavior in the elderly, an even greater problem than depression, which I will discuss in the next chapter.

CHAPTER 4

Depression

I am very grateful to old age because it increased my desire for conversation and lessened my desire for food and drink.

CATO

Why discuss depression in a book written about senility? The reason is because depression is the most common psychiatric complaint found in the elderly and can mimic dementia. It has been estimated that 20 percent or more of our older population is afflicted with depression. Psychiatrists consider the ups and downs in a mood a normal trait; however, when the mood is considerably more "down" than "up," it is called an affective disorder. The differentiation between depression and senility is sometimes very difficult in the early stages. Depression is an illness that is often misdiagnosed in the practice of medicine, and dementia is, unfortunately, being overdiagnosed. The statistics are alarming in that 40 to 80 percent of elderly patients who commit suicide are under the care of a physician, and 50 percent have seen a doctor within the week.

Volumes of books and research papers have been written about depression, but it is only recently that we have begun to understand what depression is all about. Everyone in his or her lifetime has had periodic episodes of "feeling blue." Most of us get over our minor depressions until the next episode. The older individual, however, may remain depressed for an extended period of time.

Suicide in the elderly is a devastating health problem. Twenty-five percent of all suicides occur in persons over the age of sixty-five. Depressed older men make up the largest proportion of the 10,000 older Americans who take their own lives.

Causes and Symptoms of Depression

The two major causes of depression that I have witnessed in the elderly are the threats of lack of finances to eat or pay the rent and of dependence on other people, especially their own children. People who have worked diligently all their lives, especially middle-class individuals, arrive at the time of retirement with a certain degree of confidence and peace, with financial security provided for from their savings and Social Security benefits. However, the threats of loss of Social Security benefits, increasing fuel prices, rents, and medical costs can transform even the relatively secure elderly into terrified citizens. If these people are faced with an illness that requires the purchase of medications for upwards of $200 a month, plus other medical bills, depression sets in swiftly and becomes an outstanding feature in their illness. And what of the elderly with little or no money, the poor?

The psychiatric diagnosis of depression is outlined in the *Diagnostic and Statistical Manual of Mental Disorders*, 3d ed., published by the American Psychiatric Association as follows:

A major depressive episode occurs if the following symptoms are present and if the patient is: ". . .depressed, blue, hopeless, low-down, in the dumps, irritable. The mood disturbance must be prominent and relatively persistent, but not necessarily the most dominant symptom. At least four of the following symptoms have to be present nearly every day for a period of two weeks:

1. Poor appetite or significant weight loss when not dieting.
2. Insomnia, or sleeping all the time.
3. Restlessness, agitation or retardation.
4. Loss of interest or pleasure in activities; decrease in sexual drive.
5. Loss of energy, fatigue.
6. Feeling of worthlessness, self-reproach, inappropriate guilt feelings.
7. Diminished ability to think or concentrate, slow thinking.

8. Recurrent thoughts of death; suicidal ideas; wishes to be dead; even suicide attempts."

However, older patients may not even know that they are depressed but may complain of other symptoms. Sleep disturbance is a constant finding in the depressed elderly patient. As I have described, there is a change in sleep patterns after the age of seventy. Most depressed patients will say that they have no trouble in falling asleep; however, they are awake again after two or three hours. Some will try going back to sleep but then will be awakened again. In the morning, the patients will state that they feel as if they haven't slept at all, and they will suffer from great exhaustion.

Depression is often marked by other symptoms which doctors have labeled somatic complaints—complaints which have no organic basis but which are associated with depression. Such complaints—chronic back pain, rheumatism, joint pains and headaches—often dumbfound the physician and require a skillful investigation to eliminate other causes. Symptoms, such as fatigue, loss of energy, gastrointestinal disturbances, constipation, indigestion, blurred vision, dry mouth, menstrual cycle disturbances, vaginal or rectal itch, and even worsening of skin disorders (psoriasis and excessive sweating) may be the major symptoms of depression. After a diagnostic work-up, if the physician has not found an organic cause for these complaints, it is often difficult to confront the patient with the news that his or her complaints are signs of depression. More often than not, the patient will not accept the diagnosis and will start seeking other doctors. Some patients carry their complaints from physician to physician and may find a physician who will satisfy their conviction that they are physically ill and administer placebolike medication, such as vitamin B_{12} shots. If psychiatric consultation is advised to the patient, generally the first reaction is, "I'm not crazy, and I'm not going to see a psychiatrist," and then he or she will walk out of the office, usually angry with the physician. It is these kinds of depressions which are the most difficult to treat unless the patient accepts the diagnosis.

Recently, a 75-year-old woman consulted me because of chest pain of many months' duration. The referring physician felt that she might have a cardiac problem. She described the pain in her chest as constant, not relieved by rest, by change of position, or by eating of food. She also stated that much of the pain also occurred with neck stiffness and shoulder pain. A thorough physical examination, including a cardiac exam with an electrocardiagram, stress testing, and other new complicated tests to diagnose coronary artery disease, was performed; all of the findings were normal. In addition, the patient had extensive testing done by her rheumatologist who found that her pains were not due to an arthritic condition. The patient returned to me after several weeks of testing, and further conversations revealed that she had been suffering from a severe sleep disturbance during the past six months, since the death of her husband.

"Are you depressed?" I asked her.

"Definitely not! I've adjusted to my husband's death. My mood is just fine. It is my chest pain that bothers me."

This woman was a sturdy individual who had held a managerial position in a large corporation for most of her adult life. In her mind, depression was a sign of weakness and afflicted only people of "weak" character. The very suggestion that perhaps she was suffering from depression almost prompted her to walk out of my office. She denied any difficulties in concentration, but she did admit that she did not enjoy going to the theater as before. The excuses that she gave consisted of, "it cost too much money" (she was very secure financially); "it is too difficult to get into town"; and, "the shows aren't worth seeing." Finally, I proposed using an antidepressant medication to help her with the pain, as it might have some salutary effects on muscle relaxation. She did not resist taking the antidepressant medications and was delighted to think of them as muscle relaxants. Several weeks passed and the medication began to take effect. The chest pain disappeared and her sleep pattern normalized. Only after several months was she able to admit that she had been depressed—"But how could it happen to me?"

The characteristically depressed elderly patient may not be found sitting in a rocking chair brooding or tearful. Instead, he or she may present in another fashion. For example, Mary has been a patient of mine for fifteen years and seemed to have adjusted well to her husband's death. She was always an outspoken and vivacious individual with a generous way about her and a marvelous sense of humor. The only weakness that she claimed was that she loved to smoke cigarettes, and, regardless of how many admonitions she received from friends of hers who were dying of heart disease and cancer of the lung, she decided that it was her own risk. The years had passed without much change in her life.

Although I saw her frequently, she called one day in desperation, telling me that she had to be seen for an urgent personal matter. The woman who now appeared before me was gaunt, shrunken, and untidily dressed, with heavy lines of despair in her face. On every previous occasion, she had come to my office wearing a hat, dressed elegantly in the style of the day. There was now an obvious change. She said that she could no longer stay alone in her big house. (I had told her years ago that she should sell the house and find living quarters more suitable for a single person.) She also claimed that she had lost thirty pounds, that she no longer had any appetite, and that death was imminent. She was certain that she was suffering from cancer, and the urgency of her visit was prompted by the fact that she had seen her lawyer to request that no major resuscitation measures be taken, as she wanted to die quietly and peacefully without any fuss, and not in the hands of the hospital. She came with a well-written and authenticated document, which I placed in her chart.

I asked her which illness was the cause of her urgent visit, and she replied that it was cancer. She had smoked for all these years, and now she was willing to pay the price. However, her examination was entirely normal. There were no signs of cancer of the lung, but there was evidence of a woman with loosely hanging skin who had lost thirty pounds. Exhaustive testing did not reveal any illness, except that she was suffering from depression. I proposed that she consult a psychiatrist or a psychologist. The appointment was made, but she never kept it. She wanted a different psychiatrist of the same religion and general age who would better understand her. Again, an appointment was made which she did not keep. When I saw her again one month later, she was one-half her normal size, with the appearance of a concentration camp victim. Her memory was now failing and she was confused, but, when I managed to contact her family, she threatened me with a malpractice suit for giving out personal information regarding her health, and she ordered that I was not to discuss her illness with anyone under any circumstances. It could not be proved that she was mentally incompetent, so the patient was within her rights to refuse treatment, as a Jehovah's witness can refuse a blood transfusion. This unfortunate woman refused any medication or care, and, in spite of my efforts, she finally did die at home the way she chose of dehydration, infection, and malnutrition, with her only underlying illness being depression. An autopsy performed did not reveal any pathology. Her brain was that of a 78-year-old woman with a normal distribution of senile plaques, along with neuron changes. Her depression had led to malnutrition because she stopped eating, the malnutrition helped to perpetuate her depression, and so the pattern continued in a vicious cycle.

So far, I have described to you two cases of variation in depression—in the second case, extreme weight and appetite loss, and in the first case, musculoskeletal pain. Minor forms of depression in the elderly can continue untreated for years; increasing severity, eventually coupled with anxiety can reduce the patient to an apathetic appearance, a typical picture of dementia, and finally to a vegetable state. Memory loss (short-term and long-term) may be the outstanding symptom of depression, as it is the case with brain degeneration. Depression, in itself, can be a sign of an illness elsewhere. I have known many patients who became depressed for no apparent reason, with a medical cause, such as a malignancy, becoming evident only later. In Chapter 11, I will discuss different medications which account not only for severe depression in the elderly, but also for memory loss in the picture of senility.

Dr. Schildkraut of Harvard stated the theory about 1965 in the *American Journal of Psychiatry* that too little adrenaline in the brain caused depression.

Before that time two theories as to the cause of depression were dominant in the field of psychiatry—those formulated by Sigmund Freud and Emil Kraepelin. Dr. Kraepelin (well known as the author of a textbook on psychiatry and as an investigator at the famous Kraepelin Research Institute of Munich) felt that mental problems arise because of brain damage, and he gave as an example the case of a patient suffering from advanced syphilis of the brain (paresis) who developed mental affliction. The brain became scarred and deteriorated from the syphilis leading to manic depression and schizophrenia.

Freud's theories were not based on brain damage but on the suppression of human primitive drives and the idea that the mind cannot tolerate this suppression. Emotional conflicts develop: there is a continuous battle on the subconscious level with mental illness resulting from the inner conflicts. Freud however, clearly felt that brain damage could cause disorders, and so he differentiated psychiatric manifestation originating from brain damage (organic disorders) from functional disorders stemming from psychological causes.

In 1917, Freud described depression as ". . .a profoundly painful dejection, cessation of interest in the outside world, loss of the capacity to love, the inhibition of all activity, and the lowering of the self regarding feelings. The patient emerges into a vegetative state. The diagnosis of depression must include the search for other causes, as any illness can cause depression."

Depression tends to occur most often in elderly women, for reasons we don't know yet, and may arise as a reactive emotional response to an unpleasant event, or as an endogenous response, if there is a cause such as a lingering malignancy. (As we saw in previous chapters, certain chemical neurotransmitters of the brain, when diminished, are associated with depression—in particular, serotonin.)

Depression in the elderly is somewhat similar to dementia—it is associated with chemical changes, and, as mentioned earlier, distinguishing between depression and dementia is sometimes very difficult. Unfortunately, many patients who are depressed are never discovered. They rarely see physicians and continue living in despair by themselves at home, or, once admitted into a hospital for another illness, they are often labelled as "organic" (which means "organic brain damage") or "demented."

Any elderly patient who has signs of a continuing depression should have a thorough examination to be certain that there are not underlying medical causes, some of which are especially amenable to treatment. For example, older patients develop abnormalities in their metabolism; among the most common is diabetes mellitus. Diabetes in the older person is generally not significant, and it is common to develop an abnormality in the metabolism of sugar. When sugar becomes more elevated in the blood, symptoms of high blood sugar may be fatigue, apathy, and depression. Patients living alone who have difficulty in managing their diets in the first place may continue to have elevated sugar levels and may wonder what is happening to them, and may think that this is another sign of aging. Sometimes, by proper regulation of the diet or by the addition of medications called hypoglycemic agents, the blood sugar becomes speedily controlled, a general sense of well-being returns, and the patient's depression disappears.

Eight million Americans suffer from depression, and the reason why such a large percentage occurs in the elderly is still being studied. One of the outstanding problems faced by the elderly (and perhaps by our younger generation, in whom depression is easier to diagnose) is boredom. Boredom not only arises from loneliness, but also stems from the lack of stimulating possibilities available, especially to the older person. Activities which years ago would keep a 70-year-old person active are now often either difficult or impossible in the contemporary urban or rural setting. The decision to take a leisurely walk on a busy street is frequently a cause of anguish due to the fear of mugging and rape. Visiting friends at night is a virtual impossibility for most older people, unless they are escorted. Many of my patients state that they are in bed by 8:30 or 9:00 because there is nothing further to do. They don't leave the house because of fear. In addition, the nuclear-family unit has often been shattered, a destructive sign in our society. Older persons again are left out in the cold. The occasional visit by the grandchildren is insufficient to relieve the everyday stillness and isolation, the monotony of their lives.

Formerly, the local hangouts for men night after night were around the stove in the hardware store or around a billiards table. There are now few local hangouts, except for the bar and the occasional club. The process of socialization has been undermined by separation and fear of crime. We have become, in large measure, a lonely, bored society, and our major outlet is now the television set, a one-way communicator incapable of a relationship. The ubiquitous television has contributed to loneliness and boredom, having become not only an extremely poor substitute for socializing, but having also reduced so many to passive observers. It is easier to stay home, put one's feet up, and watch a program than it is to go out on a cold wintry night to see a friend. Communist Chinese society, which has a three-generation family unit, has the least amount of mental degeneration, senility, and loneliness. Alas, this, too, is changing as they are becoming westernized.

The solutions to boredom need to be prepared years in advance. We plan for our economic survival, do our best to maintain our physical vigor, may experiment with new "prudent" diets to prevent heart attacks, or stop smoking cigarettes so as to prevent heart and lung disease and cancer, but I have not yet heard of any kind of program announced by the American Psychological Association, the American Psychiatric Association, or the government on how to mentally cope with becoming older. Just as we learn to get in shape physically, so too must we learn to get our brains in shape. Our society is so concerned with outward appearance and the outward signs of aging, that we neglect entirely that which needs to be done for our brains.

The curbing of the epidemic of boredom in the elderly and the alleviation of their apathy and depression should be one of our major priorities.

Often, I have asked friends and patients, "What are you planning to do when you retire?" Most of the time the answer is, "I'll decide that when I reach that point—if I live that long." I try to explain to them that the probability is likely they will live to retirement age and beyond. Some are fortunate and have developed or will take up new skills, such as reading, painting, sculpture, photography, and so forth. These mentally and emotionally healthy individuals will not suffer from chronic boredom. My mother-in-law rediscovered her knitting and sewing skills after I suggested to her that my daughters would be delighted to have her sweaters and skirts for the winter. The novelty struck her so positively that she now provides many sweaters for her family, each one more intricate and artistic than the previous one. She derives satisfaction from her work and is prevented from becoming bored, and we have enough handsome sweaters for at least another generation or two.

My mother has taken up many of her previous hobbies, one of which is painting. Being in front of a canvas so absorbs her that she forgets the time of day and sometimes continues working throughout the night. Another source of pleasure is in playing

cards. Any kind of card game satisfies her because it means socializing with other people, and, so, she plays cards at least three
times a week. I used to ridicule people who spent their evenings
playing cards but now I realize that this is an excellent way of
handling boredom. Certainly it is by far a better solution than
watching a television show which brings on sleep faster than any
sleeping pill.

Cooking and baking have always been a stimulating activity for
some people, if there is an appreciative recipient. I have patients
living alone who derive great pleasure from baking cookies for our
office. It gives them a sense of achievement, of being needed.

Many older patients claim disability as an excuse for not pur-
suing any other form of brain stimulation. Arthur Rubinstein, the
famed pianist who died at the age of ninety-six, lost his vision when
he was ninety and was unable to play the piano. When asked if
that meant that his life had come to a tragic halt, Mr. Rubinstein
replied, "Oh, no, not at all! Now I can listen. For the first time,
I can listen." And he continued telling us about how he had always
wanted to listen to *other* people's music. Mr. Rubinstein died in
Geneva, Switzerland, four years short of the age of one hundred

This is a book written on the aging brain, but it is also intended
to help prepare younger readers. Years prior to retiring, the reader
should plan a checklist of what to do in order to create a stimulating
environment that will last well into the eighth and ninth decades
of life. The famed behavioral psychologist, B. F. Skinner, who is
eighty-one years old, was a major speaker at the Ninetieth Annual
Convention of the American Psychological Association in Washington, D.C. It was an outstanding moment as Dr. Skinner outlined
his strategy for self-management of old age. He stated that we must
devise a stimulating environment and games and tricks for the
memory in order to meet the challenges of the failing brain and
diminished intellectual powers. Although I have great respect for
Dr. Skinner, I must disagree with his concept of diminished intellectual powers in old age. He advocates that "leisure should be
relaxing; [if] possibly you like complicated puzzles or chess or other
demanding intellectual games, give them up." I also disagree with
this concept. I think that if a seventy-eight-year-old person enjoys
playing chess and is capable of this marvelous activity, it should
be continued, and he or she should not seek out lesser gains.

However, if the playing of chess frustrates, *then* it should be given up. I have known men who have started playing chess and found that this is a way of coping with boredom.

Dr. Skinner does give sound advice which I agree with. He states that "food can be highly flavored, pornography can be used to extend sexuality into old age, and those who can't read can listen to book recordings." Furthermore, he advocates that one can promote new thoughts by moving into a new field or acquiring a new intellectual style.

If you are a man or woman soon approaching retirement, I recommend that you now sit down and make a simple checklist of what you will do with the next twenty or thirty years of your life to promote interest and prevent becoming bored. Don't use the excuse that if you had the money you'd do this and that. That is often a cop-out. And, above all, don't depend on society, your family, or your children to provide the answers for you. If you are a woman and are dependent on your husband, plan to become independent. One of my patients stated that she wants to do different things but is unable to because she does not know how to drive a car. She always depended on her husband to transport her and when her husband died, she still did not make the effort to learn "because I'm too old." There is a big difference between learning to drive and becoming financially independent, but if you exert yourself to overcome obstacles, you will exercise your brain and retain your mental energies.

Mental and physical exercise stimulates adrenaline, and high adrenaline levels in the brain will prevent depression and boredom.

Depression can be the major symptom of numerous illnesses. Below a few common ones are listed:

Adrenal disease	Multiple sclerosis
Cancer of the pancreas	Nutritional deficiencies
Cerebral metastasis	Pernicious anemia
Chronic subdural hematoma	Subacute bacterial endocarditis
Hepatitis	Systemic lupus erythematosus
Huntington's chorea	Tertiary syphilis
Hyperparathyroidism	Tuberculosis
Hypothyroidism	Chronic infections
Arthritis	Heart disease

Some drugs that can cause depression are:

Digitalis	Methyldopate
Clonidine	Barbiturates
Antiparkinsonian (Levodopa)	Benzodiazepines
Antipsychotics	Steroids
Propranolol	Alcohol
Reserpine	Guanethidine
Cimetidine	

So, if you or someone close to you is losing his or her memory due to depression, check into the medications. This list is far from complete. A more detailed discussion will follow on medications causing memory loss in a later portion of the book.

Treatment of Depression

Patients should be cared for by an expert who deals with depression, who need not necessarily be a psychiatrist. Depression is primarily a medical illness, a chemical manifestation of events which are occurring in the brain. I find psychotherapy helpful in the elderly patient, but it is most effective when used in conjunction with appropriate medication.

Antidepressant medications are extraordinarily useful in the older patient if their actions are known, side effects understood, and the proper dosage used. As Dr. Lawrence Lazarus, of Rush Medical College, states: "The chance of side effects in the elderly is several times greater than in young patients. Distribution of these medications is bound by plasma proteins, and, since elderly people have a reduced amount of plasma protein, especially albumin, there is more of the effect of free drug circulating in the body."

Several of the antidepressants with which the practitioner is familiar are generally used, such as desipramine, nortriptyline, maprotiline, or amoxapine. Patients who also exhibit manic episodes along with their depression often benefit from lithium.

ECT (electroconvulsive therapy) is still used and may be very helpful for the severely depressed patient.

Food stuffs are now being used against depression, one of which is called tryptophan, the forerunner of serotonin, which I discussed earlier. A one-gram dosage may help the patient go to sleep and possibly help his or her depression. Other amino acids, such as phenylalamine, have also been suggested.

The more we learn about chronic depression, the more we realize it may be corrected with antidepressants along with counseling, and, in the future, there may be dietary manipulations that will enhance the production of serotonin. Investigators are searching for high-protein supplements containing tryptophan that might someday be used.

In the future, we can look forward to preventing chronic depression, perhaps finding persons in families susceptible to this illness. Subjects springing from families with a history of depression may have a genetic marker, likewise, alcoholism, diabetes, and breast cancer often run amok in families. I predict that someday these family depressions will be traced to a common correctable chemical abnormality; perhaps they can be prevented by early dietary regulations in the same manner as hypertension can be prevented by restricting sodium; diabetes by eliminating sugar; cancer of the lung by eliminating cigarettes; cancer of the bowel by diminishing the fat and meat content of our diet and increasing cereals; and arteriosclerosis by starting low cholesterol diets early in childhood.

CHAPTER 5

The Lost Brain:
Brain Impairment

*I never heard of an old man forgetting where he had
hidden his money.*

CICERO

I have discussed in the previous chapters the mechanisms
of learning and memory and the concepts of short-term and long-
term memory loss, with the accompanying chemical changes in the
brain. In this chapter, I will discuss memory loss that signals significant disease, reversible and irreversible.

The unfortunate terms, "senility" and "senile dementia," have
placed another black mark on aging persons: it becomes a shameful
diagnosis for some. Consequently, many times denial of its existence makes the diagnosis belated and the possibility of finding a
treatment more difficult. The description below embraces general
symptomology which may or may not be reversible.

Again, I want to emphasize the importance of proper diagnosis
of significant declining brain function. A question frequently asked
is: "When does minor memory loss and forgetfulness of recent
events, and, for that matter, remote events signify the beginning
of a serious brain degeneration eventually leading to one of the
most dreaded of all illnesses in this country, called Alzheimer's
disease?" (Alzheimer's disease will be discussed in Chap. 14.)

There is a great deal of confusion among physicians and psychologists regarding what constitutes dementia and its causes. The
dictionary definition of "dementia," or "demented," means: "in-

sanity consisting of loss of intellectual power due to brain disease or injury." Some statistics reveal that when these specialists talk about dementia, they are referring to Alzheimer's disease. Others refer to secondary dementia with a progressive curable treatment. In a 1982 article in the *Medical Times* from the Department of Medicine of Michigan State University, there was a statement that 100,000 deaths per year in the United States occur from dementia, that 2.3 percent of the American population requires hospitalization for this reason, and that dementia affects 4 percent of all adults over the age of sixty-five.

The New York Times recently carried a piece on January 16, 1984 about Alzheimer's disease in which the author vividly described the illness in her mother and also mentioned that, according to the National Institute on Aging, twenty-five million Americans over age sixty-five, or 60 percent, suffer from dementia.

For our purposes, we will separate degenerative brain function, or brain impairment, into two groups with either known or unknown causes. The group with unknown causes includes, Alzheimer's disease, Pick's disease, and others to be described later. Those whose causes are known are reversible.

It is difficult to conclude for certain which patients have primary degeneration of the brain, or brain degeneration of unknown cause, like Alzheimer's disease, unless autopsies are performed. The number of autopsies which have been performed in recent years has markedly declined as many families, out of irrational fear, have become less willing to grant permission, and so many doctors have become less aggressive in demanding them and attempting to overcome families' resistance. Furthermore, it is not common to include a brain examination at autopsy as often the family demands that the brain and the head not be touched: "After all, Doctor, you are only interested in seeing what the heart looked like."

Most elderly people do not get autopsied after death. The cause of death as reported by the physician is usually accepted without question, and autopsies are not requested by a coroner. Families that request autopsies have to be prepared to pay for them. All in all, we have insufficient data on the number of people who are actually suffering from senile dementia. I have already described some of the findings in the normal aging brain found at autopsy, such as senile plaques, the pattern of the neurons, and the loss of cells in the hippocampus. These abnormalities are found in most, but not all senile individuals. For example, in one study done in Newcastle-upon-Tyne in England by pathologists Blessed, Tomlinson, and Roth, of 100 aged people over the age of ninety who died of different causes, nineteen did not have plaques or neuron abnormalities.

Another confusing term that doctors often use is "organic brain syndrome," which refers to abnormal brain dysfunction, confusion, memory loss, and progressive mental deterioration resulting from damage to the brain—unfortunately, another instance of grouping all elderly patients suffering from memory loss together under one diagnosis.

The earliest manifestation of a brain impairment is memory loss. Forgetting your glasses, why you came into a room in the first place, or the name of a person does not automatically signal that you are headed for brain dysfunction. The memory loss often is regarded as a consequence of "becoming older." In the early stages, it is impossible to make the diagnosis of impairment. As noted in Chap. 4, depression can be confused with brain impairment or dementia, and depression may be the first symptom that something is happening to the brain in an elderly person. In the very earliest phase, the patients themselves may not be aware of what is happening, although close members of the family or old friends may notice subtle changes. Mild forgetfulness, such as difficulty in remembering familiar faces or an appointment, may or may not be a symptom, just as chest pain may or may not be a symptom of heart disease.

The changes at first are usually very subtle—a loss of initiative, a decline in the ability to do certain things that one is used to doing, a certain apathy, the inability to understand and grasp everyday happenings, coupled with a general deterioration of intellectual ability. Above all, for such a diagnosis, there has to be a progressive and continued failure of abilities.

If the patient is progressing into dementia, memory impairment becomes severe. Neuropsychiatrists emphasize that the patient will start to exhibit strange behavior or behavioral aberrations and cognitive impairment, which means lacking the faculty of being aware, of noticing, and of perceiving—all considered important signs of dementia.

At first, the person might have difficulty in remembering certain words, the vocabulary may be depleted, and more simple words might be used for substitutes. If he or she has a great deal of ingenuity, the person will find means to compensate for the memory loss. For example, the patient will write many things down or will invent tricks to keep track of belongings and events. Eventually, as the disease progresses, those tactics will also be foiled, and the patient will have no vocabulary left at all.

The depressed person, when asked a question, may simply say, "I don't know," while the person with impaired mental function will fabricate an answer. A banker patient of mine, once an outstanding financier, developed a brain disorder, and, when I asked him, "Who is the President?" he answered, "You know, that same guy."

And, "How is the economy doing these days?"

"Like always."

"How is your good friend . . . What's his name again?"

"You know his name. I don't have to tell you."

Memory loss and depression may not be the outstanding symptoms of early dementia; instead, a distinct apathy may appear. There may be a progressive sense of unawareness, an indifference to seeing grandchildren or a favorite television program. Families and friends often interpret these feelings as selfishness or of "not giving a damn."

Eccentricities should not be confused with brain damage. Some people may be mentally alert with keen memories but will do peculiar things. The bag lady roaming through the streets may not be impaired intellectually, but might have an overriding psychiatric problem. Miserliness with aging and hoarding money for fear of loss (even though there may be millions in the bank) do not reflect mental impairment.

Dementia, actual brain impairment, is usually progressive; sometimes it can improve without treatment, but sometimes it stays about the same for years. Memory disturbance may be the prominent symptom of dementia. There may be, in the mildest form, forgetfulness in daily life. Tasks may be repeated over and over again. Sometimes, there may be hesitation in response to questions. The interruption of memory may be just temporary, and, as time passes, the name might again be recalled. In a direct meeting with a person known for a long time, the early brain-impairment patient may have difficulty at first in remembering the name, but, then, as time goes on, will say, "Oh, yes, I remember who that person is."

As the impairment gets more severe, telephone numbers, directions, or daily events are forgotten. Tasks may remain unfinished because one forgets to return to them after one is interrupted. For example, the individual might be washing dishes or cooking when the phone rings, and then he or she may forget to come back to shut the water or the stove off. As the impairment gets more severe, the names and occupations of close relatives, schools, birthdays, and sometimes the person's own name may be forgotten. Disturbance in memory may at first be short-term but eventually becomes a long-term problem.

The person may eventually have trouble coping with new tasks and will avoid situations which require learning. The patient may not be able to interpret simple ideas and situations. For example, the person will not be able to explain easy proverbs. As the disease advances, inappropriate behavior patterns may exhibit, such as laughing at tragic moments. Personal hygiene may well be neglected, social conduct may become disorderly, a cautious businessperson may suddenly pursue a reckless business speculation, one who has been sexually restrained may become seductive, and the highly moral and ethical might start shoplifting. Language may or may not be affected. Sometimes, the person may actually become mute and not talk. (As we will see in Chap. 6, the ability to copy two-dimensional figures, assemble blocks, and arrange sticks will become impaired.) There may be an inability to recognize objects or carry out simple directions. Personality changes become apparent. Some may become quite apathetic, while others may develop more compulsive, theatrical, or paranoid tendencies, irritability, severe stubbornness, or severe anxieties.

In time, some demented persons may experience delusions about the dead, imagine them to be living in their bedroom, and carry on conversations with them. Persons in advanced stages of dementia will forget from one moment to the next all previous learned skills, from using a knife and fork to turning on a light switch. The afflicted person can no longer identify any objects, such as a car, house, chair, or dog, and their existence becomes reduced to the simplest form of life—like that of a one-cell organism that breathes, ingests, excretes, and responds to painful stimuli, but is no longer able to recognize, conclude, make judgments, discuss, understand, or see any relationship between objects. In short, the person becomes devoid of all human characteristics, except for their bodily features.

What, then, should the family expect of a physician when faced with these symptoms that I have mentioned? It is the responsibility of the family not to accept these symptoms as signs of aging. If the same symptoms occurred in a 35-year-old person, help would be sought. Likewise, the family must take the afflicted older person to a physician and ask for a thorough physical examination, including a neurological examination and a mental test. The diagnosis of depression, as well as that of many other illnesses, has to be excluded before the patient is saddled with the diagnosis of dementia. Every effort must be made to find a cause.

In the *Journal of the American Medical Association* of August 1982, in an article entitled, "Diagnostic Errors in Evaluation of Behavioral Disorders," Dr. Robert S. Hoffman emphasized to physicians the importance of neuropsychiatric consultations to minimize "diagnostic errors." Dr. Hoffman stressed that there should be three stages in the evaluation of a brain condition. First, a preliminary diagnosis, which he calls an informal diagnosis, should be made. Then, the confirmation of this diagnosis should be done by careful medical assessment, and, thirdly, there should be a search for a cause. He further suggests in his study results that too large a number of patients have been diagnosed as being senile, with perhaps as many as 65 percent of the diagnoses being erroneous.

The study was conducted in the following manner. Two-hundred and fifteen patients were admitted for a fifteen-month period to a psychiatric hospital. These patients were admitted to determine the causes of and the treatments for their mental changes. Many of the patients did not fit the psychiatric criteria in the *Diagnostic and Statistical Manual of Mental Disorders,* called *DSM-III.* This manual serves as a guide for the classification of mental illness in a uniform manner. It sets criteria for diagnosis of dementia or depression which all psychiatrists can agree upon. Forty-one percent of the patients, after thorough examination, finished the study with diagnoses different from the original. This report disclosed that a 40 to 80 percent incidence of serious medical illness was the cause for these behavioral symptoms. Another 15 percent of patients with the diagnosis of dementia were suffering from psychiatric disorders. Among the conclusions from this study was that "for a population of patients with a tentative diagnosis of dementia, one could estimate that thorough evaluation would yield treatable conditions in 63 percent."

These are exceptionally optimistic figures, and perhaps they should be even higher. Furthermore, almost 30 to 40 percent may have reversible causes for their cognitive abnormal functions. It is for this reason that family members must demand a thorough diagnostic examination of the person given the diagnosis of senility before relegating them to this category of brain loss. I hope that this book will disseminate, if nothing else, the urgency of this message of responsibility to all members of families in this situation. In the next chapter, I will discuss the pros and cons of mental testing in the diagnosis of brain impairment.

CHAPTER 6

Brain-Impairment Testing

The old man keeps all his mental powers so long as he gives up neither using them nor adding to them.

CICERO

There are no specific tests to determine whether early memory loss is a sign of brain degeneration, but mental status testing *is* helpful together with the entire clinical picture. We have blood tests to determine if one is suffering from diabetes, a heart attack, or even cancer, but there are no blood tests for mental impairment. The physician relies on his or her clinical training, experience, and best judgment to diagnose senility—what we used to call organic brain syndrome. Specialists, such as neurologists and psychologists, can administer mental status tests which are of some help in making the diagnosis. Depressed people may suffer from memory loss and can appear to have brain degeneration.

A mental-status examination needs to be performed to decide if a person is simply depressed. Neurologists advocate that any person between the ages of forty-five and sixty-five who becomes depressed, a state not clearly related to any obvious event such as the death of a spouse or a business reversal, should have the benefit of mental-status testing. The primary symptom of some patients who have severe brain disease is depression. Still other patients who have severe depression may only present with memory loss. A thorough twenty-five-minute initial interview during the mental-status evaluation can save many patients from misdiagnosis and incorrect treatment. A physician needs to differentiate between a confused patient, a depressed patient, and a mentally retarded patient. It's common to find that many patients who have a pathological or organic problem of the brain have been admitted into a psychiatric hospital. These mental status tests must be interpreted along with other aspects of the examination.

Mental status testing requires of the patient mental alertness, attentiveness, and the ability to understand and visualize. People who have impaired hearing, problems with their eyes, or, for that matter, language difficulties cannot be expected to perform well on these sophisticated tests.

Recently, I was attending a 90-year-old man who was suffering from congestive heart failure. Shortly after the patient was successfully treated, the medical intern commented on the medical chart that the patient had organic brain disease, that his brain was deteriorated from aging, and, that therefore he was senile, besides being deaf. I happened to stop by the patient's room at a time when members of the family were present. They were conversing with the old man in raised voices and in Italian. The patient was alert and joking with his family in his own language. The gentleman was *not* deaf at all; he merely did not know any English and could not satisfy the questioning put to him by the intern. He was only "senile" in his comprehension of English.

Intelligence tests are a type of mental status examination which became popular in both World War I and World War II and were used by the military to screen men and women who were entering the service. Their popularity led to the standardization of the intelligence quotient, or IQ. These tests were at first used to find out about the mental development of children. These tests also concluded that the peak of intelligence was reached at the age of 18, and might continue to rise somewhat thereafter, but starts to decline after the age of 25. It was determined that people over the age of 25 maintain their verbal ability, but performance tends to decline proportionately with age.

These original intelligence tests revealed information about verbal abilities, knowledge of general information, vocabulary, and social background. At that time many researchers believed that there was little distinction between mental aging and mental diseases.

The manner in which a mental status test is administered, the setting, and the time of day must all be considered by the physician before the testing begins, as the following case study illustrates:

After being involved in an almost fatal plane crash, one of my patients was concerned about whether he had any permanent mental aftereffects. He had suffered only minor injuries, but apparently had been knocked unconscious for a period of time, as he had little recollection of the impact of the crash. (As I will discuss later, among the complications of a near-death event are not only serious posttraumatic results, but also the simulation of symptoms of brain degeneration.) He voluntarily submitted to undergo a group of psychological tests.

The testing was done at the end of the day when he was markedly fatigued after seeing dozens of patients. Not only was he bored with the test, but he had difficulty in concentrating because he was anxious to go home to dinner. The tests were started at 6 P.M. and were completed at approximately 8 P.M. on three separate evenings. A psychologist administered the tests in a professional and encouraging manner. But his fatigue caused a lack of attentiveness. As he began to perform in a manner that he was not accustomed to, he became quite anxious and his performance got even worse. He realized that the test would be totally invalid but he continued, as he was curious to learn what these tests would show and what sort of conclusions would be made. He admitted to the doctor that he had had some difficulty in concentrating since the accident and was experiencing nightmares.

The first test given is called the digital repetition test. According to the standard, a person's level of attention can be assessed by the ability to repeat certain numbers. The psychologist began the test as follows: "I am going to say some simple numbers. Listen carefully, and, when I'm finished with each set, repeat the numbers after me."

37
749
8521
29683
571946
8159362
39825147
728546739

Each time he added one more number to the group.

The patient had difficulty in repeating more than six digits, which indicated a defect in attention. When he asked his wife to conduct this same test at eight o'clock the next morning, he was able to recite ten digits forwards and backwards! At that time of day, he was alert, and at ease, and in a more suitable setting than had been the case the night before.

The ability to recall numbers in this fashion is termed by psychologists "immediate recall," and does not require long-term storage of information. This task can be performed better with practice. For example, by grouping two or three numbers together and repeating them as a unit, performance will improve. Memorization is the association of new material with material that is already stored. For example, a digital sequence that is familiar, such as an old phone number or an address, is easily recalled. The most common cause of inability to perform well on the digital examination is just lack of attention. However, inattention may also be the result of diffuse brain disease, such as that found in early senility, anxiety, and depression.

If this short-term memory fails, the examiner must be cautious in interpreting other memory tests. It could be that the person has always had trouble in remembering numbers, and the problem may represent more of a matter of intelligence of concentration than one of brain degeneration. The inability to recall numbers may be seen in patients with diffuse brain injuries, for example, in patients who have gone through a period of oxygen deprivation after their hearts had stopped. (This subject will be discussed in more detail.)

The vigilance test is another test of concentration and requires at least a thirty-second attention span from the patient. The examiner reads a series of letters and he or she asks that whenever the letter "A" is heard, the subject should indicate this by tapping on the desk. A sequence may read "A I C T D A L A A" or "L K P A U C R D F J A B A A." Subjects who have a concentration problem may either fail to tap or continue tapping on the desk.

As part of a memory evaluation test, the patient will be asked certain specific questions regarding his or her own life. The answers to these questions need to be verifiable. For example, it makes no difference to ask the patient when he graduated from high school or what she ate for lunch if neither can be verified. Patients who have memory problems may deny that they have any problem at all and may start confabulating answers which will appear perfectly reasonable to the examiner. The examiner must also learn if the patient is aware of who and where he or she is. The following questions are usually asked:

1. **Personal information**
   a. Name: What is your name?
   b. Age: How old are you?
   c. Birthdate: When was your birthdate?
2. **Place**
   a. Present location: Where are we right now? What is the name of this place? What kind of place are we in now? What city are you in now?
   b. Past location: What is your home address?
3. **Time**
   a. Date: What is the date today? Year? Month? Day of the week?
   b. Time of day: What time is it right now?
   c. Season of the year: What season is it now?
   d. Time duration: How long have you been in the hospital? How long have you been walking?

The ability to recall long-stored events requires verification, and the typical questions which are asked are as follows:

1. Personal information:
   a. Where were you born?
2. School information:
   a. Where did you go to high school?
   b. Grade school?
3. Vocational history:
   a. What do you do for work?
   b. Where have you worked?
   c. When did you work at those places?
4. Family information:
   a. What is your spouse's name?
   b. Children's names?

    c. How old are your spouse and your children?

    d. What was your mother's maiden name?

5. Historical past:

    a. Name four presidents since 1940.

    b. The name of the last war in which the United States was directly involved?

After having completed these questions, the examiner has a fair idea about the patient's orientation to time, place, and self.

It is also essential to determine if the patient can learn new material. Patients with brain impairment are unable to learn new material because they cannot understand the subject and so are unable to retain it. In this test, called a mental status examination, recognition and registration of the initial sensory input and storage information recall and retrieval are all needed. This involves the entire memory system.

The test is conducted in the following way: The examiner says: "I'm going to tell you four words which I would like you to remember, and, in a few minutes, I will ask you to recall these words." It is important that the patient hear the four words and is able to repeat them. The examiner then asks in ten and in thirty minutes for the words to be repeated. As a rule, the unaffected person who has a full attention span is able to accurately recall the four words after a ten-minute delay. During this ten-minute delay, other questions may be asked, such as word meanings and proverbs. After a thirty-minute delay, three of the four words should be recalled. Poor performance on this test reflects a deficiency in the abilities to learn and recall new material over a span of time.

Another test that is sometimes used for immediate recall is the examiner's reading the patient a short paragraph and then asking the patient to recall as many events as possible. This test requires attention and vigilance. A short story that contains, for example, fifteen or more different items is read, and the average patient should be expected to produce at least eight of those items on immediate recall. For example: "George Stern, a 42-year-old state senator from Burton County, Kansas, was planning a trip to Oregon when he experienced some chest pain. He entered the George Wilson Hospital for five days of medical tests. All his medical tests were normal, and he, his wife, Sandra, and his two sons, Harry and George Jr., went hunting together."

There are many more tests used in psychiatric testing: These have only been a few examples. Some of the tests performed can result in the physician's practically locating the part of the brain that is injured.

Most of the psychological tests, even though adjusted for age, are still based on a time element. The speed that the person responds is of utmost importance. The very fact that a time element is placed on the test in itself creates for the subject a great deal of anxiety. If the same test were given without a time limit, the paragraphs could be read and reread at leisure, questions could be slowly and carefully considered, and the performance rate would increase.

In a study by Dr. Robert Kestenbaum at Britain's Winsted University, thirty-one students between the ages of eighteen and twenty-one were involved in an experiment. Each subject had to rebuild a mock village that was destroyed by war and was given two sets of cards, one describing jobs that needed to be done, and the other describing the people available to do this job. The job had to suit the individual in terms of experience and preference. Each student was allowed five minutes to match a job with a manpower index. A bell signalled when it was time to go on to the next job. As the time grew short and they began to feel pressured, the students were found to become angry and frustrated, and some were actually unable to make any more decisions. The purpose of the study was to show that the same mechanism occurs in younger as well as in older people. If the test described were administered to the millions of American people, it would be found that the performances would be mediocre to poor for all if given in a particularly tense setting.

In western society, the idea of speed is essential—time is money. Everything has to be done as quickly as possible which is not necessarily the best method. There are few situations in our everyday lives when speed *is* essential, seen perhaps only in the hectic schedules of airplane pilots at the controls or in those of astronauts, athletes, and surgeons, where decision-making requires speed. Most activities that I know of which are performed in a carefully thought-out manner end with better results. Craftspeople, artists, musicians, and writers will perform better and more precisely if they are not distracted with the pressures of timing and speed.

One of the reasons for defects in recall and memory in the test among the older age group is the necessity of speed. Older people are usually more cautious in performing a task. Reading and interpretation is slower because the words have more meaning and are more loaded than they were at the age of twenty. Older people are often not given the opportunity to work out a task by younger people around them. For example, I so often hear my children say to their grandmother, "I will do that for you." They don't have the patience to wait for her to do the task.

The pressures of test-taking with speed and limited time begin in our earliest days when we take our IQ tests and SATs. We have become so dissatisfied with our speed of memory storage and recall that we have now moved beyond to the capabilities of the computer age. However, the computer is not improving our abilities for memory storage and recall. Simple tasks are being taken away gradually by the computer—such tasks as doing our checkbooks and our banking accounts and other procedures that we would ordinarily store in our brains. If the problem of memory loss is severe today, it will become even worse in the future if we allow the computer to take over and don't give our brains a chance to operate. Speed interferes with good performance, and, as a result, motivation and interest decline because of frustration, as demonstrated in the Kestenbaum study of the college students.

The Weschler-Bellevue intelligence scale, which was developed in 1955, inadvertently contributed to making the older patient seem an inferior mental individual. These tests concluded that there is a decline of intelligence in people beyond the age of sixty-five. They also came to the erroneous conclusion that intelligence in young adults reaches a certain plateau during their twenties and thirties, and then a decline occurs at the age of forty. Now that science had a firm conviction that intelligence declines with age, it gave license to the business and academic worlds to send individuals over age sixty-five to the retirement pastures.

Fortunately, science is always in the process of challenging concepts that have been adhered to for generations. Unfortunately, this process sometimes takes much longer than it should.

Today, the Wechsler Adult Intelligence Scale, a revised version of the original, is recognized as the standard measure of intelligence when time, one to five hours, allows its use. This test evaluates five areas:

1. Social information: i.e., What is the capital of Italy?
2. Comprehension: Why should people follow the law?
3. Simple arithmetic: A man with $10 spends $5; how much does he have left?
4. Similarities: In what way are air and water alike? Vocabulary, verbal definitions, and digital repetition.
5. Nonverbal performances: Block design construction and re-producing a pictorial design.

There is also the Wechsler Memory Scale. This is a relatively brief memory battery for clinical use. Example: In what year were you born? Who is the governor of your state?

Orientation to time and place: What is the month? What is the name of the place?

It tests memory control, for example, counting backwards from twenty to one and counting by groups of three.

Logical memory is tested by the immediate recall of a paragraph read aloud by the examiner, digital repetition backwards and for-wards, and visual memory, paper and pencil reproduction of simple designs.

Above all, these two tests must be conducted within a set period of time.

Psychologists Balts and Schaie who challenged the concept of declining intelligence. In the *Journal of Psychology*, their 1974 article, entitled "The Myth of Twilight Years," described the cri-teria and results of their own study. They found that older people increase in intelligence, in particular in verbal and numerical skills and in reasoning. Older persons tend to be more discriminating when answering a question, and the factor of speed again was one of the major drawbacks as discussed before. When a decline in intelligence was evident, it was caused by factors other than aging. Some of the reasons, which will be discussed in greater detail, include medications and certain illnesses, such as hypertension. It was found that those patients who have mildly elevated blood pres-sures exhibited a general decline in intelligence scores; hypertension, being associated with changes in the blood vessels, is considered the reason for this decline. The better one's health, the less the chance of a decline in intelligence. This study also demonstrated that people with higher intelligence live longer.

Another hypothesis which has permeated the field of psychology, with which I disagree, is that a dramatic drop in intelligence scores in an aging person indicates that death will occur in five years. In 1961, Dr. Robert Kleemeier coined the phrase "terminal drop" in a study of thirteen older people. Subjects were tested every two or three years for a twelve-year period. Those four who died shortly after the study was instituted demonstrated the greatest decline in intelligence from the beginning of the study. In Germany, the husband-and-wife team of Klaus and Ruth Reigel administered IQ tests to 380 men and women through the years of 1956, 1961, and 1966. They found that the individuals who exhibited the greatest decline in intelligence were the ones who were most likely to die. Happily, those tested individuals were not informed of these dreadful speculations.

If there is a predeath decline in intelligence, in my opinion, it is due undoubtedly to either an undiagnosed illness, an overtreated condition with improper medications, or perhaps to a lack of treatment at all. A person who is suffering from an illness cannot function properly, whether it be physically or mentally. If you have a bad head cold, for example, it is probably only through an extraordinary effort that you can accomplish any kind of high-task performance.

Some illnesses may manifest themselves for weeks and months by a single symptom such as apathy, fatigue, depression, or loss of concentration or memory loss. Any practicing physician can tell you of patients that he or she has seen who have complained of such symptoms without any physical findings. It is only later that an illness is diagnosed in these patients.

Later, I will discuss the role of slow-acting viruses (whose incubation periods last for years) which may be one of the causes of brain degeneration in such conditions as Alzheimer's disease.

CHAPTER **7**

Pressure Problems as a
Cause of Mental Impairment

*And so, from hour to hour we ripe and ripe, And
then, from hour to hour we rot and rot; And thereby
hangs a tale.*

WILLIAM SHAKESPEARE (*As You Like It*)

Atherosclerosis as a Cause of Mental Impairment

Just as senility was once regarded as an inevitable consequence of
aging, a similar myth exists today that atherosclerosis results from
aging. Five or more years ago, older patients who were confused
and disoriented with failing memories were automatically diagnosed as suffering atherosclerosis of the brain.

The term "arteriosclerosis" is commonly called hardening of the
arteries. This is a term which implies that the artery becomes thick
and hard and loses its elasticity. Atherosclerosis is a form of arteriosclerosis in which the layers of the artery become thickened and
irregular by deposits of cholesterol. These deposits, called ather-
omas, narrow the arteries and impede the flow of blood, which
then results in the symptom of chest pain, or angina pectoris, and
eventually can lead to a heart attack. Throughout this chapter and
book, I shall use the term "atherosclerosis" in referring to cholesterol.

In its most severe form, atherosclerosis of the brain causes it to look like cottage cheese and, in some patients, results in dementia and strokes; in others, there are no effects. Scientists have reported that the autopsied brain of Winston Churchill looked like "cream cheese" due to atherosclerosis, yet, his mind was sharp until almost the very end of his life.

It is not really known how many patients suffering from brain failure are affected with atherosclerosis. This is a diagnosis made at the autopsy table and can be deducted only from other findings (to be discussed later). Most people who suffer from progressive, severe atherosclerosis will show signs of it, either in the form of heart disease, kidney failure, or brain impairment. The term "lacunar infarcts" is used to describe the condition in which the brain arteries become clogged by cholesterol plaques, resulting in the dissolution of brain tissue.

What is this vicious villain called atherosclerosis, the primary killer in the United States?

The arterial wall is a busy metabolic factory, making its own cholesterol and other substances, and normally barring the cholesterol from accumulating on its surface. Then, for some reason yet to be learned, the barrier sometimes breaks down and cholesterol begins to accumulate. In susceptible persons, mostly over age twenty, the intima and the media (the inner and middle layers of arterial tissue) may become packed with cholesterol.

The normal aging artery is associated with thickening and some narrowing of the intima with minimal cholesterol deposits occurring in a diffuse way, called "diffuse arterial changes of the old." The earliest signs of atherosclerosis consist of fatty yellow streaks on the intima. This change is already seen by the age of fifteen. It may progress to the formation of plaques, the real culprit in atherosclerosis. Plaques consist of cholesterol and other tissues piled up like a small anthill. These plaques can form in the arteries of the brain or in the coronary arteries supplying the heart; the larger arteries of the blood, known as platelets, stick to the plaque, forming clots or thrombi. In time, the artery becomes blocked to such an extent that just a trickle of blood gets through until finally the blood flow ceases.

Atherosclerosis is more prevalent in the industrialized nations. The seven countries which have the highest death rate from atherosclerosis are, in descending order:

1. Finland
2. the United States
3. Scotland
4. Northern Ireland
5. Australia
6. New Zealand
7. Canada

The lowest death rates from atherosclerosis occur in Latin America and in Japan.

There are many cultural differences in dietary patterns among these nations which affect the total fat caloric intake of their citizens. In countries such as India, Brazil, Greece, and the nations of the Caribbean Islands, diets are full of vegetables which are substituted for meats, with a marked absence of fatty food intake. Finland has the highest atherosclerosis rate on record; the diet of the Finns often includes pure fat sandwiches for lunch. A university study was conducted at Stuax in Helsinki in the 1950s which demonstrated that controlling the fat in the diet changed the cholesterol level.

Further evidence of the relationship between cholesterol and heart disease was found in victims in World War II concentration camps who died of starvation and other illnesses. Some of these individuals were autopsied and found to have hardly any evidence of atherosclerosis. Similarly, autopsy studies performed on young soldiers killed in the Korean and Vietnam wars disclosed that 77 percent of these American soldiers, whose average age was twenty-two, showed signs of gross coronary atherosclerosis as compared to 10 percent of the Vietnamese men.

Who is prone to atherosclerosis of the brain? Scientists now answer this question by measuring the lipids in the blood. The lipids which are measured consist of the cholesterol, the triglycerides, the high-density lipoproteins, and the low-density lipoproteins. The higher the serum cholesterol, the greater is the incidence and the risk of developing atherosclerosis.

Cholesterol was discovered by the French chemist Poulletier de la Salle, who was the first to purify this greasy yellow substance.

Cholesterol is essential for life, for the formation of such hormones as estrogens and androgens. It is a building block for cell membranes, the principal ingredient in digestive juices, and the sheath that surrounds nerves. Most of the cholesterol in our bodies is produced by the liver, while 20 to 30 percent generally comes from the food that we eat.

Numerous studies have demonstrated that the incidence of atherosclerosis involving the heart and brain increases as the blood cholesterol rises up to 260 mg. (The normal level is below 220 mg.) Patients between the ages of thirty and forty-nine who have cholesterol levels greater than 260 mg. have three to five times more of a chance of developing arterial clots which may result in heart attacks and strokes than do individuals with lower cholesterol levels.

The level of cholesterol in the blood is related not only to dietary ingestion, but also to genetic factors, the level of physical activity, and, if present, obesity. (Cholesterol measurements should be made after the patient has fasted for at least sixteen hours.)

Controversy has been raging for years over whether altering the cholesterol in our diet will decrease the amount of atherosclerosis in our bodies. From a ten-year study conducted by the National Heart, Lung, and Blood Institute on 3806 men between the ages of thirty-five and fifty-nine, it was concluded that if cholesterol levels could be dropped 10 to 15 percent the death rate from heart attacks would decrease by 20 to 30 percent in the United States.

Dr. Charles Blueck, director of the University of Cincinnati Lipid Research Center which was one of the twelve centers included in the project, stated that ". . . for every 1 percent reduction in the total cholesterol level, there is a 25 percent reduction of heart disease risk."

I am of the opinion that atherosclerosis of the brain and subsequent dementia can be reduced or averted if our cholesterol intake is markedly reduced. The average individual's serum cholesterol in the United States is 220 mg. If we can reduce blood cholesterol to 150 mg., perhaps we can prevent atherosclerosis. A diet containing 200 mg. of cholesterol or less *is* difficult to ask anyone to adhere to. It is practically a vegetarian diet, and there is no guarantee that it will prevent atherosclerosis. I do recommend that patients with elevated cholesterol levels make a serious attempt to reduce their cholesterol intake, especially if there is evidence of diseased blood vessels. Animal experiments have already demonstrated that drastic lowering of cholesterol can reverse cholesterol deposits. Below, on pp. 100–101. is a table compiled from the U.S. Department of Agriculture that lists the amounts of cholesterol in different foods.

Progression of arteriosclerosis can be arrested and may even be reversed. There are other important factors that catalyze atherosclerosis of the brain. It has been known for years that high blood pressure is a major factor in the acceleration of atherosclerosis and can result in a stroke. The Framingham study, an eighteen-year study conducted by W. B. Kannel, reported in the *American Journal of Cardiology* in 1976, determined that middle-aged men with blood pressure readings above 160/95 were more than five times more prone to have cerebral disease than were middle-aged men with lower readings. Hypertension increases atherosclerosis throughout life. If the blood pressure is reduced, the incidence of strokes and atherosclerosic dementia is reduced. According to the National Center of Health Statistics, 20 percent of white Americans age fifty or older have hypertension.

The blood pressure reading is composed of two numbers—the upper (the systolic reading) and the lower (the diastolic reading). The systolic blood pressure is generated by the force of the blood leaving the heart. The diastolic figure refers to the resistance of flow through the blood vessels. The stiffer the blood vessels are, the higher the diastolic pressure will be.

Most scientists agree that the lower the blood pressure readings, the less likelihood there is for heart disease and strokes. An ideal blood pressure would be around 110/70. Sustained elevations of the blood pressure cause a constant pounding of forces against the arteries of the brain, eventually leading to increased atherosclerosis. In many cases it leads to hemorrhages, clots, brain softening, and, in some cases, dementia.

The previously popular concept that a high systolic blood pressure, for example, in the vicinity of 180, is beneficial to the patient as it aids the pushing of the blood through the pipestem arteries is nonsense. The disinclination of the physician to lowering the elevated systolic pressures in the elderly needs to be examined. Strokes and brain injury are most likely to occur in a patient over age sixty-five whose systolic pressure is above 180.

One of the major causes of hypertension is the overabundance of salt in our diet. There is indisputable evidence of a causal relationship between the amount of salt consumed by a population and the incidence of its hypertension. A high rate of hypertension leads to more strokes and more dementia. In the United States, the average adult consumes approximately 2 to 2½ teaspoons a day, or more than twenty times the amount of salt that the body actually needs. Salt is the catalyst of hypertension in the same manner that cholesterol is that of atherosclerosis. The elimination of the "crystal demon," as some writers term salt, would undoubtedly decrease the incidence of hypertension. (Very recent studies, however, question the role of salt in hypertension, even suggesting that additional salt may be beneficial in that it results in an increased production of calcium. We know that a lack of calcium is detrimental, but few physicians are ready to change their minds about the dangers of salt until much more concrete and complete evidence to the contrary is available.)

Japan is a country whose citizens consume an enormous amount of salt, perhaps the highest, per capita, in the world. In some villages, 40 percent of residents have high blood pressure—and Japan's leading cause of death is stroke. In northern agricultural centers of Japan, salt is used as a preservative. The average individual's intake per day might be six teaspoons or more. Japanese diets consist primarily of fish, pickled vegetables, and soy sauce, inordinately high in salt. Tribal members in New Guinea, the Amazon areas, and the highlands of Malaysia all eat very little salt, and hypertension is unheard of in these areas.

Other factors which contribute to cerebral atherosclerosis are cigarette smoking, obesity, diabetes, and lack of exercise.

Atherosclerosis causes dementia, mostly in males, and has been found in 10 to 15 percent of autopsied demented patients. Sometimes, the pathologies of Alzheimer's disease and atherosclerosis are found together. It takes many infarctions of the brain (destruction and necrosis of cells) before dementia results. When present, clinicians call this condition multi-infarction dementia (MID).

Atherosclerosis is a progressive illness which, in its early stages, can perhaps be reversed with control of hypertension, strict low-cholesterol diet, cessation of smoking, and weight reduction.

Little Stroke

The number of cerebrovascular accidents, or strokes, in the United States has decreased by 25 to 40 percent in the past twenty years, attributed primarily to the control of hypertension. It is not known if the number of "little strokes" has equally decreased. The medical term for little strokes is called transient ischemic attacks, or TIAs. These result from a temporary decrease in the flow of blood to the different parts of the brain. Some loss of motor ability occurs which may last from several minutes to a day and which then disappears entirely. The major cause of little strokes is atherosclerosis of the arteries supplying the brain. Other causes include episodes of irregular heartbeats, episodes of low blood pressure, and brain tumors.

Certain Presidents of the United States suffered little strokes during crucial times of decision-making. President Franklin D. Roosevelt was reported to have had sustained episodes of stroke during the last year of his life. The Yalta conference, held on February 12, 1945, was attended by "the big three"—Winston Churchill, Franklin D. Roosevelt, and Joseph Stalin—who negotiated the partitioning of Europe. President Roosevelt allegedly had episodes of TIAs during this conference, which might well have affected his judgment and strength, and we can only conjecture how the outcome of the conference would have differed if a healthy President had conducted our negotiations. President Woodrow Wilson, likewise, was known to have had episodes of forgetfulness and TIAs while negotiating the Treaty of Versailles.

Little strokes or TIAs can manifest as inconsequential symptoms which, at times, may even be ignored by the patient; at other times, these episodes can cause great alarm.

The location of the artery of the brain which is narrowed will determine the type of symptoms that occur. The arteries of the neck (the internal carotid arteries) supply blood to the cerebral hemispheres, and a branch goes to the artery of the eye. If the carotid arteries are critically narrowed by an atherosclerotic plaque and part of this plaque breaks off and travels to the brain, the patient may complain of a fleeting moment or two of sudden loss of vision in one eye. Doctors refer to this condition as "amaurosis fugax." Patients liken it to the experience of having a blanket suddenly fall in front of the eye. These episodes may repeat themselves several times a day. Other symptoms include brief flashes of numbness in the face and arms or sudden weakness of an arm or leg with the inability to move. It is a frightening experience, almost like being caught in a terrible nightmare and then awakening to find that the nightmare continues. Between these attacks, the patient is perfectly fine. Repeated episodes of TIA may cause MID and can lead to dementia.

The diagnosis of narrowing of the carotid artery can be suspected through the use of the stethoscope if a murmur is heard over the carotid artery in the middle or upper portion of the neck. Further sophisticated testing methods consist of digital subtraction, which is an x-ray picture taken of the artery by use of a dye and a computer. A catheter is placed into the vein of the arm and a dye is injected. The flow of the dye is traced with a computer and an image is taken. The most up-to-date technique in use today is a simple sonar examination of the carotid arteries, using a sound transmission instrument called a Doppler, which measures the flow of blood through the arteries.

Traditionally, an x-ray of the arteries, or arteriogram, of the carotids was taken by placing a tube inside the artery. Included in the diagnostic evaluation for the symptoms is an EEG and a CT scan of the brain. A CT scan of the brain is performed because a percentage of patients with TIAs may be harboring a brain tumor. Patients suffering from TIAs also need a thorough cardiac diagnostic work-up because many have associated hardening of the arteries to the heart. The cause of death in TIAs is usually myocardial infarction (heart attack).

It was discovered from a 1978 study at the Mayo Clinic that one-third of patients with TIAs will suffer a stroke within five years. Twenty percent will do so within one month of the initial attack, and 50 percent within one year. These patients should be carefully monitored by the doctors.

Basilar Artery Little Strokes

The artery at the base of the brain, called the basilar artery, furnishes much of the brainstem with the emerging cranial nerves that supply the ear, the face, and the different lobes of the brain. Patients with basilar artery atherosclerosis will typically complain of vertigo and nausea. Vertigo, or dizziness, is not to be confused with feelings of lightheadedness, giddiness, and anxiety, which are not manifestations of TIAs. Instead, vertigo is a feeling of turning around in space or that everything around one is revolving. The symptom is sometimes associated with vomiting. Patients will also complain of tingling sensations around their mouths and of difficulty in pronouncing words; sometimes there will be swallowing problems. If the entire blood flow through the artery is interrupted, the patient may have a brief loss of consciousness or episodes of falling. There may occur a loss of equilibrium, staggering, and behavior which mimics inebriation. Sometimes patients are not able to walk at all. Many of these symptoms, it should be understood, may be caused by a simple infection of the inner ear (labyrinthitis) and have nothing to do with circulatory problems.

Little strokes may possibly be playing a much more important part in memory loss than is appreciated, especially if the circulation involves the hippocampus, the seat of memory.

According to autopsy studies, the number of demented patients suffering from vascular disease of the brain has been cited to be in the vicinity of between 10 to 15 percent. The percentage may be much higher, but most patients are not autopsied, and, if an autopsy is performed, the brain examination is generally omitted.

Silent heart attacks are a well-known condition and are found either by an abnormal electrocardiogram or on the autopsy table. Silent brain destruction can result from multiple small strokes.

Symptoms of Multi-Infarction Dementia

There is general agreement among pathologists that the MID syndrome (brain-cell destruction from vascular causes) results from atherosclerosis of the blood vessels outside the brain (in the carotid artery and the basilar artery). This type of mental impairment is different from Alzheimer's disease. The MID symptoms may appear suddenly with a variably fluctuating course—at one moment progressive, and, at the next, there may be a complete disappearance of all the symptoms.

A patient who is suffering from MID may have his or her symptomatology peak between ages forty and sixty—it follows along the lines of coronary artery disease and atherosclerosis of the arteries of the lower legs (peripheral vascular disease). If the physician finds the pulses diminished or absent and coupled with memory loss, MID is suggested. The pathology of MID is described generally as irregular areas of brain softening. The majority of patients with such brain-cell destruction have had a history of TIAs and hypertension.

In Chap. 2, two types of memory loss were distinguished, short- and long-term memory. If the onset of MID is abrupt, especially after one sustains a stroke, the memory loss will involve suddenly forgetting the names of well-known persons, such as the President of the United States and members of the family, and names of towns, countries, places, and objects seen every day, such as trees and familiar flowers.

Most people have a certain degree of absentmindedness all their lives. Entering a room and forgetting the reason why one went there in the first place is a common happening in most people; yet, it may also be an early sign of brain impairment, just as forgetting telephone numbers, addresses, and the location of a restaurant may be signs as well. (Noncomprehension of a paragraph after it has been read is probably more common today than ever before, probably because people are reading less than ever before.)

The person with early MID may, one morning, not recall the name of his or her secretary, forget all the appointments of the day, and, the following morning, be entirely normal again. The person may not be aware of the fact that he or she is having some memory loss until someone brings it to his or her attention. Unfortunately, physicians often do not include a mental-testing status when they examine a patient, and so the diagnosis of early brain failure is usually missed.

The earliest signs of MID may be the inability to remember names or forgetting where one has put an object. Some people are able to remember the names of people whom they have just met, but forget things which were stored in the brain long ago. A person may not be aware of a deficit occurring because it may be indeed insignificant. For example, a physician friend of mine who sees almost twenty patients a day was asked to recall their names. He hesitated and was unable to mention more than four. He quickly added that if he saw their charts, he would immediately identify them with their appropriate faces. When I brought it to his attention that he had only recently doubled the number of his patients and was therefore understandably preoccupied, he realized that this was not a question of memory loss (this physician, by the way, is all of thirty-five years of age!).

Searching for one's car keys or glasses may be an early symptom, but, on the other hand, most people will admit that they, at times, cannot remember where they have placed an object. During periods of anxiety, we may actually forget where we put certain things that are important to us. Psychological testing of patients is also fraught with difficulties; an anxiety component may be so enormous that it might not be possible to perform an accurate test.

These are nonspecific changes and are not characteristic of multi-infarction dementia, except that the periods of forgetfulness may alternate with periods of extraordinary lucidity in this condition.

As times goes on, appointments are forgotten more often. Persons who have had very good comprehension of what they read suddenly find that when they finish an article, they have difficulty remembering its name and what they have read. Similarly, after attending a play, they find that the name and plot of the play fade quickly from the memory.

A striking example of memory loss resulting from multi-infarction dementia occurred recently during a visit to Vermont. The mother of one of my friends, who has known me since I was a child, did not recognize me. As soon as my name was mentioned, she lit up like an electric bulb and launched into a train of remembrances about me, becoming quite jovial. Several hours later, she asked her son who I was, and, as soon as my name was mentioned again, she again went through the entire exhilaration of all the years of having known me. In the course of our conversation, she said: "You see, that's what has been happening to me in the past three months. I remember something perfectly, and the next minute I don't remember a thing. That used to happen to me once in a while, every couple of months, but now it seems to happen more often." She was suffering from MID that had rapidly advanced to an irreversible state, which the family had unknowingly attributed to "getting older." In fact, she was probably having continual multiple small strokes which were destroying her brain.

Sometimes, signs of the brain failure in multi-infarction dementia may appear suddenly, after a traumatic event such as the death or illness of a spouse, or after delayed recovery from an operation which required confinement to a hospital for a long time. When the deterioration continues on to complete dementia, it is indistinguishable from other forms of dementia, such as Alzheimer's disease.

Confusion, an early sign of brain-cell destruction, may manifest itself by when patients repeat themselves in actions or while in conversation. During these early phases, patients function rather well and compensate for their mental deficits by writing things down, allowing more time to arrive at appointments, and avoiding conversations which require recall and interpretation. Most patients are aware of what is happening and suffer this heinous creeping disability in silence. Others ascribe it to a "normal" condition of aging.

Depression is present in all forms of dementia but is particularly common in multi-infarction dementia. The patients' families will bring them to the physician, stating that they have suddenly become depressed after the death of a spouse. Or elderly persons may be brought in by the family, complaining of loss of appetite, progressive weight loss, fatigue, and insomnia. A physician may prescribe a sleeping pill, which will compound the problem and make the patients even more fatigued and depressed.

A woman with MID often appears thin and unkempt, with evidence of weight loss. The physician may conduct a scrupulous search for cancer through multiple blood tests and x-rays. The observant family will tell the physician that the problem involves a recent onset of depression, loss of concentration, periods of disorientation, and memory loss. This last symptom is commonly not reported to the physician!

Stella was a hard-nosed Yankee who had raised three sons and had kept a stronghold on the family pocketbook. Her husband had died at the age of sixty-seven. She had a circle of widowed friends, who were in about the same economic bracket as she, living in a smart section of a New England town in homes that boasted of eligibility for consideration as historical landmarks. Now, at the age of seventy-four, she admitted to having periods of dizzy spells which were brief and which occurred either when she was quietly sitting and reading the newspaper, or, sometimes, while watching television. She had diagnosed herself as having eye problems and would periodically seek optometric attention to have the prescription of her glasses changed.

One morning, she awoke feeling depressed. She had no desire to make her breakfast or, for that matter, to shower or comb her hair, and she spent the rest of the day just sitting quietly in an armchair. She did not make her usual morning telephone call to check on her friend Gertrude, nor did she stroll down her long wooded driveway to the mailbox for the morning paper. It was too much of an effort for her to cook, no less to shop, as she usually did each day in her station wagon. When her daughters came to visit her several weeks later, they found a changed, disheveled woman and brought her to the family physician.

All her tests were normal, including the CT scans of her body. Her brain showed mild atrophy, as would be common at the age of seventy-four. She complained of dizzy spells, of general inattentiveness, and of having completely lost track of current everyday matters. Her family physician referred her to a neurologist. A complete physical examination revealed that the pulses of her legs were markedly diminished. The eye examination revealed that she had severe atherosclerosis involving her retina and that the carotid arteries leading to her brain were narrowed. On this basis, the diagnosis of multi-infarction dementia due to little strokes was made. After she was thoroughly questioned, it was discovered that she had experienced episodes of numbness around her mouth and occasionally had difficulty in swallowing (signs of basilar artery TIA). There were also signs of early brain failure.

After antidepressant medicine was prescribed, her appetite returned and her sleep disturbance disappeared. However, the last five years of this patient's life were punctuated by long periods of confusion, with inability to recognize her surroundings alternating with lucid moments. Her family gave her a great deal of emotional support on a daily basis, surrounding her with her friends and allowing her to continue living in her own home. She could afford full-time help, so she was not relegated to a nursing home. With guidance from her physician, the family came to understand the nature of her illness and made her life as tolerable as possible. Unfortunately, once severe advanced atherosclerosis set in, they could aim only to make her comfortable. In these advanced patients every effort should be made to give proper nutrition as discussed earlier, adequate vitamins, and ample fluid, and to avoid or treat infections promptly. Nutrition should be at its best, and ample fluid intake and good control of high blood pressure may slow down the inevitable process of decline.

Several years later, the patient sustained a massive stroke and died shortly thereafter. An autopsy of the brain revealed multiple areas of brain softening and severe generalized atherosclerosis involving the arteries of the heart and the abdomen.

This story illustrates that sometimes the onset of multi-infarction dementia can at first be marked by severe depression and recurrent episodes of dizzy spells. This unfortunate woman's illness could not be reversed, but, in the next example, another form of repeated TIA will be described whose early mental changes were reversible.

Howard was a 48-year-old successful lawyer who decided to take up jogging. He did not consult a physician, but, instead, simply bought some running shoes and books on the subject and started off. Each morning at dawn, he started to jog, and, over a period of time, he gradually increased his distance and speed. At the end of three months, he was running five miles per day and a nine-minute mile, his weight was reduced, and he had a youthful, vigorous appearance. His running accomplishments gave him so much confidence that he decided to enter a marathon.

As he increased his speed while training for the race, he found that he experienced an exhilarating "high" and a feeling of freedom that he had never before experienced, coupled, however, with lightheadedness. After running, he would return home and shower, but his lightheadedness always continued until after he ate breakfast. Although it increased in severity, he regarded it as a salutary effect of a good jog. Besides the usual ache and pains of ankle, knee, and back, he noticed that when his day at the office became hectic and pressured, the same type of lightheadedness occurred, sometimes causing him some minor confusion and forgetfulness.

One morning after a vigorous jog, he was late for an appointment, rushed into the office, and, for an instant, forgot the name of his secretary. He decided that for some reason he had simply "blocked out her name."

He fasted for forty-eight hours before the marathon, and then he ate an abundance of sweets since he had read that sugar increases one's strength and vigor in the final push of the race. He had no expectations of winning but wished only to finish the ten-mile mini-marathon in respectable time. At the end of the seventh mile, he increased his pace. He ran as fast as his legs would carry him and again got a sense of an "exhilarating high," except that this time he also lost his sense of direction. He perspired profusely, felt his heart beating rapidly, and then he suddenly collapsed. He lay unconscious for several minutes, and, when he awoke, was suffering complete amnesia about where he was and was even unable to give his name. The paramedics quickly examined him and found that his blood pressure was 280/138. In the emergency room, he was treated vigorously with intravenous fluids and medication to lower his dangerously high blood pressure.

During several days of hospitalization, a cardiologist and a neurologist were in attendance. It was discovered that during the past six months, ever since he had started jogging, he had experienced periods of confusion and disorientation and was having difficulties doing simple calculations. Several of his checks had bounced because he had improperly calculated his deposits.

A brain-wave test and a CT scan were performed, all of which were within normal limits. The conclusion of the cardiologist was that Howard had had episodes of severe hypertension which possibly may have caused tiny bleeding into his brain, contributing to the episodes of forgetfulness and confusion. (Repeated severe elevation of blood pressure can cause tiny bleeding into the brain, and, on occasion, can actually lead to hemorrhage of the brain and a stroke.) With blood pressure medications, all his symptoms disappeared entirely. After he underwent several exercise-stress tests to determine at what level he could safely jog without a serious rise in his blood pressure, he was advised to jog slowly for only one mile per day. He is now doing well.

A 62-year-old ardent tennis player, while playing a tough game of singles on a hot, sunny morning, began to experience numbness on the left side of his face and left arm and to suffer dizzy spells. Being a proud and formidible man, he would, under no circumstances, let his opponent know of his discomforts and so he continued to play. After the first set, he sat down, drank some water, and felt better. Since he had always suffered from a cervical neck problem, he interpreted the numbness as arising from a pinched nerve, and merely attributed the dizziness to the extreme heat.

He continued to play tennis throughout the summer, suffering the same symptoms. He was afraid to consult a physician, because he thought he would certainly be advised to stop playing tennis. He was quoted many times as saying, "If I'm going to drop dead, I'd rather drop dead playing tennis than doing anything else."

Five weeks after his symptoms had started, he was again playing tennis, and, in the third game of the first set, an argument ensued:

"It's 40-love," his opponent said.

"No, it can't be! It's deuce!"

A compromise was reached, but he again lost track not only of the score but also of who was serving the ball. This continued for the remainder of the set.

"I don't know what's wrong with you, Tom. I think you're getting senile," his opponent laughed. "Maybe you're getting Alzheimer's disease. I'm not going to play with you if you're going to keep arguing about the score."

Tom began to realize that he definitely had problems with his memory, along with the numbness in his arm. The memory loss was short-term, and it carried through to other daily activities. His wife noticed his problem on various occasions such as the time when he began to insist that she never told him of a dinner party to which friends had invited him.

"I told you we have a dinner tonight."

"No, you didn't! You never told me! I would have remembered it."

His doctor took a thorough history, performed a physical examination, and found Tom's blood pressure to be a satisfactory 130/70 and his pulse to be a normal 75 beats per minute. His heart sounds were also normal, and there were no murmurs. A neurological examination was also entirely normal. When the doctor listened to the arteries in the neck, he was surprised to hear a loud grating sound which is called a bruit. When he examined the back of Tom's eyes with an opthalmoscope, he found the presence of plaques.

The clinical story and the physical findings fit the picture perfectly of a case of narrowing carotid artery atherosclerosis. In order to confirm suspicions, a CT scan was taken. This revealed that the brain was within normal limits, but a specialized test, an arterial digital subtraction, disclosed that the right coronary artery was markedly narrowed. Since there is a strong association between atherosclerosis of both the carotid arteries and of the arteries of the heart, a stress test which turned out to be normal, was also included in the examination. Tom told the doctor that several members of his family had died of strokes and heart disease. A choice was given to him: either he could take several aspirins every day to prevent the clot from breaking off and traveling to the artery, or the plaque would have to be removed surgically (a procedure known as endarterectomy), obviously a much more drastic step than aspirin therapy. He sought a second opinion. Because Tom was in such excellent physical condition, it was the consensus that surgery should be performed. Prior to surgery, a more precise examination, called an arteriogram, was done. Dye was injected into the artery, and the examination verified the findings of the physician. The complications of surgery were outlined to Tom: there was a small risk of death from the operation (about 1 percent, and also there was a 3 percent chance or so of suffering a stroke (a piece of the plaque of the artery could travel to the brain and occlude one of the major branches of the arteries of the brain).

The endarterectomy, was performed. Several weeks later, the numbness had totally disappeared, and he no longer had any more episodes of dizzy spells. Prior to the operation, a minipsychological mental test consisting of recalling six numbers and four words, had been performed, which demonstrated that Tom indeed was having difficulties with his memory. Several months after the operation, Tom's memory had markedly improved, and he was again playing tennis and having no difficulties in keeping score of the game.

This story illustrates the successful treatment of carotid artery disease in order to avert the catastrophe of a stroke and further memory loss. The intermittent character of memory loss was characteristic of early MID syndrome.

The Treatment of Atherosclerosis and Stroke

Before the treatment of any medical condition can be instituted, the diagnosis has to be clearly made, and the earlier in time this is done, the more satisfactory the results will be. Unfortunately, the signs and symptoms of brain failure are not apparent to the patients. In contrast, many other diseases send out signals to let us know that there is something wrong. Inflammations are recognized because of pain. Early debilitating conditions, such as diabetes, cancer, and other, glandular disturbances, can make the patient feel weak or exhausted. Infectious diseases cause a rise in temperature. Illnesses involving the gastrointestinal tract are signalled by a change of bowel movements, weight loss, and a lack of appetite.

It is only when memory loss becomes a constant problem that the patient begins to recognize that something is afoot. Unfortunately, physicians, as a rule, do not perform mental testing. Patients who suffer from hypertension, smoke cigarettes, or have evidence of carotid artery disease, who are of an advanced age, and who have evidence of memory loss need to follow the medical treatment of these conditions carefully. Sometimes, the physician might feel that he or she is insulting the patient by asking simple questions, such as those I have listed on page 153. In this section, I will discuss how one can slow the progression of memory loss by the control of hypertension, arteriosclerosis, and carotid artery stenosis.

The Treatment of Hypertension. There are at least thirty-five million people known to have hypertension in the United States, and some are unaware that they suffer from it. Poorly controlled hypertension treatment generally results when the patients do not adhere to the program that the physician has outlined. It is universally accepted that, in the treatment of hypertension, an attempt should be made to lower blood pressure through weight reduction, strict salt restriction, and the use of relevant medications. The amount of salt intake should be reduced to approximately 1200 to 1500 mg. of salt per day. (A table which contains the amount of salt in different foods is on pp. 260–266.)

The recommendation of the Hypertensive Detection and Follow-Up Program (HDP) for patients over age sixty-five is that if they have a diastolic blood pressure of 95 or higher and a systolic pressure of 160 or higher, treatment should be instituted. The myth that blood pressure should be 100 plus your age has finally gone by the wayside. It is generally accepted that blood pressures above 160 (systolic) and above 95 (diastolic) increase the likelihood of strokes and heart attacks. In patients who are in the age range of 65 to 75, a more cautious gradual program is adopted. It is now established that patients of seventy years and older who have a blood pressure of 130/80, or lower, live longer. A patient who is seventy-five and has a blood pressure of 200/90 is a candidate for treatment. It is essential that patients who are over age seventy-five be treated in a very careful way, lest their mental state become worsened by the medication. In a younger person there is no doubt that the treatment of hypertension has to be done vigorously. Older patients do not require such severe salt restriction as younger patients, unless there is accompanying heart failure.

Appropriate weight reduction is helpful for the control of hypertension. It is unreasonable, however, to expect an older obese patient past age eighty to lose weight. In a younger person, for example under the age of sixty-five, weight reduction is encouraged along with a strict low-salt diet.

The controversy over whether or not to prescribe treatment is due to the fact that some scientists believe that a blood pressure of 200 does not necessarily reflect actual high blood pressure, but rather, atherosclerosis. It is essential that the patient's blood pressure be taken several times during several sittings before it is decided to begin a course of treatment. A patient who has rushed into a doctor's office often has temporarily elevated readings, but,

Cholesterol Content of Common Foods

MEAT GROUP
Red Meats

Food	Amount	Cholesterol (In Milligrams)
Bacon	2 slices	15
Beef (lean)	3 ounces	77
Frankfurter	2 (4 ounces)	112
Ham, boiled	2 ounces	51
Kidney, beef	3 ounces	315
Lamb (lean)	3 ounces	85
Liver, beef	3 ounces	372
Pork (lean)	3 ounces	75
Veal (lean)	3 ounces	84

Fowl

Chicken (dark meat, no skin)	3 ounces	77
Chicken (light meat, no skin)	3 ounces	65
Eggs (whole or yolk only)	1 large	252
Turkey (dark meat, no skin)	3 ounces	86
Turkey (white meat, no skin)	3 ounces	65

Fish

Clams, raw	3 ounces	43
Crab, canned	3 ounces	85
Flounder	3 ounces	69
Haddock.	3 ounces	42
Halibut	3 ounces	50
Lobster	3 ounces	71
Mackerel	3 ounces	84
Oysters, raw	3 ounces	42
Salmon, canned	3 ounces	30
Sardines	3 ounces	119
Scallops	3 ounces	45
Shrimp, canned	3 ounces	128
Tuna, canned	3 ounces	55

MILK GROUP

Butter	1 tablespoon	35
Buttermilk	1 cup	5
Cheese, cottage (4% fat)	½ cup	24
Cheese, cottage (1% fat)	½ cup	12
Cheese, cream	1 ounce	31
Cheese, hard	1 ounce	24–28
Cheese, spread	1 ounce	18

Cholesterol Content of Common Foods *(continued)*

Food	Amount	Cholesterol (In Milligrams)
Chocolate milk (low-fat)	1 cup	20
Cream, heavy	1 tablespoon	21
Ice cream	½ cup	27
Ice milk	½ cup	13
Milk, skim	1 cup	5
Milk, 1% fat	1 cup	14
Milk, 2% fat	1 cup	22
Milk, whole	1 cup	34
Yogurt (low-fat)	1 cup	17

BREAD GROUP		
Angel food cake	1 slice	0
Chocolate cupcake	2½-inch diameter	17
Cornbread	1 ounce	58
Lemon meringue pie	⅛ of 9-inch pie	98
Muffin, plain	3-inch diameter	21
Noodles, egg	1 cup	50
Pancakes	7 tablespoons batter	54
Sponge cake	½₂ of 10-inch cake	162

after he or she rests quietly for several minutes, the blood pressure may return to normal. In the quieter environment of the patient's house, the blood pressure tends to be lower than in the doctor's busy office.

When early memory loss is detected, a vigorous approach to the treatment of high blood pressure is essential.

Once the decision has been made to treat an older patient suffering from hypertension, it is the experience of many physicians that it is best to start with a small dosage of a diuretic perhaps three times a week, accompanied by some sodium restriction. If other medications are needed, some doctors recommend in treating elderly persons (75 to 90) that either clonidine (0.1 or 0.2 mg. at bedtime) or Aldomet (125 to 250 mg.) be used to start. These medications are given in a step-by-step fashion; the blood pressure is carefully monitored before changing the medication or increasing the dosage.

Diuretics are the mainstay for early treatment but lead to the major complication of potassium loss in the body. Patients are advised to consume potassium-containing foods, but it has been my experience that an entire truckload of bananas would have to be eaten to replenish the amount of potassium lost. If a diuretic is used that causes potassium loss, I strongly recommend a potassium supplement. Potassium loss can cause sudden abnormal heart rhythm and even death. A low level of salt in the blood can result from diuretics, causing another disabling problem in the elderly (which will be discussed further on).

It is important that, during each visit, the blood pressure be taken in each arm, while the patient is seated and standing. The older patient may have atherosclerosis involving the arteries of only one arm, which will show a lower reading, while the blood pressure of the other, normal arm will be much higher. The doctor can swiftly assess this by feeling for the pulse at the wrist. A reduced pulse in the arm or wrist might indicate atherosclerosis or a small clot of long duration, and the blood pressure in that arm will be much lower than in the normal arm. The blood pressure that is highest is the one that is treated. Treatment must be monitored. If, for example, standing up causes the blood pressure to drop too low and makes the patient dizzy, the medication needs to be adjusted. The golden rule is to fit the drug to the patient rather than the patient to the drug. In spite of all the publicity about the treatment of hypertension, patients still have a tendency to omit medications, and blood pressure is often poorly controlled.

A fashionable and effective treatment of hypertension consists of a group of medications called beta-blockers (propranolol, etc.), which have a notorious reputation for affecting patients' mental status (often causing depression and sometimes memory loss) and are usually avoided in the older patient, since they are not as effective in the older person over age seventy-five.

The purpose of treating hypertension is not only to prevent the calamity of stroke or heart attack, but also to reduce the incidence of atherosclerosis. If we are to diminish brain damage from atherosclerosis (and perhaps avoid it), we have to control hypertension.

Treatment of Carotid Artery Disease. When carotid artery disease is found through the tests described and the patient is in good medical condition and does not have any heart disease, surgery called endarterectomy is recommended. The surgeon selected, however, should be especially well-trained and experienced in this operation. The death rate from this surgery is low, below 1 percent, with good results expected in at least 95 percent of patients.

In males, when symptomatic carotid artery stenosis is detected and the patient is not otherwise in good medical condition, aspirin can substitute for surgery. For women—we don't know why—it doesn't help, though it is often prescribed anyway. In the United States, 12,000 tons of aspirin per year are used by the public. The use of aspirin is increasing since it has been widely reported to prevent heart attacks and strokes by impeding the formation of clots. This remarkable drug dates back 2000 years, since the time of Hippocrates, and has been used for pain throughout the centuries. Derived from the bark of the willow, its chemical name is acetylsalicylic acid; it was refined for general use by Felix Hoffman, a German chemist who was looking for a remedy for his father-in-law who was suffering from arthritis. He brought his discovery to the director of the Bayer Company, Heinrich Dresser, and it was Dresser who labeled the product "aspirin."

The mechanism of clot formation is still a mystery. Some recent research discloses that a metabolic derangement occurs in the arterial walls, causing platelets to stick together and form a clot. Aspirin seems to prevent the platelets from sticking together by interfering with the actions of enzymes. A small dosage of aspirin prevents the clot; larger dosages actually may encourage the clot to form in the first place. At the present time, scientists are still trying to decide the proper dosage. One to two aspirins per day are generally prescribed for the prevention of stroke, and one-half aspirin per day is prescribed for the prevention of heart attacks in patients of all ages. Undoubtedly, patients who have ulcers or other GI upsets should not be taking aspirins until they first check with their physician. Many cardiologists, including myself, take one-half aspirin per day in the hope of averting strokes and heart attacks.

I recommend aspirin to patients who are found to have atherosclerosis of the carotid artery, even though they may have no troublesome symptoms in hopes of averting a stroke.

Patients who are over age forty, expecially if they have a history of diabetes, hypertension, or cigarette smoking, should have a careful evaluation done of their carotid arteries. If there is the presence of a bruit or a decreased pulsation of these arteries, an ultrasound exam should be performed to detect early hardening of these arteries. The ultrasound principle involves no radiation; rather, it uses sound waves. The detection of atherosclerosis of the carotid arteries may not mean that automatically there is any impairment of blood flow to the brain, but perhaps further deposits of cholesterol can be prevented and even reversed in the early stages.

Treatment of Multi-Infarct Dementia (MID). As I have stated earlier, patients who are prone to develop multi-infarction dementia are: 1) those who are suffering from previous heart attacks, angina, and other cardiac conditions, 2) those with hypertension, 3) those who have transient ischemic episodes, or "little strokes," 4) those suffering from diabetes mellitus, 5) obese patients, 6) cigarette smokers, and 7) patients who have other evidence of atherosclerosis, such as poor circulation of their legs (peripheral vascular disease).

It is disheartening to open a current textbook on pharmacology and find only one paragraph on the treatment of senile dementia. This reflects the current frustration that physicians have to live with when faced with a patient with progressive dementia. In the near future it is hoped that this will change.

A group of medications called sympathomimetic amines has been used for years for treatment of brain arteriosclerosis. These medications relax the smooth artery muscles and dilate the arteries of the brain to some degree. These drugs, which have different names such as isoxsuprine (or Vasodilan) and nylidrin (or Arlidin), are called cerebrovasodilators. They are derivatives of a powerful substance called ergotamine and are classified as dihydroergotoxin, which comes from a fungus grown on rye bread. They have been used to increase blood flow to the brain and allegedly to treat hardening of the arteries, but may actually have the opposite effect in patients with MID. The arteries in this illness are narrowed and cannot expand. The vasodilators divert the blood to arteries that can dilate and diminish the blood flow through the narrowed arteries, which worsens the problem. Most doctors are disappointed with the results of these drugs.

The vasodilator which has received the greatest publicity is Hydergine. It is used extensively in nursing homes, and it seems to have a favorable effect in patients who are suffering from a mixed type of dementia, which includes Alzheimer's disease. In nursing homes, patients who are demented very often have advanced atherosclerosis and Alzheimer's disease. Doctors administer Hydergine to demented patients with the hope of benefitting those patients whose problems are largely those of Alzheimer's disease rather than of atherosclerosis. Throughout the country, doctors and families have reported that some patients who are receiving Hydergine have become more alert and have increased attention spans and memory improvement, and that the progression of their illness seems to be markedly slowed down. Those patients who have only atherosclerosis of the brain, in contrast, do not generally benefit from Hydergine.

Hypotension

In the previous sections, I discussed how high blood pressure can be detrimental to the brain. Unaccustomed low blood pressure in an elderly patient can also be responsible for a variety of brain syndromes. However, blood pressure is essential for life. It is produced by the contraction of the heart which propels the blood along the arteries (this is the systolic blood pressure), before relaxation (the diastolic pressure) which is needed for blood to travel throughout the brain to the kidneys and to the other vital organs. Some patients who experience a lack of blood arriving to their brains will faint. Sometimes, the experience of having blood taken from a vein can cause a frightening reaction—the blood pools into the abdomen leading to a sudden drop of the blood pressure, which causes the patient to faint.

There are many factors that regulate the blood pressure: the amount of water that is in the body, the force of contraction of the heart, the salt intake, metabolic forces generated by the kidney (the renin system), and still other forces yet to be determined.

Low blood pressure can be caused by chronic blood loss, inadequate fluids, excessive vomiting, heart attacks, heat exhaustion, endocrine diseases of the adrenal glands (to be discussed later), and abnormalities of the thyroid gland. The older patient has such a remarkably sensitive balance of water and electrolytes that this can be upset by excessive urination, too much overheating, and, above all, too much medication and an inadequate amount of fluid intake.

Elderly patients who live alone and who are partially disabled by arthritis often have a markedly diminished intake of fluids. The reflex desire to drink water may be diminished in the older person because the sweating mechanism is impaired. If the environment is hot and humid, there is a greater requirement for fluid intake. Water is an essential for life—90 percent of the cells are composed of fluids—and they cannot tolerate having inadequate hydration for long periods. Doctors see the consequences of inadequate fluid intake in the emergency room, in the coronary care unit, and in the general hospital. Decreased amounts of fluid in the body cause the kidney flow to diminish and can result in kidney failure. The red blood cells of the body in cases of dehydration will have a tendency to clump and form clots.

The sensitive brain is unable to tolerate water loss: it needs a certain amount of blood pressure, oxygen, and fluids. The elderly brain has diminished brain cells and may already be suffering from some other chronic insult. It can swiftly decompensate and produce the syndrome of dementia. Disorientation and confusion, marked lethargy, and a chronic languid feeling can all be symptoms of low blood pressure. Periodic episodes of dizzy spells, fainting, and lightheadedness may be the only symptoms, along with a chronic feeling of weakness, inattentiveness, and the desire to sleep.

A casual physical examination might disclose no abnormalities unless a special effort is made to consider episodes of low blood pressure as the cause of chronic brain dementia syndrome, dizzy spells, and weakness.

A 79-year-old woman was having episodes of weakness and dizzy spells which increased in severity over many months. A thorough brain work-up was conducted, which included an EEG, a CT scan, and multiple blood tests, all of which were within normal limits. The patient even had a heart monitor to discover if there were episodes of heart irregularities. There being no significant findings, it was concluded that the patient was suffering from a progressive type of brain degeneration, either of the Alzheimer type or from multi-infarction dementia, described before.

During one of the office visits, a young nurse fresh out of training recorded the blood pressure, when the patient was seated, to be 110/70 in the right arm and 120/80 in the left arm. The patient was then instructed to stand with the help of the family. The blood pressure, when taken in the standing position, dropped to 80/80 in the right arm and to 90/70 in the left arm. The nurse had been taught during her training period that the patient should stand for at least three minutes in order to accurately assess the blood pressure. Within a period of three minutes, the patient began to complain of dizziness and began to stagger. The nurse took the blood pressure again in the left arm and found it to be 70/50 and then could not hear it at all. The patient staggered and then sat down, and, in a few minutes, the blood pressure in the left arm returned to its level of 120/80. During all her previous examinations the patient had been either lying down or just sitting, traveling back and forth in a wheelchair during her hospitalization since there was fear of her falling.

It became evident to the physician that the patient was suffering from low blood pressure, or orthostatic hypotension (a fall of blood pressure which occurs when the erect position is assumed), which undoubtedly accounted for her episodes of dizzy spells and contributed in part to her mental slowing and exhaustion. (Younger patients may have a similar type of symptom, especially young women.) Fluid intake was encouraged, since it turned out that the patient was drinking inadequate amounts of water, and salt was added to the diet. In spite of the increased fluid and salt intake, the patient continued suffering from severe episodes of low blood pressure, and she did not improve. A chemical hormone called desoxycorticosterone acetate (DOCA), which functions to retain salt and water, was added. A minimal dose of Florinef Acetate was given, and, in subsequent weeks, the patient's blood pressure rose to 140/70. Her dizziness almost disappeared, and her mental state improved. Fatigue was replaced by her normal activities. Her memory improved and she no longer had episodes of confusion and disorientation.

Episodes of severe low blood pressure can occur with patients under treatment for congestive heart failure or for high blood pressure. Too vigorous a treatment can cause dehydration, chronic brain dysfunction, loss of water from the body, and periodic drops in blood pressure.

Patients complaining of dizziness and weakness and showing signs of memory loss may be suffering from low blood pressure. This can be discovered only if the blood pressure is taken while the patient is seated and then stands for three minutes. (Pressure may drop long before three minutes, but three minutes is recommended for accuracy.) Once discovered, the low blood pressure should be treated by increasing the fluid intake and, sometimes, by prescribing medications.

Cranial Arteritis

The arteries of the brain can suffer a smoldering inflammation and eventually close as if clogged by cholesterol. This condition, known as cranial arteritis, occurs mostly in older women and has no known cause. Often, it is associated with rheumatism of the upper arms and shoulders (polymyalgia rheumatica). The muscle problems of this strange illness may be the first predominant symptom; later, there may be the further complication of arterial affliction. However, arteritis may be the only symptom.

The rheumatism element of this condition has a bizarre presentation of marked pain on elevation of both arms. Weakness and fatigue may be present with little evidence on physical examination. When this illness strikes, it can completely disable the patient. It was originally described in Czechoslovakia and then in England, and I had the occasion to write in 1964 one of the first papers on the subject in this country, entitled, "Polymyalgia Rheumatica." The diagnosis of the rheumatism portion is made through a blood test (a measure of the pace of blood cells falling in a tube, which is quickened by most infections) entitled the sedimentation rate which is generally found to be markedly elevated. Many times, these patients are considered neurotic, and the diagnosis will remain obscure for months.

If the arteries are attacked by this illness, the patient will complain of a throbbing, pulsating headache. In describing pain, the patient will place the palm of the hand over the artery on the front side of the skull, which may be found to be knotty and markedly inflamed. It may be evident only at night when the patient cannot lie on the side of the inflamed artery, lest he or she feels pain. Cranial arteritis can cause depression, intellectual impairment, confusion, poor judgment, and memory loss. Some patients may complain of sweating at night and often are found to have an associated anemia. The diagnosis is made by a biopsy of the artery. The clinical presentation is very characteristic, and the response to cortisone treatment is dramatic. The sedimentation rate is a sensitive test for inflammation. If this test is markedly positive, cortisone must be given, as the patient can suddenly go blind. Treatment is given even if the biopsy is normal, when the clinical picture is so characteristic. Unfortunately, the patient's first symptom of cranial arteritis is sometimes a stroke or sudden blindness, preceded by many months and sometimes years of headaches, confusion, and dementia. Not only are the arteries of the brain afflicted, but sometimes even the arteries of the heart as well, causing a heart attack.

A 78-year-old woman had complained of intermittent headaches for a four-month period. Her daughter noticed that she had begun to squint a great deal and had developed marked forgetfulness and confusion. During this four-month period, she suffered a heart attack, from which she completely recovered. Her headaches, after discharge from the hospital, increased because she was receiving nitroglycerine tablets, which often cause severe headaches. The astute physician questioned her further regarding the pain and found that it occurred primarily at night. When she located the exact point of pain, an inflamed, bumpy artery was found. A biopsy was performed which confirmed the diagnosis of temporal arteritis. The patient was placed on cortisone medication for a period of six weeks. Her headaches and also, interestingly, her periodic episodes of chest pain disappeared. Her memory markedly improved. She no longer suffered from confusion and no longer seemed senile.

This is another example of confusing a diagnosis in an elderly patient who often complains of rheumatic pains and headaches; it should *not* be assumed that all people who have pains in their shoulders, who cannot raise both arms, and who have headaches have temporal arteritis. The important point in the diagnosis is the relatively recent onset, combined with a disabling pain in the head and in the muscles, and the blood-test results of an elevated sedimentation rate, which respond swiftly to cortisone medication.

In an article written by Dr. George Paulson, in the *American Journal of Psychiatry* in August 1983 and entitled "Steroid-Sensitive Dementia," there appears a discussion concerning the occasionally favorable response of patients with dementia to cortisone therapy. A case in point is how patients may respond to cortisone treatment. The author emphasizes that some of the patients who develop a sudden onset of dementia may be suffering from an arteritis. The first patient he describes had a TIA and other neurological findings that responded dramatically to steroids. The second patient was a 56-year-old woman who was admitted into the hospital because of confusion, memory loss, and difficulty with manual dexterity (in doing her crochet). She became progressively more demented in the hospital, and, when she was placed on cortisone, had a dramatic improvement. The third patient described was a 42-year-old man who was admitted because of an organic brain disease of "unknown cause." This patient had a brain biopsy performed, which confirmed the diagnosis of an arteritis, and the patient responded dramatically to cortisone. Paulson recommends that, in the case of a fulminating dementia of unknown cause, corticosteroids should be tried. Paulson said: "It is hazardous to suggest that every patient with smoldering, chronic, and unexplained dementia should be given a trial of steroids, but it is equally unwise to withhold steroids from patients with possible vasculitis (arteritis). . . . If steroids do not lead to an obvious benefit in a demented patient in a few weeks, the medication should be discontinued."

There are 400,000 strokes per year in the United States. The majority of them are closely linked to hypertension and atherosclerosis. The percentage of those who may also be suffering from arteritis is very small.

For the families of afflicted persons complaining of severe throbbing headache on the side of the head, difficulty in raising the arms, or memory loss, the advice of a physician must be sought.

Today, physicians are well-acquainted with cranial arteritis. If a careful search for inflammation of the arteries of the brain is made in every patient suffering from cerebrovascular disease, the diagnosis is rarely missed.

CHAPTER 8

Heart Sounds

*My heart has remained so young that I have the
continual feeling of playing a part.*

ANDRE GIDE

Cardiovascular Causes of
Reversible Mental Deterioration: Slow Pulse Rate

Just a few years ago, prior to writing this book, I met a delightful,
vigorous 75-year-old man who was a retired president of the company that he had founded a number of years before. He was far
from being inactive, having continued consulting and making major
decisions for his firm, and he was looked upon by his corporate
cronies as the wise old fox. As a matter of fact, they had labeled
him "the silver fox" because his hair had grayed at the age of forty,
although his brain was still sharp as a tack.

On a hot summer night, I got a frantic call from my next-door
neighbor telling me that Will had suddenly collapsed after finishing
his dinner and a few drinks.

With my tattered doctor's bag, I rushed to the scene, and, in
the darkness, saw Will lying on the ground. Swiftly, I examined
him and found his blood pressure to be 150/90 and his pulse to be
85 beats per minute. He was perspiring profusely, and he suddenly
arched his body forward and vomited. It seemed that his affliction
might be nothing more than an acute upset stomach. However, I
still chose to admit him to the hospital to rule out a heart attack
(myocardial infarction).

In the coronary care unit, he was somewhat disoriented for the
first twenty-four hours. His pulse and blood pressure showed no

signs of change. I did manage to get a complete history from him, since I had not seen him in several years and was not his regular physician. I asked if he had noticed any changes in himself, and his wife said, "No, except that he forgets things."

I said, "Will, forgetting things? I don't think it's possible. I've always admired Will's incredible ability to recall everything, and his retention of recent events and names that I have trouble with has always amazed me."

"Well, for example," she said, "I said, 'Will, we're going out to dinner tonight at the club.' An hour later, Will asked me, 'What are we doing for dinner tonight?' "

Will did admit to the fact that he was having moments of forgetfulness which he attributed to aging. "Well, what do you expect? Will is now age seventy-five," his wife said.

I had a strong suspicion that his problem was *not* due to aging (especially since I was in the midst of research before writing a book on the subject).

All the laboratory tests, including those for heart attack, returned with normal results. His monitor remained unchanged, and it was decided that he should be discharged. I gave him instructions to quickly call me if the event should occur again.

An aide arrived and placed him in a wheelchair, which he refused, saying, "I can walk. I'm perfectly fine." Hospital rules, however, for a patient in his condition made it mandatory for him to leave in a wheelchair, so Will *pushed* his own chair. As he started towards the exit of the hospital, he suddenly collapsed directly in front of me. I discovered his pulse to be about 23. He was readmitted and again placed on the monitoring system. I carried out some simple tests, such as asking him who the President of the United States was, to which he indignantly replied, "It's none of your business! You know damn well who's President, and stop making me look like a fool!" I asked him what year it was, and he said, "The year it's always been."

"And what are the names of your grandchildren?"

"They haven't changed either."

We continued in this banter, with Will pretending that his intellect was intact by dodging my questions. It became apparent that he had lost not only his ability to recall recent events but also important facts of common knowledge, such as who discovered America.

It was found that Will's pulse was too slow, and an artificial pacemaker was inserted. Will's heart rate increased to 60 beats per minute as soon as the pacemaker began to operate.

Approximately six weeks later, when I saw Will again, he was dressed neatly in his usual banker's dark suit, and he was again his old self. "You know, I don't know what the hell happened to me, but I was really out of it for the past eight months. I can remember everything now; fortunately, I don't have those dizzy weak spells and that fatigue any more." This story illustrates that if the heart does not pump enough blood to the brain, the brain will suffer from oxygen starvation. If the pulse is very slow, below 40 beats per minute, the heart does not pump enough blood to the brain and dizziness, fainting, and memory failure can result.

The heart is a muscle like no other muscle in the body. It has its own inherent electric system. All other muscles require for their contraction a supply of nerves from the brain. The heart muscle has its own intricate electricity and its own pacemaker, which makes it possible for the heart to contract in an orderly fashion. The pacemaker has its origin in the atrium (the first chamber on either side of the heart, which receives the blood from the veins), called the sinoatrial (SA) node. Signals are then sent down special conducting tracks into the midportion of the heart, and then they divide into branches, supplying the right and left ventricles. The impulses may be affected by a variety of agents, such as coffee, cigarette smoking, alcohol, or an inadequacy in the arterial supply. Atherosclerosis of the arteries can cause a slowing of the pacemaker. The normal transmission of the impulses causes the heart to contract between 60 to 85 beats per minute. This pulse rate may vary from person to person; some people have normal pulses at the rate of 45 all their lives. Athletes, for example, tend to have much lower pulse rates.

If the pacemaker becomes diseased from atherosclerosis or other causes, it may cause a marked delay in the impulse, or it may become unduly activated, causing a rapid increase in the pulse rate. A delayed pulse rate is reflected by a heart rate that slows down to 35 or even 25 beats per minute, to the point of actually disappearing. Cardiologists speak of a "sick sinus syndrome" when the pacemaker that begins in the SA node is diseased, causing an undue slowing of the heart. The result of the heart's not contracting and releasing blood from the left ventricle is that parts of the body may not receive enough oxygen, especially the brain.

Symptoms of a slowed or diseased pacemaker may vary from feelings of undue fatigue, episodes of dizzy spells, fainting, and, in the older person, impairment of brain function. It is not often recognized that a slow pulse rate can cause memory loss and other abnormalities of brain function since patients rarely undergo psychological testing.

It is sometimes quite difficult to determine whether someone has an abnormally slow pulse rate. Even a method of recording a twenty-four-hour heart rate, called a Holter monitor, may be inadequate. More specialized techniques of electrophysiological testing are now being used that can measure the conduction rate of the inherent pacemaker system in the heart. These tests are performed in medical centers and can advise the physician as to whether the patient needs a pacemaker. Electrophysiological testing requires the patient to be admitted into a hospital. It is performed only if there is a strong suspicion of an abnormally slow pulse rate, causing the symptoms which I have described such as fainting and dizzy spells, and, above all, if the Holter monitor does not demonstrate a slow pulse. It is not necessary to do this test if the Holter monitor or a routine electrocardiogram displays a pulse rate below 40, and the patient has dizzy or weak spells.

Heart Valve Disease

Aortic Stenosis

There are numerous heart conditions that prevent the blood from leaving the heart and circulating to the brain. The aortic valve, located on the left side of the heart, keeps the flow of blood moving from the left ventricle of the heart, through the aorta and into the rest of the body. This valve may become progressively narrowed in the older person, whose symptoms might be some memory loss, fatigue, exhaustion, episodes of fainting, chest pain typical of angina, and a low blood pressure. This condition—a narrowing of the diameter of the passage or orifice—is termed "aortic stenosis." A sound called a murmur is produced from the narrowed valve, which is the sound of blood being forced through a narrowed orifice. This murmur when heard by the examining physician, may be very loud or may be so soft that it can be missed.

The signs and symptoms of aortic stenosis may mimic those of angina and coronary artery disease. An alert physician will detect a murmur with the stethoscope and will suspect that the problem lies in the valve and not with the coronary arteries. When other symptoms, namely heart failure, arise from the aortic valve and it is determined through cardiac catheterization that the valve is critically narrowed, replacement of the valve is mandatory. A new valve can pump blood to the brain, and dizziness, fatigue, and memory loss may disappear, or at least be alleviated, by the new supply of oxygen that brain cells now receive.

Patients with chronic valvular disease or aortic stenosis are rarely screened for mental impairment or given psychological testing. The overriding cardiac problems of shortness of breath, chest pain, and dizzy spells cause the other worries to be secondary to the patient. Increasing memory loss and lapses in mental judgment, often attributed to aging, may, in reality, be arising from inadequate blood supply from a diseased aortic valve.

A retired 75-year-old German, a mathematician and engineer by profession, had begun to "slow down," according to his family. There had been a progressive loss of interest on his part in reading the newspaper and in keeping up with current events. A strongly opinionated man, once a martinet at his profession, he prided himself on having a thorough knowledge of European history, especially of the events of World War I. It became clearly evident to the family that something was amiss when Walter confused the American General Pershing with General Rundstedt, the German officer who launched the invasion of Poland. He began to muddle the dates of World War I and World War II and, in addition, exhibited signs of recent memory loss. When the first day of June arrived, Walter seemed unaware of it. He did not dress up in his blue suit to make his visit to the bank to cash in his bond coupons, a ritual he strictly adhered to every month.

"Aren't you going down to the bank this morning? It is the first of June," his wife asked him.

"You know, I forgot, but I really don't feel like going anyway."

His wife did not realize that Walter had forgotten where the bank was located, and that he feared that he would not know which route to follow downtown.

"I have also been awfully tired," he said. "I just would like to stay home."

His wife tactfully suggested that perhaps he ought to have his blood pressure checked, as it had been a while since he had seen the physician. Actually, it had been almost *ten* years. The traditional family doctor had since passed away, and a new younger doctor had taken his place.

When the young doctor took a careful history, he realized that Walter had difficulty in remembering anything about his past and had only some vague notions of his previous occupation. The doctor inquired whether these changes occurred over a number of years or just in the past six months.

"It's very recent," his wife told the doctor, "because this is the first month that he didn't go down to the bank himself."

Walter's physical examination disclosed that his blood pressure was 120/70 and that his pulse was 75. The heart examination disclosed a loud murmur that was present in the region of the chest called the aortic area, and this gave the doctor a clue that he might be suffering from aortic stenosis. The electrocardiogram and chest x-ray results were abnormal, both showing an enlarged heart. A special new test, called an echocardiogram, which sends sound waves to the heart in order to image the motion of the valves was performed. The doctor found that the valves moved very little and that Walter was suffering from severe aortic stenosis; little blood was leaving his heart.

The doctor explained that the valve could be replaced and that Walter could still have a useful, functional life, but his wife insisted that since his mental status had so badly deteriorated there might not be a point to the operation.

"It is possible," the doctor explained, "that his mental status results from the aortic valve's being so narrowed, and that there isn't enough blood perfusing to the brain. It's going to be your decision because he is unable to make the decision for himself."

After discussing the procedures with the rest of the family—two sons, both chemists, and one daughter, a physician—Walter's wife agreed that he should undergo cardiac catheterization to replace the very tight, narrowed aortic valve.

The surgeon informed the family that the operation was dangerous at his age, but that Walter had an 85% chance of surviving; without the operation, there was a 70% chance of his dying that year. The operation was a success and a new valve was inserted. Immediately after surgery when Walter awoke, he was confused and disoriented. He had a vague idea that he was in the hospital but remembered little of the surgery. The family and the physicians were all discouraged with his markedly deteriorated mental state. In the ensuing days, however, when Walter was moved from the intensive care unit and placed on a regular floor, he became more lucid. His mental alertness progressively returned. Two weeks after the operation, on the day of discharge, he called his wife in panic and informed her that he had just realized that it was far past the first day of the month and that he *must* immediately go to the bank.

This is a dramatic illustration of how aortic-valve replacement can improve a patient's mental status and quality of life. Walter is still alive and well, at the age of eighty-eight, still taking his daily walks and keeping a sharp eye on his accounts. This story also illustrates that all is not lost when one is faced with severe memory loss. There is more hope in 1985 than ever before. There *are* reversible causes of dementia, and Walter's story is a perfect example of the *myth* of senility.

Mitral Stenosis

Another heart valve that is frequently diseased—the mitral valve—can also be the cause of brain loss. The mitral valve of the heart separates the upper chamber (the left atrium) from the lower chamber (the left ventricle) and directs the flow of blood in one direction. It looks like a bishops's cap, or miter—hence the term "mitral." It is a complex structure that is suspended in the left ventricle like a parachute with long cords (the chordae tendineae), which attach to the papillary groups of muscles. By the cords' pulling and tugging of the muscles, the valve with its two leaflets opens and closes—opening to allow the blood to flow forward and closing to prevent the flow of blood from going backwards into the upper chamber of the left atrium. This entire mitral apparatus can become destroyed by rheumatic fever or other infections, which prevent the valve from properly closing.

When the valves cannot properly open, the flow of blood is impeded, a chamber behind the valve enlarges, and the heart can begin to beat erratically, a condition known as atrial fibrillation. Clots tend to form in these chambers, become dislodged, travel to the brain, and cause strokes. Repeated showers of these clots to the sensitive brain tissue can result in MID.

A few years ago, I met Mary Ann, a 58-year-old woman who was diagnosed as having had a rheumatic heart as a child. She had been one of the first patients on whom Dr. W. Glenn of Yale Medical School had performed the famous heart operation in which a finger was stuck through a mitral valve to widen it. The operation, called a commissurotomy, was performed in 1961. She did rather well for five years until, one day, she awoke with paralysis of her left arm and left leg. She also had difficulty in speaking. A thrombus from her heart had traveled to her brain and caused a stroke. In subsequent years, she continued to have recurrent little strokes and became progressively demented. There were times when she had lucid moments and was able to converse with her children, but finally she lapsed into complete oblivion, diagnostic of MID. She became a permanent tenant of a nursing home and lived until the age of eighty.

An autopsy was performed which disclosed that her brain had been almost completely destroyed by the repeated clots. Mary Ann had unfortunately refused repeat heart surgery ten years prior to her death and had also rejected taking any medications to prevent her blood from clotting further.

The diagnosis of mitral stenosis is not difficult, initially being made with the stethoscope and then confirmed by echocardiography or a sonar device. Symptoms of a diseased mitral valve include shortness of breath, swelling of ankles, a rapid heartbeat, and a great deal of fatigue. If these are present, visit your doctor. Prevention of dementia, when possible, is still easier than its treatment.

Brain Impairment After Open-Heart Surgery

It is often the case that after open-heart surgery, there are cerebrovascular complications that may last for months. It has been estimated that approximately 5 percent of patients may suffer a stroke and that up to 30 to 40 percent have some mental aberrations, such as confusion, depression and memory loss. Older patients function on a limited and critical number of brain cells, and any surgery can cause some deterioration of the brain. Mental deterioration is often not recognized by the physician, but by the family when the patient returns home. Depression, lack of awareness as to time and place, and nonrecognition of family members have been described in younger patients as well.

Prior to open heart surgery, some patients may have vascular disease of the brain which has not been recognized, and the surgery can further compromise the blood supply to the brain. Some patients may actually suffer strokes. Luckily, this does not often occur. Patients are informed of this risk before surgery. Although there is no way of actually predicting who will suffer a stroke, patients who are prone are those who have long-standing hypertension and those who are smokers and diabetics.

Placement in the unfamiliar surroundings of the recovery room with an uncomfortable breathing tube and resulting disruption of the circadian rhythm of the body can cause temporary brain impairments or sometimes permanent injury. Night and day become merged into one. The patient's sleep is continually interrupted with examinations, medications, sounds, and noises. This intensive-care-unit syndrome occurs in 30 percent of postoperative heart patients.

Scientists recognize that patients who are in a coma, whether it be from a head injury or other causes, recover better if their nutritional status is adequate. It has been shown by Howard Kaufman, an Associate Professor and neurosurgeon at the University of Texas that patients with head injuries have increased metabolic needs. He has been quoted as saying that: "They [the patients] are not getting anywhere near the caloric and nutritional needs, so we are starving them when they have an excessive need." With this new information available to doctors, patients are receiving extra nourishment if it seems that a long treatment period lies ahead. Extra calories are given in an IV infusion called hyperalimentation, which consists of proteins and vitamins.

After injuries, patients also have profound changes in their hormonal activities, coupled with metabolic stress and diminished circulation of blood to the brain. The patients are starving from impaired nutrition after the operation, and perhaps this is responsible for some of the psychiatric problems that occur. It is certainly responsible for slow healing.

Most patients completely recover and suffer no lasting brain impairment. Some patients may need an entire year to regain their previous mental abilities; most improve in the first two months.

Once at home, patients are advised to have a high protein diet from meats and fish, as well as vitamin supplements. Plenty of fresh vegetables are encouraged. Patients are advised to eat three regular meals, not to skip any meals, and not to rely on snacks and "junk foods."

Endocarditis

A diseased heart valve can become the site of an infection called endocarditis. Infections of the valve have been known to result from an innocuous dental visit for a simple cleaning. Patients who have valvular disease are always forewarned to receive prophylactic antibiotics before visiting the dentist, lest an infection should arise. When patients do not know they have a heart murmur from a diseased valve and do not receive prophylactic antibiotics, bacteria can implant themselves on the valve. The infection is called subacute bacterial endocarditis (SBE) because it is an illness of slow insidious onset and is characterized by a chronic low-grade fever. Sometimes, the only sign felt by the patient is sweating at night. The bacteria organize themselves into clumps which pathologists call vegetations, which progressively bore into the valve, as does a mole into the ground, causing further destruction and leading to heart failure.

Symptoms of SBE may first appear either in the form of heart failure or in the breaking off of the vegetations which travel in the bloodstream throughout the body, occluding arteries which supply different organs. If these infect the brain, they can cause severe mental impairment and stroke. Memory loss, depression and confusion, can be the first signs of endocarditis after sweating—but may be blamed on aging!

The diagnosis of subacute bacterial endocarditis is made by culturing the blood for bacteria. Sometimes, these warty bacterial vegetations are seen by the sonar examination of the valve; in other cases, the diagnosis may never be made, except on the autopsy table.

The course of the illness can extend for months with a generalized feeling of malaise, weakness, depression, weight loss, and lethargy. Bizarre symptoms can occur, such as momentary numbness in an arm, a pain in a leg, a sudden tingling sensation of the hand, and the constant nightly sweats resulting from fever. If the temperature is taken during the day when the patient feels well, it may be normal; it is not often that patients take their temperatures in the middle of the night.

Prior to the discovery of penicillin, patients with SBE invariably succumbed to the illness. In 1985, we can anticipate that the majority of patients will survive if SBE is recognized early enough and treatment with IV antibiotics is given.

A 76-year-old antique dealer had for years suffered from mild hypertension but had no other serious illnesses. He had recently retired and had become depressed from the boredom of staying home. He missed making the appraisals and travelling around the country to bargain for rare pieces before selling them to his customers.

When George arrived at my office, he did not look his usual energetic self; he looked crestfallen, walked in a stooped fashion, and did not carry on in his usual colorfully bantering tone. His wife whispered to me, "I think he is fading. He sits around all day. He is not interested in any of the antique magazines, and his memory is failing dreadfully. I recently took him for a drive to some antique stores just to see if I could revitalize him a bit. There was an English linen press that he examined, but he had forgotten its provenance and, no less, was unable to date it. Doctor, I can assure you, if George can't tell what a linen press is and the date which belongs to it, then I *know* he is failing!"

George's physical examination revealed that his blood pressure was 120/70; the heart examination was unremarkable, except that there was a heart murmur which he had developed in recent years from his long-standing hypertension. There were no other findings and the laboratory examination results were all within normal limits.

Because of the recent onset of memory loss, a CT scan was performed of his brain which showed some early atrophy of brain tissue—this generally is not clinically significant. A brain-wave test was within normal limits, as was an electrocardiogram. An entire gamut of testing of every organ of his body was normal. A sonar examination of his heart was also done which showed that the valve was slightly damaged but still functioned well.

I reassured the patient that all was well and advised more exposure to intellectual stimuli; one of the causes of depression and its accompanying memory loss is just plain boredom. Psychological testing had not shown any gross impairment. He was able to remember four names, recall several numbers, count backwards from seven, and was totally oriented to time and place. In retrospect, I realize that more detailed psychological testing might have revealed that there was indeed a serious memory impairment problem.

When he returned to his house, he dressed himself in a conservative blue suit, and he and his wife went out to dinner; on the following day, they went to an art gallery in New York. This took a great deal of effort because he felt drained—he would have much preferred to go home to sleep.

Several weeks later, while standing in the kitchen, he suddenly began to feel woozy and fell to the ground. His wife called the emergency squad, but the paramedics found that his blood pressure and pulse were normal. He was admitted into the hospital for several days to assure that he had not suffered a heart attack. He was then discharged and given antidepressant medication. He was advised to seek a psychiatrist or a social worker to help him manage his retirement depression. In spite of the medication and psychiatric assistance, he continued to do badly, and, for the first time, complained of a great deal of sweating at night. It was an unusually hot summer and so his sweating was attributed to the hot weather. He had several more episodes of faintness, and he progressively retreated into his own world, sitting in the chair, uninterested in his grandchildren or anything else. A neurologist was consulted who diagnosed the possibilities as either early Alzheimer's disease or MID.

Three months later, George showed progressive signs of depression and brain failure. His son would not accept the diagnosis and was sure that there must be something else wrong.

"He sweats so much," his wife continued to say, "that you have to see it to believe it."

"Have you taken his temperature?"

"Everytime I take his temperature, it's always normal and sometimes is below normal."

Because of the insistence of his son, the patient was hospitalized when he had another episode of near-collapse.

More x-rays were taken in the hospital, causing him to have greater exhaustion since he was not allowed food or drink in order to prepare for them. Each day, however, there was a slight rise in the temperature to 99.9°; on the third day of hospitalization, the temperature suddenly rose to 102°. As is the common medical practice, further blood cultures and chest x-rays were taken to locate the source of infection. Four days later, bacteria were located growing in his blood of the type called *Streptococcus viridans*. The diagnosis now became clear: the antique dealer was suffering from subacute endocarditis.

When his medical history was reviewed, it was discovered that three months prior to his illness, George had undergone some minor dental treatment. Because he was given no penicillin prior to dental work, the bacteria from his traumatized mouth entered through the small mouth wounds and settled on his deformed valve.

For the next four weeks, George received intravenous penicillin. Forty-eight hours after the treatment had begun, he became more alert as his temperature dropped. By the end of the first week his strength had returned, and it became obvious that his demented state was rapidly subsiding. Now, five years later, George is once again active, and his only infirmity is some loss of vision from degeneration of the macula in back of his eye. His memory is as sharp as ever, and he no longer has any other signs of dementia.

This story illustrates a not uncommon cause of brain failure. Elderly patients are unable to respond in the same manner as younger people to a rise in temperature. Their immune system is impaired as well as their temperature regulatory mechanism. For

George, the temperatures of 99° to 100° were the highest that could be discovered until he arrived at the hospital when it became apparent that he was also having periodic episodes of temperatures of 101° to 102° which had been missed. When he started perspiring, his temperature dropped; his wife took his temperature at home after he began to perspire and so the higher temperatures were missed.

There was a time when endocarditis was predominantly seen in younger people before penicillin was known and its administration given prophylactically. It now can be called a disease of the elderly, since it is seen more frequently than before in the group aged between sixty and eighty. It is also predominantly seen in males. In younger people, endocarditis is seen in drug addicts, who bring the bacteria into their systems through intravenous injections.

The diagnosis is often delayed, as the symptoms are so insidious and subtle. Many elderly patients do not have a thermometer at home, and, if they do, they are unable to read it because of poor vision. A temperature taken in a doctor's office setting may be normal.

Other patients who have infected emboli (vegetations) traveling to the brain may show periods of complete disorientation and hallucinations. For example, one elderly man consistently conversed with his dead wife during several hours of the day and also experienced memory loss. Episodic mismatching of words and ideas with a scrambling of incomprehensible sentences and phrases can occur for hours at a time. Patients who have a chronic brain insult sometimes fabricate their own language that is incomprehensible to others and even to themselves.

The symptoms of dementia from SBE may go on for more than three months. It is currently acknowledged that when patients exhibit three months or more of a brain disorder associated with memory loss, it is a form of dementia.

Congestive Heart Failure

Other cardiac disorders can cause brain dysfunction. The elderly patient is, in some ways, as helpless as an infant. Younger people suffering from a general illness usually can express themselves more specifically. Many times, however, the sickly elderly patient's only cry for help is a retreat into his or her own shell, suffering from severe exhaustion, appetite loss, and no longer wanting to communicate with the surroundings. He or she will have no desire or ability to retain any new information and will be barely able to recall old knowledge.

Recently, I received a phone message from a daughter of a patient that I have been caring for through the years. The conversation went as follows:

"I just want to let you know, Doctor, that mother is failing badly. I know she is eighty-five. I'm afraid we now will have to send her to a convalescent home, because we cannot manage her, and we would like very much for you to fill out the papers and help us to make the arrangements."

The daughter gave me the usual brain-failure story and had already attributed it to old age. Because there were no complaints of pain or obvious signs of illness, an attempt had not been made to find a medical cause for the "failing."

I answered, "You're probably right, but I think that it is only fair to your mother to have her examined to be certain there are no illnesses that are causing this."

"You know very well yourself, Doctor, that she's been healthy, but I would certainly be happy to bring her in."

The next morning the patient arrived, assisted by her daughter; she had a stooped appearance and was barely able to walk. As she walked across my large waiting room, I observed that she was actually panting. The dear lady, whose name was Lucille, greeted me with a weak voice, but there was still a slight sparkle in her eyes; she was neatly coiffured and was wearing a neat light blue dress with a white collar.

"Did you know that she is short of breath?" I asked the daughter.

"No, I never noticed, because she has been sitting around for so long, and we really haven't been taking her out at all. Now that you mention it, she did seem to pant as she walked across your waiting room."

The examination of this woman disclosed that her lungs were filled with water, her heart was markedly enlarged, and her blood pressure was low—in the vicinity of 100/70. It became obvious that she was suffering from chronic congestive heart failure which can set in insidiously in elderly patients, especially if the underlying cause is a valve that is degenerated, or a chamber that becomes enlarged as a result of a silent heart attack. With treatment of her congestive heart failure, which included diuretics, digitalis, and salt restriction, she dramatically improved in the ensuing days and her mental status cleared.

The classic symptoms of congestive heart failure that we see in younger people—marked shortness of breath, swelling of the ankles, a slight cough—may not occur in the older person. The older person usually compensates for the illness not by sending out signals to the doctor or to the family, but by resting quietly and becoming immobile. Middle-aged individuals are forever expending energy, requiring their hearts to work, and, if a heart that is not able to pump properly is forced to work, the water backs up into the lungs, causing congestive heart failure.

Older patients have, alas, a tendency to sit around, especially if there is accompanying arthritis. If there is arthritis of the hips or knees, they sit a good part of the day, with a commode placed at their side. They never move except to go from bed to chair, and occasionally to the bathroom. Swelling of the ankles is a common result of just sitting about, and their families, used to seeing their older members with swollen ankles, simply ignore the symptom.

Many older patients with very large hearts caused by a heart attack, long-standing high blood pressure, or chronic valvular disease function remarkably well. These "big heart syndromes" are poorly tolerated in the younger person. Older patients with controlled congestive heart failure may do rather well for years with minimal symptoms, until a dietary indiscretion, excessive physical activity, or a heart attack for example, pushes them into more serious heart failure. Increasing the salt intake can be very subtle but just enough to cause this acceleration of heart failure and mental impairment.

An 80-year-old woman who had been functioning moderately well at home with her family developed more memory loss than before, which again was attributed by the family to natural aging. At Christmas the patient received a large can of Polish ham from

Warsaw as a present from a member of the family. (During Christmas and holidays, dietary rules very often are broken just to make an exception for a special treat.) When she arrived in my office with heart difficulties and with enormous mental depression and memory impairment, the family denied any change in her diet. As always, they had been "very careful." Her electrocardiogram did not show a heart attack, and her blood pressure remained unchanged. I could conclude only that her aortic valve had degenerated more, furthering the course of her heart failure and requiring extra medication.

Just as they were about to leave the office, I again inquired, "Are you sure she hasn't been taking in salt of any kind or salty foods?"

"We do not add any salt to our diet, Doctor. We told you that."

Finally, one of the younger daughters said, "What about that ham that mother received from Warsaw?"

In both of these patient situations, the gentle treatment of heart failure was necessary, as more vigorous treatment could cause further brain damage (I will discuss this in a later chapter). The current medications which physicians are using in the United States are a diuretic to release the water from the body and digitalis, if the heart is beating erratically (in atrial fibrillation). Both of these drugs can raise havoc in the elderly brain so caution and moderation are advised with their prescription.

CHAPTER 9

Chemical and Blood Deficiencies

What the retired need isn't leisure, it's occupation—
two weeks is about the ideal length of time to retire.

ALEX COMFORT

Hyponatremia, or Low Salt

Nutritionists and other members of the medical profession have rightfully urged us to curtail the amount of salt that we take into our bodies in order to avoid or treat high blood pressure. The normal sodium level in the blood is measured at 135 mEq per liter. Younger patients are able to tolerate a low sodium, in the vicinity of 130 and 125. However, a chronic low sodium, or even a sudden onset of low sodium (termed "hyponatremia") can cause serious central nervous system disorders, depression, mental impairment with the loss of concentration, and even seizures. If the sodium salt in the blood gets too low, it can actually cause death.

In an article in the January 1984 edition of *Geriatric Medicine*, written by Daniel Bichet and entitled "Hyponatremia in Geriatric Patients," the author tells us that even levels as high as 130 can cause symptoms in the older person.

When the salt level of the body is too low, the brain can swell. As a rule, a prolonged period of low sodium is better tolerated than is a sudden withdrawal of salt from the body. If the onset is sudden, low salt can cause swelling in the brain (brain edema), with the characteristic of abnormal breathing (Cheyne-Stokes respiration), a rhythmic waxing and waning of respiration.

The symptoms of very low salt in the blood can be predominantly gastrointestinal—nausea, vomiting, and loss of appetite—as well as signs of sleep disturbance. There are multiple causes for low-salt syndrome, including medications. The major cause of low salt, resulting in disorientation, muscle cramps, and agitation, can be that too much salt is being lost through the kidneys as the result of excessive diuretics for the treatment of heart failure or high blood pressure, or as a result of hormonal deficiencies of the adrenals, chronic kidney disease, and heart failure. Inadequately nourished elderly patients in nursing homes and even in the hospital setting, who do not receive enough fluids, may suffer from a low-sodium syndrome. The patient may have characteristic low blood pressure (there are the telltale findings of orthostatic hypotension on standing), the temperature may be below normal, and the skin is often dry.

An illness that is seen in the elderly which causes an impairment of water loss and a low-sodium concentration is the syndrome of inappropriate antidiuretic-hormone secretion (SIADH). This is a complicated metabolic disorder, resulting from numerous causes, which is characterized by the patient's retaining too much water. The doctor determines the cause of low salt through various tests— for example, the determinations of how much urine is put out by the kidneys, the salt content of the kidneys, and the concentration of the urine. Patients who lose salt through the kidneys because of kidney disease will have a high salt in the urine. As a result of vomiting, diarrhea, or injuries, the salt in the urine may be low; however, in the SIADH syndrome, the salt of the urine is actually high, above 20 mEq per liter. Below is a list of diseases that cause the SIADH syndrome:

1. Cancer of the lung
2. Lung disorders, such as pneumonias or tuberculosis
3. Central nervous system disorders, such as infections of the brain, strokes, tumors, abscesses, and head injuries

Sometimes, medications can cause a low-salt syndrome, stimulation of the antidiuretic hormone, or the SIADH. Below is a partial list of such medications:

1. Nicotine
2. Chlorpropamide (Diabinese)
3. Clofibrate (Atromid-S)
4. Morphine
5. Barbiturates
6. Indomethacin (Indocin)
7. Acetaminophen (Tylenol)
8. Cancer drugs such as cyclophosphamide (Cytoxan); isoproterenol; and carbamazepine
9. Antidepressants, such as doxepin, imipramine, nortriptyline, and trimipramine

An outstanding example of a case in which chlorpropamide (Diabinese) caused dementia follows. It is another case of a patient's having been labeled as having senile dementia when, in reality, she was suffering from a low-salt syndrome, resulting from low salt in her blood caused by her diabetes medication.

An elderly 74-year-old woman was confined to a nursing home; at the age of seventy, she had suffered a stroke which left her paralyzed on one side. Prior to her stroke, Mimi had suffered from hypertension for twenty years. Her children, of modest means, were unable to provide home care for her. Their widowed mother had lived alone and had functioned marginally in terms of her finances until she developed the stroke and was forced to sell her house. The monies collected from the sale of the house, coupled with her entire savings, were spent on her nursing-home care, and now she was a ward of the state. Her sons visited with regularity, and, on weekends, brought her to their homes. Her grandchildren were, of course, a great joy for the lonely woman, and every attempt was made to make her life tolerable. She was a mild diabetic who did not require any insulin. Her physician prescribed an oral medication, Diabinese, to control her blood sugar, which ranged in the vicinity of 180 to 220 (the normal blood sugar being 110).

After she spent several years in the nursing home, her grandchildren were the first to remark that "grandma was acting funny." The 18-year-old grandson who visited her on a regular basis told his mother that, "Whenever I go to visit, Grandmother seems to be sleeping. Don't they ever take her out of the bed? I have to shake her to wake her up, she barely recognizes me, and it's getting worse."

The nurses were questioned and admitted that she had become a little more lethargic, but believed that it was not uncommon for patients in a nursing home to periodically go through such periods.

Wednesday was bingo day, which was one of the favorite pastimes of Grandma Mimi. One day, Grandma Mimi found that she had difficulty in remembering the numbers which were being called out and she also had no idea where on the board to find them. Too embarrassed to tell anyone, she decided to tell her friends that she was too tired to play when the next bingo Wednesday arrived. When the weekend arrived and Grandma Mimi went to her son's home, she just sat silently all day in her chair, offering an occasional smile.

The physician of the nursing home was notified of her change. He then immediately ordered tests, which included a chest x-ray, and suspected that perhaps her blood sugar was too low. All the test results were normal, except that her serum sodium was 130. The physician informed the family that she was probably suffering from progressive little strokes in her brain and that there was little that could be done for her, except to give her as much attention as possible and to surround her with familiar possessions. He added that he would give her a trial of antidepressants. Family photographs were brought to the nursing home. Her children visited several times per week, and, as the weather turned warmer, she was taken out for strolls, but her condition remained unchanged, and, if anything, worsened. Her appetite decreased, as did her food intake, and it became clear that Grandma Mimi was deteriorating rapidly.

One of her sons had heard that Norman Cousins, the editor and essayist, had helped to enhance his recovery from a heart attack with the salutary effects of laughter, and so he rented a movie projector and some Laurel and Hardy movies. Grandma Mimi watched them, smiled briefly, and soon fell asleep.

"Isn't there some kind of a stimulant that you can give her? She's sleeping all the time. How about some vitamins?"

After reviewing her entire history and physical and ordering numerous blood tests, the physician found that her sodium was too low and that she was receiving Diabinese. He discontinued all her medications and instructed the home to put her on the American Diabetic Association diet because he suspected that the Diabinese was causing an SIADH syndrome, resulting in a low-salt level.

Within a period of ten days, the serum sodium returned to normal, the patient's blood sugar was well-controlled through her diet alone, and her mental status improved remarkably. The oldest son had in the interim found a better job, and it was decided to take Grandma Mimi home after a small addition was built onto the house. Although Grandma Mimi is still in a wheelchair, she is not receiving any medications: she is living at home, being cared for by her family and is doing very nicely.

In Mimi's case, some of her symptoms were obviously worsened because of her previous stroke and the mental degeneration was thought to be secondary to the stroke. However, in view of the excellent improvement that followed once the Diabinese was discontinued, the staff realized that in this case Diabinese was the cause of her accelerating deterioration.

In essence, this story lends insight into one of the reversible causes of senility. An energetic approach is necessary to find the cause of memory loss, along with a broad knowledge of medicine. (In a separate chapter, "Medications and Chemicals," there will be a detailed description of commonly used medications that can cause this problem.)

Diabetes

This is one of the ancient earliest known diseases; it was recorded in the Ebers Papyrus papers of ancient Egypt before the year 30 B.C. The most obvious symptom of the illness is excessive urination and thirst. In the first century A.D., Aretaus coined the word "diabetes," from the Greek term for "passing through." His description remains appropriate today:

> The nature of the disease then is chronic and takes a long period to form, but the patient is short-lived. Moreover, life is disgusting and painful; thirst unquenchable; excessive drinking,

which, however, is proportionate to the large quantity of urine, for more urine is passed and one cannot stop either from drinking or making water. Or, for a time, they abstain from drinking, their mouths become parched and their bodies dry, their viscera seem as if scorched up, they are affected with nausea, restlessness and a burning thirst, and at no distant term, they expire.

The relation between sugar and diabetes was recognized in the sixth century by the Indian physician Susruta, who wrote of diabetes as the "honey urine disease."

Dr. Thomas Willis, in the seventeenth century, added the tasting of urine to the time-honored practice of urine-gazing, a testing of urine for color, odor, and texture, discovering diabetic urine to be "wonderfully sweet." It was later discovered in 1775 by Matthew Dobson that the sweet material in diabetic urine is sugar.

Prior to the discovery of insulin in 1921 by Dr. Frederick Banting of Toronto, the natural course of severe diabetes was death. Some elderly patients can still recall how members of their family appeared before the era of insulin—progressively emaciated, with eyes pushed back into their sockets, the skin hanging over their bodies from weight loss and dehydration, completely mentally disoriented, confused, and no longer able to function. Clinicians could recognize a diabetic by just walking into the room and observing the patient's gaunt look and smelling the odor of acetone.

In the younger person, the onset of diabetes can present with an explosive picture of acute nausea, vomiting, dehydration, the smell of acetone on the breath, and, finally, if untreated, coma and death. Patients still die from diabetic coma, although it is now rather uncommon.

The elderly patient is unable to send out signals of the classic picture of diabetes. The major symptom may be lethargy, a generalized weakness, memory loss, and a progressive deterioration of mental faculties. Once the diagnosis is made and agents prescribed to lower the blood sugar, the mental process may become completely reversed, if not too much brain damage has already occurred.

Diabetic patients, regardless of age, can have progressive elevation of their blood sugar levels with the symptomatology consisting of weakness, inability to concentrate, prolonged fatigue, and increased thirst. There is no definite numeric level of the blood sugar synonymous with the onset of mental symptoms. Most patients who have blood sugar of 400 will start exhibiting signs of some mental impairment. However, some patients may do so at a much lower level such as 300. A normally controlled blood sugar may rise for many reasons: excessive anxieties, infection, a sudden ingestion of sugar, or medications such as diuretics and cortisone. Diabetics who are receiving medications such as thiazide or furosemide for heart failure and treatment of hypertension may show a progressive rise in their blood sugar with the resultant symptomatology of diabetes, which, at times, may be thought due to heart failure or hypertension. A quiet indolent infection of the urinary tract can cause an elevation of the blood sugar. Diabetics are more prone to infections, especially of the kidney, as organisms proliferate in a diabetic environment. In diabetic patients who exhibit mental changes with elevation of blood sugar from an unknown cause, a urine culture should be performed to look for an infection. *Any* kind of infection, whether it be of the skin or of the lung, can cause a precipitous rise in the blood sugar.

Diabetic experts now classify diabetes into two forms—Type 1, which is called insulin-dependent diabetes, usually found in younger people and indicative of the fact that there is not enough insulin being produced by the pancreas, and Type 2 diabetes, the type usually seen in older people, which does not result from an absence of insulin, but from a blockage of insulin, which renders it ineffective in regulating the blood sugar.

The elderly person who develops diabetes has adequate insulin stores; the insulin, although available, is blocked from lowering the blood sugar. At present, with our knowledge of diabetes, adequate control can be achieved with the help of weight reduction and oral agents called hypoglycemic agents to lower the blood sugar—chlorpropamide (Diabinese), acetohexamide (Dymelor), tolazamide (Tolinase), tolbutamide (Orinase), etc. If the diabetes is more severe, insulin is given in a long-acting form. The current trend in insulin administration is to simultaneously give the patient two types of insulin for 24-hour regulation—a short-acting insulin (two- to four-hour duration) with a long-acting one (ten- to sixteen-hour duration), or a long-acting one coupled with an intermediate acting insulin (five- to eight-hour duration).

More vigorous control is achieved with an insulin pump which gives a 24-hour-insulin injection by an automatic implanted system. There is a trend today which allows patients to ingest a moderate amount of sugar in spite of their diabetes because it seems to have little effect on their control. However, this new concept remains controversial and I, for one, cling to the old-fashioned notion of restraining sugar intake.

One of the methods of controlling the patient's diabetes is the monitoring of the urine glucose. It is actually a relatively crude method, since the blood sugar may be very high although the sugar may not appear in the urine. On the other hand, the blood sugar may be moderately elevated and the sugar will appear in the urine. Patients have varying thresholds for excreting the excessive sugar in their blood, although urine sugar, if high, is a useful warning sign that better control is needed.

Complications of diabetes such as detrimental effects on the kidneys and the eyes are well known. Diabetes is one of the major causes of blindness and can adversely affect the circulatory system, causing atherosclerosis. Deposits of the atherosclerotic plaque, which cause the coronary arteries to harden, often resulting in heart attacks and strokes, are of the same kind found in nondiabetics, but diabetics generally have even greater plaque formation than usual.

One of the purposes for the treatment of diabetes is to give the patient relief from chronic excessive thirst and urination, weight loss, and general debility. Some diabetic experts claim that excellent control of diabetes may avert the vascular and kidney complications. On a more practical basis, the treatment of diabetes in the elderly should prevent the blood sugar from rising too high, or, for that matter, dropping too low, as the result of the treatment.

If blood sugar levels fall too low, prolonged dementia can result. The patient may complain of chronic dizzy spells, headaches, clouding of vision, confusion, bizarre behavior, and memory loss, and the condition could be mistaken for multi-infarction dementia or Alzheimer's disease.

Elderly patients are particularly prone to the development of hypoglycemia because of tremor and poor vision, which may cause them to accidentally self-administer too many insulin units. The most common cause of an excessive insulin reaction is the failure of the person to eat breakfast, lunch, or supper. Food must be taken when insulin is given. The maximum effect of a morning administration of long-acting (NPH) insulin is at 4 P.M., though the dosage may last for twenty hours. If the person fails to eat lunch, a 4 P.M hypoglycemic reaction occurs (or reactions can occur in the middle of the night if supper is not eaten). The common insulin reaction is the sudden onset of weakness, sweating, faintness, and actual unconsciousness. These hypoglycemic reactions are quickly reversed with the administration of sugar. In the older person, symptoms of hypoglycemia may often be more subtle. If the hypoglycemia is prolonged and recurrent, there may be no sweating episodes, but the patient will appear listless, apathetic, and will experience periods of hallucinations, memory loss, and loss of cognition.

Sam, a 78-year-old male, developed Type 2 diabetes at the age of sixty-four. He sustained a heart attack at the age of sixty-seven, followed by an excellent recovery. His blood sugar varied, in the range of 200 to 350 mg., and he was placed on a long- and short-acting insulin program. Each morning, a half-hour before breakfast, he placed 45 units of NPH and 10 units of the short-acting insulin into his syringe. For the next three years, his daily insulin requirements remained the same. Periodically, through the next few years, he had episodes of dizzy spells and occasional numbness of his lower extremities. The dizzy spells were attributed mostly to improper blood circulation to his brain, probably arising from the basilar artery, and the numbness was seen as a classic example of diabetic neuropathy, one of the complications of diabetes involving the nerves. He was a conscientious patient and went to see his physician every three months to have his blood sugar and blood pressure tested and to have his heart examined.

His wife died suddenly but Sam refused to move in with his children. He wanted to maintain his independence. He did his own cooking and shopping, as well as his own housecleaning. Unknown to the doctor or his family, Sam experienced periods when he felt a great deal of exhaustion, and he was afraid to tell anyone that at times he was confused. Sometimes, after falling asleep in his chair he awoke several hours later to find that he was drenched in sweat. His memory failure became evident to his children when he did not call them on a regular basis and when he began to forget his grandchildren's names. He forgot the name of the President of the United States and sometimes lost his way when shopping for food.

The family brought Sam to the family physician who found that his blood pressure was 150/70. His heart examination was normal, except for a slight heart murmur. All the laboratory examinations were also within normal limits. A spot blood-sugar test was 140 (normal being in the range of 100 to 130, depending on the laboratory). The doctor had strong suspicions that the memory loss had a definite physiological cause. He continued to go through a diagnostic detective search, including an EEG (which was normal), as well as a CT scan of the brain. A neurologist was called in consultation and did some psychological testing, finding that Sam had brain failure, probably of the multi-infarction type. As he was a diabetic, Sam had a propensity toward atherosclerosis of the brain. The family physician, however, was still not satisfied and considered one more possibility. Was it possible that Sam was injecting himself with too much insulin and that his sugar was dropping too low? He asked the family to bring Sam into the office in the morning and again at 4 P.M., and, to take him to the emergency room at midnight.

Sam was brought to the doctor's office in the morning; his blood sugar was found to be over 200. At 4 P.M., his blood sugar was 130, and, when his family brought him to the emergency room at midnight, the blood sugar was 50. It was at this time that he was most confused and disoriented. It became clear that Sam was having prolonged episodes of hypoglycemia, which were causing his brain to become more damaged. The insulin dosage was halved; part of it was given in the morning and the other part given at night, and the blood sugar moved to a controlled range of 160. Furthermore, Sam was instructed to have a snack at bedtime to prevent any further hypoglycemic reactions. In the course of the next two weeks, he became more mentally alert and his memory improved. Undoubtedly, he still suffered from some multi-infarction early dementia, which had been worsened by the severe hypoglycemic episodes. He finally was convinced to move in with his family, and his mental status improved greatly because now his insulin was even more carefully regulated, as were his eating habits.

Patients who are taking beta-blocker agents for the treatment of hypertension and coronary artery disease may have less of a requirement for insulin and can suffer insulin reactions. Beta-blockers are sometimes poorly tolerated by the elderly patient and are less effective for the treatment of hypertension than would be the case in younger persons.

A 77-year-old woman who needed insulin for the control of her diabetes was given a beta-blocker to help control her hypertension, which was in the range of 200/110. She was also receiving 40 units of NPH. Her blood pressure was moderately controlled, but it became clear to the family in the ensuing months that she had begun to change and was going downhill.

"I think mother will have to be put in a home soon. We will not be able to take care of her," her daughter lamented.

She made arrangements for her mother to be hospitalized in a nursing home, but, upon the insistence of her physician, her mother first had a complete examination. Her diagnostic work-up disclosed that she was having severe episodes of hypoglycemia, resulting in mental retardation and intellectual failure. When the beta-blockers were discontinued, her insulin adjusted and her memory improved. She is now doing well and is still living at home.

Alcohol in large quantities can also cause hypoglycemia. Diabetics taking insulin and consuming large quantities of alcohol are prone to develop hypoglycemic reactions. Excessive alcohol by itself can cause mental deterioration, and, if coupled with hypoglycemia, can be a cause for reversible dementia.

A 69-year-old man who had been a severe diabetic all his life suddenly lost his wife to a heart attack, and, now, living by himself, was drinking much more than usual. Whenever he arrived at the doctor's office, he was fully alert, but there was evidence that his mental status had changed. It was reported that he smiled and cried at inappropriate times and exhibited bizarre behavior, such as getting up at 4 A.M. and walking aimlessly through the streets. During these walks, he sometimes would buy dozens of lobsters at the fish market, but then forgot how to find his way home. It was not known that he was an alcoholic, and, when he was brought totally disoriented to the emergency room one day, his blood sugar was found to be 35, instead of in the normal range of 90 to 100. He received an infusion of sugar and very quickly reacted and became mentally oriented. He was advised to decrease the amount of insulin that he was taking. His dosage was reduced to 60 units in the morning and 25 units at night. However, things changed little. He continued to have his periods of disorientation and confusion and complete memory lapses regarding time and place. Once when he was hospitalized for a myocardial infarction, he was completely oriented during his entire hospitalization, until he again returned to his home. During his stay in the hospital, the intern, resident, medical student, and attending physician all asked him whether he drank, and he said, "Occasionally, on the weekends."

Several months later he was again admitted into the hospital in a stupor, and an intern on duty measured a series of toxic substances in his blood, including alcohol which was markedly elevated. Alcohol, it was discovered, was never smelled on his breath because he used a great deal of garlic (which, he had read in a health magazine, prevented strokes). He finally admitted that he had been drinking heavily since the death of his wife because he no longer found life to be worthwhile. After he was placed in a rehabilitation center and was cured of his drinking and depression, his diabetes came under excellent control, and his mental status returned to the level it was at prior to the death of his wife.

Pancreatic-Tumor Hypoglycemia

The entire subject of hypoglycemia has received widespread publicity, being used to explain the cause of depression, weakness, tiredness, inability to concentrate, loss of sexual desire, bad breath, and sagging skin. There are still thousands of patients who carry the diagnosis of hypoglycemia because a blood sugar of 60 was found on one occasion and they were then placed on high-protein diets and given vitamin injections. The hypoglycemic fad continues and is still a fashionable diagnosis that charlatans use to explain a patient's symptoms. There are, however, times when hypoglycemia is the genuine illness, but this is not very common. Some patients run low-blood sugars (as low as 25 mg.) with no symptoms. True hypoglycemia can have numerous causes: 1) liver disease, such as cirrhosis or hepatitis; 2) certain drugs, such as alcohol, beta-blockers, and aspirin; 3) enzyme deficiencies; and 4) hormone failures. Some patients become hypoglycemic as the first sign of diabetes (this is reactive hypoglycemia) or from intake of too much insulin, as previously described.

The diagnosis of hypoglycemia is considered if the blood sugar falls below 50. True hypoglycemia can cause brain degeneration, and the diagnosis is made after a 72-hour fast. Blood sugars are drawn, and cortisone levels and other tests are taken. If, during this 72-hour fast, the blood sugar falls far below normal and the patient become symptomatic, then the diagnosis is confirmed. A casual five-hour glucose tolerance test sometimes gives the answer. The patient is given a known quantity of sugar and then blood is drawn on a prescribed half-hour or hourly basis. At the end of five hours, a blood sugar of 35 is strongly suggestive of true hypoglycemia.

There are patients with true hypoglycemia who suffer memory loss and dementia. Every medical house officer has had the occasion to see such a case at least once during his or her training career, presenting with disorientation, confusion, confabulation, and total brain dysfunction.

When I was a resident physician at a city hospital in New York, I met Gordon, who was brought into our emergency room. He had been picked up while semiconscious on the street—unshaven, unwashed, and wearing shabby clothing. After injection with intravenous fluids, he became conscious after several hours but had little recollection of what had happened to him. A thorough investigation disclosed that he was a 43-year-old formerly successful electrical engineer who had lost his job. He stated that he had since become markedly depressed and suffered a great deal of fatigue, and he had also noticed that his memory was failing. He denied ever drinking any alcohol, and now, homeless, he wished that we had not saved his life.

After numerous tests, we found no evidence of brain tumors and no definite cause for his unconscious state, except, possibly, malnutrition. In the hospital, after being maintained on a proper nutrition program, he became alert and turned out to be a very intelligent man. In the ensuing months, however, Gordon was brought into another emergency room and went through similar types of tests with no findings. He became a patient in our out-patient clinic, and it became clear that Gordon was gradually deteriorating mentally.

On one of his visits, when he had to wait for almost four hours to be seen, the nurse found him sitting in the chair and staring up at the ceiling, not knowing where he was. He was unable to give his name, and it was only by pure chance that I happened to look out towards the waiting room and saw him sitting there, totally immobile. We swiftly brought him into the examining room and I drew several blood samples for tests, including those for sugar levels, kidney function, and blood count. As he sat waiting—conscious but totally unaware of his surroundings—the laboratory technician called and told me that his blood sugar was 20 mg. I thought it was a laboratory error and so I drew another blood sugar; in the meantime, I inserted an intravenous tube and began to administer sugar. Within one hour, Gordon was fully awake and alert, and we realized that we had been missing a case of severe hypoglycemia. It was not necessary to go through a 72-hour fast because we had our diagnosis—now we had to determine the cause.

Through complicated testing, we discovered that he was suffering from a tumor of the pancreas called an insuloma. The diagnosis of an insuloma of the pancreas was confirmed by an arteriogram (an x-ray of the arteries) of the pancreas. An operation was performed and a large tumor was found and removed from the head of the pancreas. Several weeks later, Gordon was discharged from the hospital, totally cured, and there have been no further episodes of hypoglycemia.

As I reviewed his history when he was fully lucid, it was apparent that he must have been suffering from this illness even when working as an engineer, and that he had lost his job because, unable to concentrate and suffering from memory loss, he had made many mistakes. He is again working as an engineer and lives a normal life.

All these cases serve to illustrate that dementia and brain failure may have curable causes for which a diligent search must be made, as many of these problems are relatively uncommon causes of brain failure.

Calcium Abnormalities

As a result of the current health-food craze for vitamins, their sales have been rising astronomically, and unknowingly, patients may very well be overdosing themselves. I know some patients who take 40 to 50 pills per day because of quackery regarding prolongation of life with megavitamins. In trying to correct a deficiency, sometimes we overcorrect and cause an excess, with long-term, serious detrimental effects.

Calcium is now in the limelight as a recommended preventative of bone destruction and hypertension. Doctors are urging female patients to take calcium supplements to prevent osteoporosis. Calcium is the fifth most abundant element in the body and makes up most of the bone. We need calcium for the function of nerve, muscle, and heart, and for the normal clotting of blood. Our skeletons contain 90 percent of the calcium of the body. The average American diet contains from 250 to 2500 mg. of calcium per day. Calcium is absorbed through the intestines and its absorption is enhanced by the addition of vitamin D. We lose approximately one gram of calcium per day through the excretory systems. If an excessive amount of calcium and vitamin D is ingested for a long time, there can be too much calcium in the blood, with deposits in the kidneys, arteries, and soft tissues.

Excessive levels of calcium can result from either excessive ingestion or from an overactive parathyroid gland. Calcium abnormalities can be responsible for dementia. Excessive calcium can also cause gastrointestinal symptoms, such as diarrhea, constipation, nausea, vomiting, loss of appetite, and weight loss. In the chronic high-calcium condition, the major symptoms may be psychoneurosis and dementia.

A 65-year-old widow, Agatha, living with her daughter, had always been regarded as a high-strung individual. She suffered from mild diabetes which was being treated with an oral hypoglycemic agent, from mild hypertension (160/110) for which she was receiving a diuretic, from chronic arthritis of her lower back (osteoarthritis), and from chronic obesity. Her daughters were extraordinarily devoted, and they were always available when she needed them. A slight headache, a little gas bubble, an aching joint—all received immediate medical attention. In recent years, her daughters had noticed that she was complaining more often of indigestion and had marked episodes of depression, coupled with anxieties and memory loss. The daughters, being health-food faddists, made certain that each morning Agatha took 100,000 units of vitamin D, 1½ g. of calcium, and at least 15 other pills. The calcium, the daughters explained, was necessary to prevent her bones from breaking and to help arthritis. Although the instructions were to give her only ½ to 1 g. per day, her daughters felt that if one was good, then two must be better. They changed their mother's physician frequently, especially if he or she did not understand "her problem," even though Agatha might have been quite satisfied with the physician. Each physician she saw performed a thorough physical examination and numerous blood tests. In some of the screening blood tests, a calcium test was not included. In others, the calcium had returned to borderline limits; sometimes her calcium was found to be 10.5 (the upper limit of normal being 10). This slightly abnormal calcium level was considered to be the result of her taking calcium pills.

Soon Agatha's depressions, anxiety, and memory loss increased to the extent that she had to be seen in consultation with a psychiatrist. Psychiatric care continued for a period of four months, with little improvement. In spite of antidepressant medications and antianxiety pills, she was clearly becoming worse. The daughters decided that her first internist had been the best one and made an appointment for her to be seen again on a Thursday morning.

The internist was quite surprised to see her. Her blood pressure was under control, but her mental status had changed dramatically. Unlike her previous presentation, this time she wore no lipstick, her hair was uncombed, and she had gained a great deal of weight. Agatha could barely converse with the physician.

"What year is this?" he asked.

She answered, "1963." (It was 1984.)

"What time of the year is it?"

She answered, "It's January." (It was in the heat of July.)

Her daughters were surprised to see how seriously altered her mental state had become because no one had actually tested her in this way before. She had difficulty in retaining five numbers and could not recall four words.

Unknowingly, her daughters had aggravated her condition by their overprotective attitude. Wherever the mother went, she was always accompanied by a daughter because they believed that she was unable to drive her own car. She no longer did her own cooking because her daughters wanted her to "take it easy." All responsibilities had been taken away from her, including the writing of her own checks. It was because of this excessive indulgence, all this "help" she was getting, that there was no possibility of realizing that she was indeed deteriorating very badly.

The entire physical examination was essentially unchanged from the previous one, with a borderline blood pressure reading; however, the blood tests this time disclosed a serum calcium of 13.0 (above normal). The alert physician had the patient discontinue all her medications, including the vitamin pills, repeated the calcium level again, and found it to be even higher, at 14.0.

The perceptive physician searched for causes of Agatha's high calcium, one of which could be cancer. There was no evidence of cancer, and it seemed likely that the patient was suffering from hyperparathyroidism (a condition of high calcium and low phosphate). (The diagnosis of hypercalcemia from an overactive parathyroid gland is a difficult diagnosis. Other endocrine disorders should also be looked for, such as an overactive thyroid or an underactive adrenal gland.)

Many patients with an overactive parathyroid gland may not need to be operated on if the calcium level is minimally elevated and causes no symptoms. This patient did have an operation, and a parathyroid-gland tumor was found and removed. Her serum calcium level dropped within a day and then remained normal. In the ensuing months, her senility dramatically reversed. Her anxieties, however, remained, as did her periods of depression. The physician counseled the daughters to give her more responsibilities—for example, allowing her to do housework or to cook. After becoming involved in local retired-citizen groups, her life dramatically changed; she even got her own apartment with another elderly woman, and is, now, at the age of seventy-eight, carrying on a productive and vital life, visiting her daughters once every two weeks.

It is essential for the patient to tell the physician about every medication being taken and *not* to forget to mention the vitamin pills. Most people do not regard vitamin pills as medications because they are bought over the counter. (In Chap. 11, on page 180, I will discuss many of the medications bought over the counter that can cause chronic senility.)

If excess calcium in the blood is suspected, several calcium blood levels need to be drawn as the level of calcium may vary from day to day. The combination of symptoms of senility, depression, and nausea, sometimes coupled with duodenal ulcers or kidney stones, should make the physician suspect an overactive parathyroid gland.

Another dramatic example of an excessive calcium store in the body is described in the next, 42-year-old patient.

Alice had exhibited extraordinarily bizarre behavior throughout most of her life, which intensified as she approached the age of forty. She continually sought medical attention for a variety of symptoms that were described as "something crawling up my back," "a bad taste in my mouth," "a hot feeling going down my throat," and "a continual pulling of my privates." She noted that, "I never eat anything and yet I gain weight. I am always thirsty and I'm always urinating."

All of her examinations had been normal, including multiple laboratory tests for various glandular disorders. During one blustery winter night, she developed a high fever and chills and was diagnosed as having severe bronchopneumonia. After she was admitted into the local hospital, treatment was started with antibiotics, and the next day her blood chemistry results showed an extremely elevated serum calcium level of 20 (the normal range is 5 to 10). It was repeated several times because it was thought to be a laboratory error. A scrupulously diligent investigation by the physician did not disclose a cause for the unusually high calcium level. All the x-rays and laboratory examination results were normal. Alice was treated vigorously for the high calcium level, which remained normal for the rest of two weeks.

Prior to the patient's discharge, the nurses noted that Alice showered at least eight times a day, violently scrubbing her body until she became as red as a lobster. In addition, she brushed her teeth at least seven times during the day. She asked the nurse for bicarbonate of soda to remove the "pollutant stains" from her teeth. A psychiatrist was called in to observe this behavior and Alice told him that a devil lived in her body and that the only way to get rid of it was to cleanse her body scrupulously. The devil, she said, caused the burning in her stomach and in other areas of her body, as well as her blurred vision. The psychiatrist asked her what she did to get rid of the burning.

"The only thing that will make it better," she stated, "is taking antacids."

"And how many antacid pills do you take per day?"

"Sometimes up to 200."

It was thus clear that Alice was psychotic, even though she had seemed normal and was married and had raised children. The doctors concluded that because of the excessive ingestion of antacids, Alice had developed a classic syndrome, called the milk-alkali syndrome, which caused her calcium level to rise inordinately. The psychiatrist performed some mental testing and found that she had a marked brain deficit, equivalent to an IQ level between 50 and 69, which, if she were older, would classify her as senile.

In the ensuing months, Alice was hospitalized in a psychiatric ward and was no longer provided with antacid medications. Her serum calcium level returned to normal, and she experienced a remarkable return of her memory. Her periods of hallucinations diminished. She became convinced that the devil was no longer inside of her, that the high fever and pneumonia had pushed him out of her body, and that now she was completely cured, except for the occasional "devil visit on religious holidays."

This patient's story illustrates a case of hypercalcemia resulting from ingestion of too many antacid pills. Although she probably had been a borderline psychotic for many years, she had suffered severe mental aberrations coupled with memory loss, as her calcium level increased. It had never been apparent to her husband or doctors that she suffered from hallucinations, as one does not usually ask an apparently normal woman, "Do you ever hear voices or see animals walking on the ceiling?"

The opposite condition to an elevated calcium problem is an abnormally *low* calcium, a rare condition. It can result from surgery to the parathyroid gland, which is located in the neck, or the thyroid gland. A patient can develop brain disorders from too low a calcium level in the blood. It occurs rarely—if the parathyroid gland becomes underactive, or if family members have been shown to have an illness called familiar syndrome of hypoparathyroidism. It is considered to be an immunological illness in which antibodies are being formed against the patient's own parathyroid gland. Low-calcium levels can also occur because of the improper absorption of calcium through the body, as in certain illnesses of the gastrointestinal tract. The illness, called malabsorption syndrome, consists of a group of disorders, such as celiac disease which prevents the absorption of calcium and other imporant nutrients, that result in a seriously malnourished individual. Brain dysfunction, memory loss, and mental impairment can result from the loss of important nutrients such as amino acids, sugar, proteins, blood electrolytes, and fats—material which are needed for the synthesis of brain chemicals. In essence, the chemistry of the brain can become altered.

Borderline-to-low serum calcium levels are frequently found in the elderly patient, resulting from nutritional inadequacies, but these rarely become so critical as to cause mental impairment. It is common to have associated softening of the bone, or osteoporosis, in patients with low calcium levels.

A common disorder of the bowel that causes poor absorption of proper nutrients, such as calcium, is an infection called giardiasis which is transmitted by the parasite *Giardia lamblia*. This parasitic infection usually results from the drinking of well water which is contaminated with the parasite. In certain areas of the world where well water is used—Switzerland, the Virgin Islands, and sections of the United States including parts of Colorado—this giardiasis infestation is common. More recently, it has become an illness common among homosexuals. It is a strange illness that has an insidious onset and is sometimes explosive, with bouts of diarrhea, fatigue, and weight loss. The diarrhea may at first be just some loose stools which occur three or four times a day. The symptoms can continue for years; the longer the illness is present, the harder it is to diagnose. The surface of the small intestine becomes denuded and flattened, losing its fingerlike projections called villi which aid in absorption. Undigested fatty material then appears and makes the stool odorous, bulky, and fatty in appearance.

Some of the symptoms that result are a progressive slow weight loss, extreme fatigue, the inability to concentrate, and memory loss. It afflicts the young and the old. As we have seen in the earlier portion of this book, important foodstuffs are necessary for brain function. If the amino acids are not properly absorbed and converted into the neurotransmitters and neuropeptides, brain dysfunction can result. Even though there may be adequate food intake there is still inadequate absorption; it is essentially a state of starvation.

The diagnosis of giardiasis is made by finding the parasite in a stool culture. Unfortunately, culturing techniques are sometimes inadequate, and many times the parasite is not recovered from a stool specimen. In due time, the intestine may have the appearance of a lymphoma or cancer of the bowel. The conclusive method of diagnosing this illness is to have a biopsy done of the small bowel, using proper staining techniques to find *G. lamblia*. A biopsy of the bowel which is not focused on a search for this parasite by staining technique will usually miss the diagnosis.

This illness, which can cause a dementialike picture, is remarkably amenable to treatment and cure. A medication used for the treatment of malaria—Flagyl—is used in cases of giardiasis and can result in improvement in a few days.

A 49-year-old executive vacationed each winter in the Virgin Islands. After returning from one of his trips, he noticed that his bowels became loose and he attributed it to the food on the plane. This continued for many months, along with diarrhea, lack of concentration, enormous fatigue, and memory loss. Finally he consulted a physician.

The entire examination was normal. Stool cultures were taken and were also within normal limits. His symptoms were believed to result from tension, and he was given tranquilizers and medications for too-frequent bowel movements.

He did not improve and remained in about the same condition. He started to lose his appetite and felt extraordinarily bloated. His sleep became impaired, with early morning sleeplessness coupled with depression, and, in addition, he became impotent. The combination of symptoms of sleep disturbance, impotence, and weight loss pointed to a severe psychoneurosis.

Stool cultures were repeatedly normal. Blood-chemistry analysis showed that the executive was not absorbing proteins and other substances. He was suffering from malabsorption, but the cause had yet to be discovered. Was the cause cancer or a parasite?

A GI series was taken which suggested cancer. A small-bowel biopsy showed the villa of the bowel to be completely destroyed with lymphoma. The doctor asked the pathologist to do special stains of the specimen for giardiasis. Much to the joy of the patient and the doctor, giardiasis was demonstrated on the specimen. After one week of treatment with Flagyl, the diarrhea disappeared, and, after several months, all the physical and mental symptoms had subsided, never to return. If you have prolonged diarrhea and have recently traveled abroad, tell your doctor—you may have a parasite in your bowel.

Diseases of the Thyroid Gland

It has long been known that impairment of the thyroid gland is a well-known cause of dementia. This gland, first described by Vesalius in the sixteenth century, is butterfly-shaped and located in the neck, straddling the windpipe, and is surrounded by nerves that help to control the movement of the voicebox. The parathyroid glands, described earlier, are meshed in its center.

The thyroid gland secretes hormones called thyroxine and triiodothyronine which regulate the metabolism of the body. The gland depends upon a supply of iodine, obtained from foods, to manufacture these hormones. Formerly, if one traveled to the mountains of Switzerland where iodine was not found in foods, he or she would have found an extraordinary number of alpine villagers with large goiters in their necks. The condition in which the gland works overtime is called hyperthyroidism; inadequate secretion results in the condition of hypothyroidism.

"Underactive thyroid," another fashionable diagnosis, is too often the label used to describe a patient who is excessively fatigued and overweight. Unfortunately, thyroid medication has long been used as a panacea for weight loss along with appetite suppressants and B_{12} injections. Prior to the discoveries of thyroid replacement and thyroid suppression, a disease of the thyroid often resulted in death. For centuries, terms such as "thyroid storm" and "myxedema madness" were well known to the physician.

Dr. Carl Basedow was a nineteenth-century expert on thyroid disease and established a fashionable elite rest home for affluent Victorian ladies outside of Wurzburg, Germany. The following is an abstract from some of Dr. Basedow's notes describing the overactive thyroid:

The year is 1849, in the castle of William II. The tall windows are barred and it is snowing. In some of the rooms, the windows are flung open as elegant women parade naked, screaming, prancing back and forth, wringing their hands in despair, complaining of the heat as a snowflake enters. The eyes are popping, they are shouting obscenities, completely disoriented and demented. In other rooms, women are lying in bed with their wrists and feet strapped down, covered by ice blankets as they lie in delirium with temperatures of 104°. Attendants dart over to them to prevent them from injuring themselves.

In the parlor, women are talking in loud explosive voices, their thoughts racing ahead of them, forgetting the names of knives and plates, confusing names of objects, suspicious and paranoid that someone is about to kill them. They eat off elegant plates, using their fingers as they forgot how to use knives and forks.

All of these elegant ladies, coming from aristocratic homes, slowly develop severe anxieties and nervousness with uncontrollable appetites, and some with lewd behavior could no longer be kept at home.

The treatment for the overactive thyroid consisted of baths, relaxation, and ingestion of seaweed and burnt sponges, as they contain iodine until the storm of their illness subsided and their gland returned to a normal or euthyroid state. Many of these poor women died; others were spontaneously cured.

Today, an overactive thyroid is readily diagnosed with the characteristic findings of tremors, weight loss, increased appetite, bulging eyes, prominent swelling in the neck, excessive nervousness, and psychoneurotic behavior. Patients rarely die from this illness, although there are times when the "thyroid storm" still occurs, with temperatures of 105°, delirium, confusion, and dementia.

In the elderly patient, this is a difficult diagnosis to make because the classic symptoms of hyperthyroidism may not be present. Besides the subtle mental changes that the overactive gland manifests, older patients can present with the predominant symptom of heart failure: the heart may not be pumping enough blood, causing shortness of breath, or there may be a common irregular rhythm (atrial fibrillation) or, less commonly, a heart attack. Among cardiologists, there is universal agreement that in a person who is found to be in atrial fibrillation with no apparent heart cause, such as rheumatic fever or enlarged chambers, hyperthyroidism should be considered.

In the elderly patient, an overactive thyroid can cause reverse symptoms! This is the reason doctors call the condition "apathetic hyperthyroidism." The patient may show signs of brain failure, be poorly responsive to anyone speaking to him or her, be unaware of his or her surroundings, or not recognize the family or physician. The excessive thyroid hormone can make the patient look starved, due to loss of muscle tissue. The routine thyroid test may be normal, or just slightly elevated, and the physician will proceed to perform a sophisticated thyroid-function test, called the TRH-stimulating test. This test stimulates the thyroid to produce hormones. If its function is impaired, the stimulation with TRH (thyrotropin-releasing hormone) will have no effect. The picture of apathetic hyperthyroidism may appear as symptoms of an underactive thyroid (which I will discuss later). Patients who are labeled as "demented" should have thorough thyroid studies.

A 75-year-old woman was escorted by her husband to a doctor's office because of continual weight loss and lack of desire for food. Ella sat quietly in the examining room with her hands on her lap. Her hair was neatly combed. She had a pale grayish complexion. Her eyes sat back in their sockets, dull and staring, indifferent to her surroundings. She had been married nearly fifty years, was childless, and had always been a fragile, taciturn lady.

"What is your name?" the doctor asked.

"Ella."

"Do you know where you are?"

"I think I'm in a doctor's office."

"What is your husband's name?"

"Stanley."

"Have you noticed anything different about yourself?"

"No."

"Have you lost any weight?"

"I don't think so."

"Do you feel like eating?"

"I never have any appetite."

"Who is President of the United States?"

She sat quietly, fidgeted a while, and said, "I don't know. I used to know."

Ella was never much of a reader and had never finished high school. She had worked as a sewing-machine operator until the age of sixty-five. Her husband informed the doctor that she had always been a quiet woman—"not much for words." She was now showing signs of uninterest in food and just sat quietly all day in her chair.

She was diagnosed as having dementia of the Alzheimer type after she had complete x-ray studies of the upper and low GI tract. A CT scan of the brain showed brain atrophy. Her examination revealed that she had low blood pressure, a slow pulse rate, dry skin, cracks at the angles of her mouth, and a sore tongue—all suggestive of a vitamin deficiency and malnutrition. Routine thyroid tests were all within normal limits, but her triiodothyronine, or T_4, was borderline, on the upper limits of normal. A TRH test was performed, which pointed to the diagnosis of an overactive thyroid. Using a pediatric dosage plan, the patient received antithyroid medication over a period of four to six weeks, and her entire mental status progressively changed. She became more alert, her appetite returned, and her demented state completely reversed.

It is not possible to determine how many patients carry the diagnosis of apathetic hyperthyroidism because it is not a common illness, but it *is* one that needs to be considered in the patient suffering from dementia, especially if there is some enlargement of the thyroid gland in the neck.

In one study published in the *New England Journal of Medicine* in 1983, it was discovered that of all elderly patients who entered into the hospital with an abnormal heartbeat of no apparent cause, 10 percent were suffering from hyperthyroidism, which was discovered by the TRH testing.

When I had the opportunity to spend a year working at St. Mary's Hospital in London, the chief of the medical service was a British medical sleuth par excellence. He delighted in solving difficult cases using sheer deductive reasoning—finding subtle clues and gluing them together into a solid diagnosis. He presented me with the problem of a 68-year-old gray-haired woman who was brought in by her family since she showed signs of "being out of her wits." She was a heavyset woman who looked like Tugboat Annie; she was wearing a cap on her head, a long-sleeved dress with a sweater, and woolen stockings rolled up to her knees. A worn sweater was thrown over her shoulders. She had a face of strong character which lacked any luster, eyes with swollen eyelids, sparse eyebrows, and skin that was weatherbeaten and coarse in appearance. Her lips were prominent, puffy, and crusted, covering tobacco-stained teeth. Every once in a while, she rolled a mound of tobacco and pushed it against her outer jaw and asked for a wastebasket to spit out the juice.

When I interviewed her, she spoke slowly, in the tone of an old phonograph record that was about to stop playing. Her voice was low and hoarse. I could barely understand her muttering, not only because of her strong cockney accent, but also because her words were confused and inappropriate.

She was the owner of a two-family house in which she rented out flats, her daughters said, and, at one time, had done work on a coal-carrying barge on the Thames.

When I examined her, I found her blood pressure to be 90/70, her pulse to be 50, and her temperature to be 94°. I took the temperature several times rectally and found it always below normal. Her skin had a peculiar coldness and was coarse and extraordinarily dry and almost felt like the skin of an alligator. She was pale, obviously anemic, and exhibited an unusual skin condition below her knees, where she wore woolen socks in the heat of summer. There was a brown crisscross pattern on both legs below her knees. The mental test revealed that she was unaware of the time of day, the year, and her location, and had lost track of recent daily events although she did recall events of World War I.

The hospital registrar and I then discussed the possibilities of her condition.

"She obviously feels cold. She is wearing a sweater."

The registrar said, "Oh, many English women like to wear sweaters. It is not so unusual."

I said, "Even in the heat of the summer?"

"She's demented and she's cold," I continued, "her skin is like that of an alligator. She is slow in her speech which is slurred and sounds like she's had too much to drink."

"What about her legs?"

I said, "I haven't got the slightest idea of what that could be caused by."

"You would have to be English to know," the registrar said. "Here you have to put a shilling into the heater to warm up your room, and, because she was so cold, she placed her legs against the grate and didn't mind one bit the great heat against her legs. The grate of the heater left marks on her legs."

"Her skin also had a peculiar swelling along with the roughness."

"This, young man," the professor said, "is the classic sign of myxedema, or an underactive thyroid gland."

"Tugboat Annie" remained fixed in my memory through the remainder of my medical training and since then into practice, and I have seen many patients since with the same disorder.

Some hypothyroid patients may have the physical characteristics of Down's syndrome. Eyebrows, characteristically, are sparse, the outer third of which may be missing. Patients do not sweat. They may have, in addition, pain in all their joints (knees, ankles, wrists) and deafness.

Brain degeneration is a prominent feature of advanced stages of this disease, and with appropriate blood tests, the diagnosis of hypothyroidism myxedema can be made.

In contrast to an overactive thyroid, patients with myxedema cannot tolerate the cold, their pulse is slow, their hearts tend to be enlarged, and their reflexes are markedly delayed—all their activities are in "slow motion." The diagnosis, however, is not so easily made if it is superimposed on other illness, such as a previous stroke, diabetes, or an already partially demented condition. Many older people may have degeneration of their brain cells on a vascular basis, and then if an illness such as myxedema is superimposed on this, they may become completely demented.

"Tugboat Annie" received thyroid replacement, and, after several months, her voice improved, her skin became less coarse, her hair grew, and she was able to return to renting out her flats to the students.

A much less evident case of myxedema was seen in our ward at Yale–New Haven Hospital. A 74-year-old heavyset woman had suffered a stroke and remained partially disabled. Her speech had barely returned and her convalescence was extraordinarily slow. A sharp resident physician noticed the characteristics of her sparse eyebrows and her dry skin, and performed thyroid blood tests which disclosed that, in addition to her stroke, she had severe hypothyroidism.

This illness can proceed slowly over many years, ending in a coma which may have the appearance of a cerebrovascular accident or stroke. With the administration of thyroid hormones, the patient can have a complete recovery.

An underactive thyroid is seen frequently in people who have been treated for an overactive thyroid, either by radiation, medication, or thyroid removal. Many patients will develop an underactive thyroid twenty years after receiving radiation. Doctors, patients, and their families should be aware of this as a possible cause of reversible senility.

Adrenal Gland Failure

A 54-year-old insurance salesperson became markedly depressed in the spring of 1970 because he had become impotent. Since the age of thirteen, he had had a daily erection. With marriage had come an extraordinarily active and enjoyable sexual life.

With his depression came a great deal of exhaustion. He lost his appetite, and, after he had his checkup with his doctor, he was advised to go on a three-week vacation to the seashore. The Cape Cod air was invigorating and the long walks on the beach were very relaxing, but his exhaustion continued and his penis remained limp.

When he returned again to see his physician, a thorough examination was performed and it was decided that he was suffering from a midlife crisis and needed some antidepressant medication. He looked so well that four months later his neighbor remarked, "I don't know what's bothering Bill. He looks so healthy, yet he feels so lousy."

Frustration with his marriage was replaced by anger and resentment. His wife was even seriously thinking of a divorce because her husband wanted to do nothing but sit at home. "He is always too tired to do anything. I think he is getting senile," his wife told one of her friends. "I've heard that some men age quickly, and I fear that Bill is an example. Not only has he lost all interest in sex, but his memory is also failing and he is beginning to look old to me."

With one last glimmer of hope, Bill's wife literally dragged him to another doctor who examined him thoroughly and discovered that his blood pressure was low, his pulse rate was slow, and he did indeed have evidence of progressive memory failure.

"It looks like you just came home from a vacation," the doctor said, "because you're all tanned."

"No, Doc. Some months ago, we went to the seashore for three weeks in the summer and I haven't lost my tan yet."

His skin looked dirty, as if he had stopped washing, especially around the genitalia and nipple area. When the doctor examined his mouth, he found brown spots inside the cheeks. The combination of exhaustion, feebleness, the brown coloration of the skin, and the brown spots in the mouth were the clues that the doctor needed to make the diagnosis of adrenocortical insufficiency, or failure of the adrenal glands. In reviewing the family history, the physician learned that one of Bill's sister's was suffering from an overactive thyroid, another from pernicious anemia, and a third from an underactive thyroid. All these illnesses, including adrenal failure, are related.

The laboratory tests confirmed the diagnosis that the patient was suffering from adrenocortical insufficiency, or Addison's disease, which is a rare illness, occurring in 1 patient in 100,000, and often is associated with other endocrine abnormalities seen in families. The illness is thought to belong to a group of diseases having an autoimmune cause—patients develop antibodies to their own cells.

In the nineteenth century, Dr. Thomas Addison described both diseases—pernicious anemia, called Addison's disease, and adrenocortical insufficiency. Both diseases are linked together by having common antibody abnormalities.

I had the opportunity of diagnosing this patient as having Addison's disease and Addisonian anemia (two separate diseases, though linked together often), and, with cortisone replacement and B_{12} injections for the anemia, Bill quickly returned to his vigorous self, and his sexual appetite and vigor were also restored. Today, ten years later, he is still alive and well, and, when I see him periodically, he informs me that he can tell when his illness is starting to get out of hand: he starts to feel lethargic and his mental faculties begin to fade. He then increases his medications and recovers within a day. Unfortunately, other patients, although rare in number, have periodic adrenal failures in spite of medications, if they perspire too much, have a severe infection, or develop an associated illness. These patients should be under constant treatment and must be informed that, if they develop an infection, they must notify their physician. The physician will then instruct them to increase their medications by a certain amount until the infection is cured.

Kidney Failure

The kidney is an indispensable organ for the maintenance of life. It is the organ that recycles waste materials and it also, as a sideline operation, manufactures hormones. The kidneys keep in balance the concentrations of proteins and salts. This organ has a remarkable capacity to withstand the insults which are continuously directed against it.

The nondiseased kidneys in a person over age sixty-five do not function as efficiently as do those in the younger person. The body can readily withstand diminished function, but, if there is disease, the organ can, unfortunately, fail. The patient needs only one kidney to function, but most diseases affect both at the same time.

There are numerous causes for uremia or kidney failure, such as chronic infections, immunological disturbances, abnormal deposits of amyloid, calcium, and uric acid, injuries, a compromised blood supply, and cancer.

Once the kidney fails, it affects every organ in the body, including the central nervous system. The earliest signal that the kidney is failing may be a generalized fatigability. Kidney specialists state that a certain percentage of patients with kidney failure lose their ability to concentrate, suffer memory loss, and may not be able to perform simple skills of arithmetic. Uncorrected kidney failure finally causes complete chaos of the entire metabolism of the body, resulting in disorientation, coma, and death.

It can easily be ascertained that kidney failure is present by simply measuring the creatinine and the BUN, which are kidney-function evaluations tested through the blood.

Some medications can actually cause kidney failure in particular, some of which are listed below:

1. Kanamycin
2. Gentamicin
3. Polymyxin B
4. Coly-Mycin
5. Streptomycin
6. Vancomycin
7. Para-aminosalicyclic acid
8. Amphotericin B
9. Amikacin
10. Tobramycin

When these antibiotics are given, kidney-function tests have to be carefully monitored.

Other antibiotics require that the dosage be carefully monitored in patients who have renal failure, lest the failure becomes progressively worse.

1. Penicillin G
2. Cephalothin
3. Lincomycin
4. Clindamycin
5. Isoniazid
6. Ethambutol
7. Rifampin
8. Cephaloridine

Many medications are excreted by the kidney, and, if the kidney is not functioning properly, they can accumulate in the blood and cause toxic symptoms.

In elderly patients who have marginal kidney function, dehydration from a chronic infection, diuretics, or inadequate water intake can worsen their kidney failure.

Patients who take an excessive amount of over-the-counter pain-killers called analgesics for prolonged periods of time can develop a chronic kidney condition called interstitial nephritis. The analgesic kidney disease accounts for at least 6 percent of all patients with chronic kidney failure.

A 58-year-old woman who had suffered from migraine headaches for most of her life had been using acetaminophen (Tylenol) for a period of ten years. She took an average of eight to ten pills per day, sometimes even twenty. She arrived at her physician's office with a chief complaint of extraordinary weakness, difficulty in concentration, and a progressive severe memory loss. The physical examination disclosed a woman who was 5'4" and weighed 98 pounds, had a scrawny, gaunt appearance, and looked chronically ill. As the physician was taking the history, he noticed that she also had a slight facial twitch and that her color was gray. The examination was entirely normal, except that she was clearly malnourished and her blood tests indicated that she was anemic and that there was kidney failure.

The patient was admitted into the hospital and denied taking any sorts of medications. The cause of her renal failure remained a mystery until the toxicological blood tests were performed, demonstrating that she was ingesting acetaminophen, phenacetin, and aspirin. She had the appearance of an elderly Alzheimer's patient—erect, alert, yet somewhat depressed, with progressive memory loss. Since she no longer received any further analgesics, a kidney biopsy demonstrated the diagnosis of interstitial nephritis, with the most probable cause being the excessive painkillers that she had been ingesting over a period of at least ten years. With proper fluid balance, her kidney failure improved. She no longer took any analgesics. In subsequent months, her brain impairment did not worsen, and, at the end of one year, it had begun to show improvement. Specific antimigraine medications were prescribed by her physician.

Kidney failure should be suspected in an elderly individual suffering from chronic disease, a worsening of mental symptoms such as memory loss and loss of concentration, and increased fatigue, and appropriate kidney tests should be conducted by the physician.

In this section, I have discussed the endocrine and metabolic causes for reversible memory loss. Families of victims so affected should insist upon having certain tests performed to attempt to uncover a course of dementia. They should ask the physician the following questions:

"Is my mother suffering from too little salt in her blood? Will you get a serum sodium determination?"

"Is my mother a diabetic? Is it possible she is getting too much insulin, causing her blood sugar to be too low? Should she have a blood sugar determination in the morning, afternoon, and night?"

"Is her calcium level normal? Too high or too low? Should we order a serum calcium level?"

"What about her thyroid gland? Is it functioning right? Should we order thyroid tests in the blood?"

"Are the other glands working, like the adrenal glands? Can you get adrenal function tests?"

"Is the liver working properly?" Early liver coma can cause dementia.

The searching, conscientious doctor will gladly order these tests for dementia and may thus find a way to reverse a patient's mental deterioration.

CHAPTER 10

Lung Disease

*Every man desires to live long but no man would
be old.*

JONATHAN SWIFT

Low Oxygen

We have seen in previous chapters that different nutrients are
needed for the brain to properly function—blood protein, sugars,
etc.—and that, above all, the brain needs oxygen.

In 1772, Joseph Priestley (1733–1804) discovered that oxygen
was needed for the growth of plants. The deprivation of oxygen
(hypoxia) has many causes. This chapter follows the discussion in
Chap. 9 of chronic alcoholism as a cause of dementia because lack
of oxygen in many ways simulates the effects of excessive alcohol.

Lack of oxygen can be caused by:

1. Insufficient oxygen being present in the air
2. The oxygen's not arriving at the respiratory tract because
   something is interfering with the ability of oxygen to be
   moved to the lungs—for example, muscular weakness, certain neurological disorders, or medications called neuro-
   muscular-blocking agents
3. The oxygen's inability to pass through the lung tissue into
   the artery because of chronic lung disease (smoker's lung)
4. The capacity of the blood to carry oxygen being decreased,
   as in anemia or carbon monoxide poisoning
5. Insufficient oxygen arriving into the tissue because the body
   as a whole requires more. This happens especially in cases
   of high fever.

A sudden deprivation of oxygen to the brain can result from drowning, strangulation, sudden hemorrhage after surgery, paralysis of breathing muscles, and, most commonly, from cardiac arrest after a heart attack or respiratory failure.

A mild degree of oxygen lack (hypoxemia) causes some inattentiveness, poor judgment, muscle incoordination, and lethargy, but generally does not have lasting effects. In the case of cardiac arrest, when consciousness is lost within seconds, recovery can be complete if the heart starts to beat again in three to five minutes. Permanent brain injury almost always occurs if the cardiac function is not restored during that time. However, this is not an ironclad rule; there are some individuals, even after ten minutes of severe cerebral oxygen lack, who suffer little or no brain damage.

The extreme form of oxygen lack to the brain results when there is no longer any brain activity, as seen by the electroencephalogram (EEG). This state is called "brain death." Some patients who have prolonged hypoxemia continue surviving in a vegetative state, and the question of deciding what is death is a medical, legal, and moral issue. Most authorities believe that if the pupils do not react to light and if there is paralysis of eye movement for 24 to 48 hours, with marked slowing of the EEG, this signifies that there is irreversible brain damage. Patients who have lesser injuries and regain consciousness may retain some confusion and memory loss.

The lack of oxygen to the brain causes the entire brain chemistry to become upset, with resulting accumulation of lactic acid, destruction of neurons, and the blocking of metabolism.

Some patients suffering from chronic lung ailments, such as bronchitis and emphysema, have a chronic low oxygen level and an elevated carbon dioxide level in their blood. These patients may present with the symptoms of a progressive dementia, not unlike patients with excessive alcohol intake. Many of these patients become more alert as soon as oxygen is administered. The patient with low oxygen may show signs of muscle incoordination, fatigue, and inability to concentrate. Patients suffering from chronic lung disease complain of shortness of breath at the slightest effort, coupled with mental changes. If the patient is elderly, these symptoms are aggravated, especially if certain medications (such as too much theophylline) are being given, which, in themselves, can cause confusion.

Confusion, disorientation, and mental impairment may be more profound during the night when the patient's entire metabolism slows and the brain suffers from lack of oxygen. Oxygen given during the night can alleviate these symptoms. If the lung disease is complicated by the combination of heart failure and improper medications, the mental failure can be aggravated.

Just as oxygen deficiency can cause symptoms of brain failure, too much carbon dioxide, which accumulates in chronic lung patients, can also cause central nervous system symptoms, such as confusion, drowsiness, brain dysfunction, and memory loss. Sometimes, symptoms from lack of oxygen can even simulate a brain tumor.

Adequate treatment of chronic lung disease can alleviate the symptoms of chronic-oxygen lack through a physical therapy program entitled "bronchial toilets." Cessation of smoking is essential in this program. The therapist will attempt to clear secretions that form in the lungs by various back-slaps and taps, which encourage coughing. The patient will also have breathing treatments, in which he will inhale humidified and warm air. Adequate fluid intake is necessary. Certain medications given as part of another treatment, bronchodilator therapy, also help to clear these excessive secretions that accumulate in the chronically infected lung.

A respiratory tract infection can quickly cause an acute exacerbation of the lung problem with further oxygen deprivation and more mental deterioration. Breathing exercises are taught and the periodic inclusion of antibiotics for infections is necessary. If there is increased shortness of breath, the turning of the sputum's color from white to brown to yellow signals an infection present in the lungs.

Chronic bronchitis, which afflicts millions of Americans secondary to cigarette smoking, is defined as "the production of sputum occurring on most days for at least three months of a year for at least two successive years." The mucus plugs the lungs and prevents the oxygen from traveling into the blood and eventually to the brain. Chronic bronchitis can become exacerbated by infection, especially in the elderly patient confined to a wheelchair who has little opportunity for motion of the lungs.

A 78-year-old woman, a chronic smoker who had suffered a

stroke, was confined to a wheelchair in a nursing home. She had smoked incessantly for years and had a chronic cough. At least three times a year, she developed a respiratory tract infection which forced her to be hospitalized, and her oxygen level was found to be so low that intubation was necessary (an oxygen tube had to be placed into her trachea). During the time of her illness, she was totally disoriented. After her illness was treated and the tube removed, her mental state improved, although she could not remember how many days she had been in the hospital.

Sometimes, oxygen deprivation to the brain can cause a patient to become clearly psychotic and to exhibit violent behavior.

A 72-year-old robust man who was a chronic smoker suffered from emphysema and chronic bronchitis. He was admitted into the hospital because of great difficulty in breathing. His oxygen level was found to be dangerously low; his lips and fingertips were blue. As the medical officers rushed to place a tube into his throat to force oxygen into his lungs, he became violent and pulled the intravenous needle from his arm. As the nurses came to restrain him, he swiftly tore the belt from his pants and wrapped it around the neck of one of the nurses. Several guards were called in to restrain him, as he surely would have strangled the young nurse. Several days later, after oxygen treatment, he had no recollection of his behavior. His mental status had returned to normal. It was later learned that the patient often became confused and disoriented at home. Once home, he received oxygen throughout the night and there was no repetition of his violence or his breathing difficulty.

Sleep Apnea Syndrome

The Nobel Prize winner, Gabriel Garcia Marquez, in his brilliant novel *One Hundred Years of Solitude*, gives us the opportunity to envision a village whose members develop a lethal illness that causes insomnia and memory loss:

"But the Indian woman explained that the most fearsome part of the sickness of insomnia was not the impossibility of sleeping, for the body did not feel any fatigue at all, but its inexorable evolution toward a more critical manifestation: a loss of memory."

She meant that when the sick man whom she had observed became used to this state, the recollection of his childhood began to be erased from his memory. Next, the names of things, the identity of people, and, finally, even the awareness of his own being was erased, until he sank into a state of dementia.

A particular condition called sleep apnea syndrome can cause serious chronic neuropsychiatric symptoms during the daytime and make the patient appear demented. He or she may continue daily life for years without recognizing that a serious fall of the oxygen level in the blood is occurring during sleep. Sometimes, school-children and obese patients may have this problem, as well as those with chronic lung disease, neurological disorders, or nasal obstruction. This is a phenomenon different from sudden infant death, however.

Sleep apnea is a condition in which air no longer flows into the nose or mouth for more than ten seconds because of an interruption. Later the flow will start again. It is not to be confused with periodic cessation of airflow, lasting a few seconds, which can occur in normal individuals.

This condition is particularly common in older overweight men. During the day, the patient is chronically fatigued and has difficulty with his or her concentration and memory. During the day, the patient may want to sleep all the time and will doze off at inappropriate moments, when talking, driving, or even eating meals. Sometimes, there may be a mechanism in the brain which causes the respiration to temporarily stop while sleeping. The patient may, for years, have been a chronic snorer, with the snoring interrupted by periods of complete cessation of breathing. During the night, the patient may move his or her legs restlessly and fling the arms violently. The patient may sleepwalk and may have difficulty in awaking. Usually, the bed partner moves into another room because of the chronic annoyance of the patient's violent snoring and restless acrobatics.

These patients tend to be overweight with short necks. Their condition is the Pickwickian syndrome, named after the kindly and endearing (but also corpulent and short-necked) character in Charles Dickens' *The Pickwick Papers*. Many have hypertension, and there may be some obstruction either in the upper airways of the nose or in the larynx. Some, during their abnormal sleep pattern, develop irregular heartbeats with slow rates, which compound the disorientation, since not enough blood is arriving at the brain.

This does not mean that every patient who snores has the sleep apnea syndrome, but snoring accompanied with behavioral changes during the day, memory loss, disorientation, and the continual desire for sleep should make the physician suspicious. Some authors have called this "Ondine's curse," which refers to the revenge that Ondine, a river nymph, took upon the nefarious mortal who deceived her. His punishment was that he was to be aware of all the simultaneous activities of his bodily functions (the beating of his heart, the contracting of his muscles, etc.) and that when he fell asleep, he would stop breathing and die.

The diagnosis sometimes is made by the spouse or other family members. In the middle of the night, the spouse's sleep is suddenly disturbed by sudden and violent arm swinging, followed by the sudden arrest of breathing. Hundreds of episodes of complete cessation of breathing may occur during one night with a marked drop in the oxygen level and a rise in the carbon dioxide. As the carbon dioxide rises, it stimulates the breathing to start again.

Many times, the cause of the sleep apnea is not determined and it is considered a central problem, namely, one arising from the brain. The diagnosis of this condition is often made after first being suspected by the physician and then confirmed in a sleep laboratory by monitoring the oxygen levels in the blood and by observing the breathing mechanisms of the person. The treatment may consist of correction of an obstruction, coupled with vigorous weight reduction or the administration of oxygen through the night.

Shirley is a divorced 72-year-old woman who looked at least ten years younger than her stated age. She had worked as a sewing-machine operator for many years and had little personal life other than her devotion to her children and her grandchildren. She had been a "chronic wreck," as she described herself, and was still "extraordinarily nervous, fatigued, and depressed."

After she retired, her mental outlook worsened and she sought further medical attention for a string of symptoms throughout her body, including headaches, dizzy spells, numbness of extremities, back pain, burning tongue, and a bad odor in her mouth. And there continued to be the incessant problems of fatigue, yawning, and falling asleep at inappropriate moments.

"Are there some vitamins you can give me for always being so tired?"

Vitamins were given—and antidepressants, too—which did not give her any relief. Numerous x-ray examinations and CT scans of her brain did not disclose any abnormalities. She was advised to be as active as possible, to enter into an exercise program, make some new friends, enlarge her horizons, and rid herself of her continual reproaches of self-deprecation and her complaints about feeling poorly.

On this occasion when she went to see her physician, she stated that she was now not only terribly tired *all* day, but that also her memory was going. "The end will come soon. My brain is now deteriorating." Furthermore, she stated that her sleep disturbance had become even worse.

"When I wake up in the morning, the covers are on the floor and the pillow is on my feet. I couldn't keep a boyfriend if I wanted to," she said. "My husband used to complain of my snoring, which probably drove him to leave me."

A careful history this time revealed that she had experienced difficulty in awaking in the morning, and that, throughout the night, had dreadful nightmares and sometimes walked in her sleep. Her snoring was so explosive that it often woke her.

Careful examination of her upper respiratory tract revealed that she had a marked chronic nasal obstruction from a polyp, and, in addition, an abnormality of her larynx that caused it to close off at night, resulting in a picture of classic sleep apnea syndrome. Surgery was performed for removal of the polyp and a markedly deviated septum. Early in her stay in the hospital, it was discovered that the oxygen in her blood had dropped to critical levels. After surgery, follow-up studies revealed that the oxygen level had returned to normal. She was no longer snoring and found that when she awoke in the morning, her fatigue had disappeared and her memory had improved. Her other complaints—the muscle aches and headaches—remained.

This patient illustrates an extreme case of early symptoms of dementia with forgetfulness and depression, which may very well have progressed and eventually led to the diagnosis of the onset of Alzheimer's disease. Now that she is more alert during the day, she has become more energetic and less fretful.

CHAPTER 11

Medications and Chemicals

Youth longs and manhood strives but age remembers.
OLIVER WENDELL HOLMES

Since antiquity, doctors have used some form of medicine to put back into order the chemical chaos caused by disease. The body itself, with its intricate abilities to keep the internal milieu in harmony, is the best pharmacist. Hormones, enzymes, and blood cells battle scavengers every second to keep the body healthy. When the external forces that invade the cells overcome the internal defense mechanism, medication is often needed to help the natural mechanisms cope.

The purpose of medications is to destroy the invader, whether it be a bacteria, a virus, or a noxious agent, and to allow the body time to survive the insult and reestablish defenses and the natural healing process.

At times a pill may have an effect that is worse than that of the original disease. The further that scientific research has advanced, the more evident it has become that some of the best medications are formed by the body itself. For example, endorphins, the strongest painkillers known, at least ten times more powerful than morphine, are produced in the brain. The most powerful enzyme systems that prevent and dissolve clots of blood are manufactured within our own bodies. Every organ seems to be able to manufacture its own important hormones. Even the heart has recently been found to produce a hormone from the atrium of the heart, that has important regulatory functions.

The concept that each illness should be treated with a specific medication was advocated by a Swiss-born doctor named Paracelsus (1493–1541). He is considered by many to be the "father of modern pharmacology." A fearless and controversial physician, he challenged all the older concepts of therapeutics and was the first to advocate the use of chemicals in medicine. He is famous for preparing ether as an analgesic for pain. In the late nineteenth century, French writer Guy de Maupassant used Paracelsus's ether during his migraine attacks.

Within the past fifty years, there has been an incredible development of medications for the cure and control of illness that has resulted in a prolonged life expectancy and a more bearable life for multitudes of suffering individuals. Today, we are only beginning to understand what happens to the medications once inside our bodies. Only a portion of the medication—the active portion—circulates in the plasma; the other parts become bound to proteins. Drugs bound to the protein plasma are inactive; only when they are in the free form are they able to exert their effects.

In the older person, medications have a different effect than that in a younger person. Many of the medications pass to the liver where they become partially inactivated. Others are excreted through the kidney. In the older person, the mechanisms of excretion and deactivation are diminished.

In the United States, a total of approximately twenty billion dollars per year is spent on pills. Patients over age sixty-five receive 25 percent of all the drugs prescribed—this adds up to five billion dollars worth of prescriptions annually! The average elderly person receives about thirteen prescriptions each year. A drug that is given to an elderly person may produce concentration in the blood that is twice as high as that in a younger patient. Absorption of the drugs may be delayed in the older person, and the distribution of the medication may be altered.

As we age from 40 to 80, muscle mass decreases by 35 percent, the fluid in the cells decreases by 40 percent, and the total body water decreases by 17 percent. The body fat increases by 35 percent, and the amount of the protein that carries the medication, albumin, also decreases.

Since the ability of the heart to pump blood decreases by 25 percent after the age of forty, the distribution of the medication in the body is decreased. The kidney function also diminishes, and medications will not be excreted to the same degree. If, in addition, the patient has illnesses of various organ systems, such as congestive heart failure, kidney failure, or liver disease, there is further impairment of circulation of the medication to the brain. The acidity of the stomach diminishes and may be totally absent in 30 percent of patients over age sixty, further resulting in decreased absorption of the medication. As the stages of the aging process differ from individual to individual, so too will be the effects of medications taken. It is impossible to predict one's reaction to different medications. However, an example of a *predictable* drug reaction is that following alcohol intake. Older people become drunk more quickly because of decreased water in their cells, and alcohol exerts a greater effect on them, and for a much longer period of time. The older patient can get drunk faster, with half the amount of alcohol needed to intoxicate a younger person. Some optimistic souls regard this, tongue-in-cheek perhaps, as one of the most positive effects of aging.

In one study by Dr. J. Williamson in *Aging*, it was discovered that at least 20 percent of the patients taking medication had no knowledge of why they were taking it, and 40 percent omitted the drug prescribed. Another 10 percent increased the dosage on their own initiative and 70 percent used over-the-counter medications.

It is extraordinarily difficult for older patients to keep track of the multitudes of medications which are prescribed. The average older person takes a minimum of 3.5 drugs per day. In nursing homes, the number may be as high as ten. In one study, reported in *Geriatrics*, May 1984, it was shown that 20 percent of patients over age sixty exhibited a drug reaction.

Cortisone

Our bodies struggle constantly to maintain a balanced chemistry. Complicated chemical compounds formed by different glands circulate throughout, exerting important effects on every organ. Our hormones keep a balanced homeostasis. The physiologist Claude Bernard (1813–1878) summarized this beautifully in his thesis entitled, "Le Milieu Intérieure."

The hormones give us our identities, differentiating the characteristics of male and female. Their secretions are intermittently linked to what occurs in the brain: the master gland sends messages to its subordinate glands when stimulated by anger, fear, a change in environment, or accidental or deliberate ingestion of different materials.

Cortisone is one of these hormones essential in keeping our water, salt, fat, sugar, and protein metabolism balanced. The cortisone steroids have their effect on the central nervous system. Cortisone is manufactured by the adrenal glands situated above the kidneys. The adrenals secrete a number of important products, classified as steroid hormones. Excessive production or deficiency of cortisone has major life-threatening effects on every organ system, notably on that of the brain.

Dr. Harvey Cushing (1869–1939), a brilliant surgeon and professor of neurosurgery at Johns Hopkins University, discovered a collection of symptoms resulting from excessive cortisone production, now called Cushing's syndrome. Cushing's syndrome is not a common illness: it occurs in 1 of 10,000 people.

An excess of these hormones gives a characteristic obese appearance to the patient. The face becomes ruddy with bluish striations. A round "buffalo hump" of the back develops, as well as a protruding belly and thickening of the fat pad. Often there are also multiple abnormalities, including softening bones, generalized muscle wasting, diabetes, memory loss, agitation, depression, delusions, and manic behavior. These patients also suffer from hypertension and kidney stones. Menstrual disorders are common in women, as is facial-hair growth.

The diagnosis of this condition is not easy and requires expert laboratory analysis to measure the cortisone level in the blood during various times of the day: these are the diurnal variations. *Most* obese patients with diabetes, hypertension, and mental impairment do *not* have Cushing's syndrome.

A 76-year-old obese woman was admitted to a psychiatric service for evaluation of her severe depression, memory loss, and suicide attempts. The patient was found to have a long history of psychiatric problems, with chronic depression, hallucinations, and memory loss. Diabetes and high blood pressure were also present. The cortisone in the blood was extremely high, and a CT scan of her abdomen showed markedly enlarged adrenal glands. From this evidence, the diagnosis of Cushing's syndrome was made. The patient was promptly treated, and, within a period of several months, her grotesque appearance had disappeared and her mental state had improved dramatically.

Cortisone is a commonly used medication for a variety of illnesses, notably bronchial asthma, rheumatoid arthritis, and systemic lupus erythematosus (SLE). It makes the lives of asthmatics bearable and makes it possible for some patients with rheumatoid arthritis to function.

Rheumatoid arthritis is a "mean disease," according to Steven Vincent Benet who was a sufferer. This is an illness that affects every organ of the body, not only the muscles and joints. It causes widespread destruction of the joints, which results in a terribly disabling illness. Many patients are fortunate and have excellent responses to gold injections, which lead to complete control of their arthritis. When the arthritis becomes resistant to aspirin and other anti-inflammatory agents, cortisone is used.

P. S. Hench made the observation in 1949 that pregnant rheumatoid arthritic patients went into complete remission—the arthritis actually disappeared! Hench concluded it was the excess cortisone formed during pregnancy that caused such improvement. He made similar observations in jaundiced patients who had increased cortisone levels; those who were rheumatoid improved.

At first, cortisone was hailed as the "miracle drug" for arthritis sufferers. It soon became apparent that sometimes the side effects were worse than the disease! The chronic use of cortisone, even in small dosages, can cause widespread complications in the body. Increased softening of bone, or osteoporosis, is a common complication which can cause more pain in the patient, but can, however, be partly averted with adequate calcium and vitamin D. The subject who is on cortisone is more prone to infections and diabetes. A particular complication not obviously apparent is its effect on the brain. Psychiatrists can recognize "cortisone madness"—depression, hallucinations, psychosis, and even dementia in some patients.

The excessive effects of cortisone are more apparent in a hospital setting when patients may suddenly become psychotic for no apparent reason except that they are receiving intravenous cortisone for a life-threatening situation. Elderly patients who received even a small dosage of cortisone for bronchial asthma or for arthritis for many years can sometimes suffer symptoms of brain disorders. The most dangerous situation arises if the patient suddenly stops the cortisone that he or she has been taking for years. Patients on cortisone treatment must be carefully supervised and must not take it upon themselves to suddenly stop the medication. Withdrawal symptoms of cortisone stoppage can cause not only severe mental impairment but can also create a life-threatening situation which can even result in death. Patients deciding to stop cortisone must do so *only* under the strict supervision of their physician. It may take weeks or even months to properly discontinue the cortisone medications.

Some elderly patients when admitted into the hospital may fail to tell the house physician that they have been taking cortisone medications. After taking a medication for many years, it becomes almost a natural element of their diet (as does a vitamin pill). This oversight can lead to problems, as seen in the following patient's story.

A 74-year-old widow was admitted into the hospital because of pneumonia. The patient was receiving medications for hypertension and angina which were continued in the hospital but she was also taking a small dosage of cortisone (Prednisone) for rheumatoid arthritis. The small dosage of cortisone kept her arthritis in check, and so there was little deformity of her joints. After several days, her temperature had dropped and her pneumonia had improved, but she also became disoriented and confused, and started to talk in a completely demented fashion. She could no longer identify objects and used inappropriate words and phrases, such as "I have to go to school," when she meant that she needed to use the bathroom.

Thanks to an astute physician who suspected a metabolic disorder, a blood test revealed a low level of cortisone. The physician also suspected that she had been taking cortisone for her arthritis and that she had failed to tell him this. The replacement of the deficient cortisone resulted in rapid improvement of her mental and physical state.

Beta-Blockers

Medications given to an older person must be carefully monitored and a smaller than "normal" dosage given. Currently fashionable medications used for the treatment of angina and hypertension are called beta-blockers. Beta-blockers perform an excellent job of controlling chest pain that results from coronary artery disease and hypertension, but, unfortunately, can cause some unpleasant mental symptoms in patients, especially in older patients. For example, the ability of a person over age sixty-five to metabolize a single oral dose of propranolol is far diminished from that of a younger person. Ninety percent of beta-blockers are inactivated by the liver. A lower dosage of propranolol needs to be given because the circulation to the liver is decreased in the older person. In the older person, the level in the plasma or in the blood can be two or three times higher than that in a younger person. In addition, the number of receptors on the cells to which the medication adheres is decreased, and this explains why untoward effects of propranolol are more evident in the older person.

When fatigue begins to set in, coupled with memory loss and depression, older patients receiving beta-blockers assume "that the end is near and the heart is failing." If these older people have additional problems, such as some hearing and visual loss and musculoskeletal abnormalities which cause them to be less active and viable, they can readily present the picture of a demented patient. Elderly patients taking propranolol who find that their memory is decreasing, that they are depressed, or that they feel tired and weak will not volunteer this information readily unless specifically asked.

Although beta-blockers are excellent medications, they can cause a chronic lethargic state even in younger persons. In the male, impotence is a very common unpleasant side effect, which compounds the fatigue and depression and may actually aggravate the angina. The most common complaints in the male who is taking beta-blockers are impotence and exhaustion.

A 47-year-old vigorous male was found to have hypertension and had also developed some angina. His family physician prescribed a beta-blocker and a tranquilizer for his great anxieties.

The angina disappeared, the blood pressure was controlled, but the patient's mental status began to change. At work, it was found that he was not as productive as before and that he had some periods of memory loss. His employer felt that perhaps he should take a rest from his job because his performance had deteriorated. Once the medications were changed, he returned to his old self. The combination of a tranquilizer and a beta-blocker had compounded the effects on his brain.

Sometimes, tranquilizers and sleeping pills used by the elderly can cause brain impairment. At one time, phenobarbital was used extensively in the practice of medicine to calm patients to help them fall asleep. Phenobarbital was known to cause lethargy, fatigue, and brain impairment.

Drugs can become toxic to the brain when they are incorrectly combined—for example, the combination of cimetidine (Tagamet) and beta-blockers can lead to mental deterioration, fortunately reversible. Cimetidine by itself can cause memory loss, fatigue, and depression.

When the kidney function is poor because of chronic kidney disease, careful attention must be given to the dosage of medication.

Tranquilizers

Rauwolfia drugs, like beta-blockers, comprise another family of medications once actively used in the control of hypertension. We have discovered that these drugs tend to decrease the amount of adrenaline in the brain, which leads to depression.

An example of the complications surrounding the use of these medications is the case of my own mother-in-law.

She took the death of her husband as best she could and was able to adjust to her widowed life by finding many outside activities and community interests. She was found to have hypertension by a family physician who prescribed a once-popular drug called Serpasil. It controlled her hypertension effectively, but there was a gradual simultaneous change that occurred in her entire mental outlook. Her interests dwindled, she gave up her community commitments, and her loquacious and gregarious manner changed: she became withdrawn. She interfered less and less in our lives and became uninterested in her grandchildren. One day she finally volunteered that she felt very blue and she couldn't understand the cause. The psychiatrist who saw her felt that now facing the reality of being alone with the prospect of another marriage slim, she was having a delayed reaction to the death of her husband. She began to age rapidly in appearance. She was treated with antidepressants but was unable to tolerate the side effects.

One day, she casually mentioned that her blood pressure was now controlled and she wondered whether she should stop the pill that she was taking. As soon as my mother-in-law stopped her medication, her depression disappeared, and she returned to her old ways, much to our delight.

Serpasil had been a "miracle" drug introduced into this country about 1940, derived from the rauwolfia plant in India. The drug originally was thought to cure schizophrenia but was also used for snakebites and diarrhea. An entire family of medications was then born from this original source, and these were known as tranquilizers. It was later determined that depression is one of the outstanding side effects of these medications. Even today, similar medications such as Aldomet can cause depression.

Digitalis

Digitalis is one of the drugs longest known to humanity. It is derived from a group of plant extracts called cardiac glycosides, which have been used throughout the world as arrow poisons. To the ancient Egyptians, squill was a digitalis preparation. The Romans used digitalis as a heart tonic, rat poison, and also as an emetic. Sir Thomas Frazier discovered the action of digitalis in 1890 when he studied African arrow poisons. The dried skin of the toad has been used as a drug by the Chinese; it contains digitalislike properties. The digitalis that we know is derived from the beautiful purple foxglove plant and is called *Digitalis purpura*. The dried leaf and seeds of the foxglove contain the active ingredients.

At one time, charlatans used digitalis as a means of losing weight; it was given as a primary diuretic. It is now used for the treatment of heart failure and irregular heartbeat. This is one of the most commonly used medications in the elderly and can cause serious side effects—in some cases even death. It is well-established that 20 percent of patients taking this medication can have side effects.

In elderly patients, digitalis toxicity occurs more frequently than in younger patients because the ability of the kidney to excrete digitalis is impaired. If there is present, in addition, some decreased kidney function, then digitalis intoxication occurs more readily. Digitalis can accumulate in the blood because of kidney failure, but also because of adverse interaction with other medications. For example, another drug that is used for irregular heartbeats, quinidine, can increase the plasma concentration of digitalis. The side effects of digitalis can be gastrointestinal—nausea, vomiting, and loss of appetite. In the elderly, it can cause a generalized poor feeling. Less common side effects may consist of visual blurring, double vision, and neurological manifestations, such as drowsiness, headaches, fatigue, numbness, and "pins and needles." Many elderly patients are already suffering from atherosclerosis of the brain and digitalis may contribute even further to their disorientation, memory loss, and confusion. Today, there is less likelihood of digitalis intoxication because a blood test can measure the digitalis level and signal to the physician that there is already too much in the blood.

A 74-year-old man had been suffering from heart failure for many years and was being treated with digitalis. He became progressively more lethargic and apathetic and lost much of his powers of concentration and memory. A physical examination disclosed that he had heart failure and that his blood pressure was normal. There were no other abnormal findings. The digitalis level in his blood was found to be elevated. Once the digitalis was restricted for a week until its level returned to normal, he began to brighten up and his fatigue lessened. Half the amount of digitalis was thereafter prescribed along with diuretics.

In addition to cortisone, beta-blockers, and digitalis, there are numerous medications known to cause reversible dementia, many of which are listed below.

Medications and Chemicals That Can Cause Reversible Mental Impairment

Methyldopa and haloperidol
Clonidine and fluphenazine
Disulfiram

Lithium carbonate
Phenothiazines
Haloperidol and lithium carbonate
Bromides
Phenytoin
Mephenytoin
Barbiturates
Clonidine
Methyldopa
Propranolol hydrochloride
Atropine and related compounds
Serpasil

Drugs *commonly causing confusion in the elderly are:*

Digitalis glycosides
Sedatives/hypnotics
    Benzodiazepines (Librium, Valium, Dalmane)
    Barbiturates
    Chloral hydrate
    Antihistaminics
    Glutethimide (Doriden)
Antidepressants
    Tricyclics (imipramine, amitryptyline, desipramine)
    Lithium (uncommon)
    MAO inhibitors (uncommon)
Antipsychotics
    Phenothiazines (Thorazine, Stelazine, Mellaril)
    Butyrophenones (haloperidol)
Minor tranquilizers
    Meprobamate
Antihypertensives
    Beta-blockers (propranolol)
    Methyldopa
    Guanethidine
    Mecamylamine
    Reserpine
Alcohol
Antiparkinsonian medications
    Levodopa

Drugs *commonly causing confusion in the elderly are: (cont.)*
    Anticonvulsants
       Dilantin
       Mysoline

Over-the-Counter Medications

Self-medication with over-the-counter preparations can be an important overlooked source of reversible dementia. Over-the-counter
medications, although benign in appearance, can have a cumula-
tively deleterious effect on the individual, especially antihistamines, sleeping preparations, mild tranquilizers, and even analgesics.
Often, the patient denies taking over-the-counter medications because he or she does not consider them to be "real" medications.

An elderly woman with chronic sinus infection was taking medications for her blood pressure and for heart failure. For her chronic
sinus condition, she was using a nasal spray which was an antihistamine preparation. The physician suspected that some medications were possibly accounting for her memory loss and
disorientation. All the medications were discontinued. She, however, still had the same symptoms. Multitudes of tests were performed, including total neurological examinations, and the conclusion
was reached that she was probably suffering from early Alzheimer's
disease. A member of the family called the physician and informed
him that she was taking a nasal spray every three or four hours
and had been doing so for a number of years. When the nasal
antihistamine spray was discontinued, the patient progressively
became more alert, and the diagnosis of Alzheimer's disease was
revised.

Pertinent to this discussion is the case history of a 78-year-old
woman who was a diabetic and had suffered a heart attack. She
was receiving multiple medications, consisting of beta-blockers,
diuretics, digitalis, insulin, and a blood-thinner called Coumadin.
She fared well, and, at each office visit, seemed content and had
minimal complaints. A typical conversation went as follows:

"Do you have any chest pain?"
"No."
"Any shortness of breath?"
"No, I feel fine."

"Is there anything that's bothering you?"

"I feel fine."

She brought a list of her medications with her, and the examination results remained the same during each visit. However, her son came with her on one occasion and stated that she would have to be placed in a nursing home in the near future because, on numerous occasions, she had left the stove on and had forgotten that she was heating water. He feared that she was going to harm herself. All her medications were temporarily discontinued. She still, however, had evidence of brain degeneration.

It took several weeks to make the arrangements for her to go to a nursing home, and, one morning, she was found unconscious on the floor. The emergency squad arrived and gathered up all her medications, and, by pure accident, found a large bottle that must have been at least thirty years old which contained hundreds of phenobarbital pills prescribed for her husband all those years ago. Her son searched the apartment and found several other large empty phenobarbital bottles. It became apparent that she had been taking this medication along with all the others. Phenobarbital, even in small dosages, causes fatigue, decreased mental alertness and, in continual usage, mental confusion. Because of her confused mental state, she took more medications than were prescribed. She was detoxified in the hospital, progressively, because there was fear of phenobarbital-withdrawal syndrome. She experienced a good recovery with some brain impairment and was even able to take care of herself once again without supervision.

This story illustrates a common occurrence in the older patient. Medications prescribed years ago continue to be taken and refilled without the updated knowledge of the physician. Sometimes, a patient will take pills belonging to the spouse for an ailment that sounds similar to theirs.

If there is some brain impairment, the person may forget when the pill was last taken and may take an extra dosage. Some patients completely forget to take their medications and suffer adverse reactions from omission rather than from overmedication. For example, the omission of a blood pressure pill can cause severe hypertension and signs of brain failure.

The chief of a local emergency room informed me that one of the reasons patients go into congestive heart failure is because they have either taken too many pills or else have failed to take those prescribed totally or in the proper manner. Older diabetic patients receiving insulin sometimes develop hypoglycemia because they skip their essential lunch if they spend the day shopping in town.

Anyone who has ever taken prescribed medications has had the experience of forgetting the conventional doctrine "three times a day." My 21-year-old daughter, when she was told to take penicillin three times a day, omitted at least one of the dosages each day. My father—a sophisticated and alert man—had an eye operation, and antibiotics were prescribed after surgery. When I went to visit him in the hospital, I opened his night-table drawer and found *all* the antibiotics which he should have swallowed. I asked him why he hadn't taken the antibiotics and he simply replied, "I don't need them and I'm not going to poison myself with these pills when I am not sick." Luckily, he did not develop an infection.

It should be emphasized at this point that patients should never discontinue medication (especially after reading this portion of this book) unless they consult their physician. Any change of medications, in dosage or amount, needs to be carefully regulated by the physician.

One of the causes of brain impairment in the nursing home is medication given either to calm the patient or to lessen pain. Too often, the nursing staff will prescribe a sleeping pill for a patient because he or she is agitated and has to have "something on hand" for discomforts and pain. Unfortunately, many times the origin of the agitation is not sought or discovered, and it is much easier to prescribe a sedative than to spend the time finding alternatives to such "treatment."

There were 1.3 million residents in nursing homes as of 1982. In one study cited in *Annals of Internal Medicine*, 1982, it was estimated that 50 to 70 percent of the residents of nursing homes were intellectually impaired. In a particularly poignant article in the 1982 *Annals of Internal Medicine* entitled "Dementia in the Elderly: The Silent Epidemic," the authors alert us to the enormity of the problem. Sometimes, for example, an agitated patient needs to be sedated for his or her own safety, and the consequences of sedation can further aggravate brain abnormalities.

In the United States, a great deal of improvement is needed in the management of older patients. Funds are desperately needed, auxiliary help is often lacking, and adequate facilities are frequently sparse. The treatment or lack of treatment that so many elderly people are subjected to is far too often simply degrading. An improperly supervised older patient may be forced to live a life inappropriate to his or her physical and mental states of fitness. This is especially evident in the oversedated, confined patient who is barely aware of the surroundings and barely functioning—*but* there seems to be no present alternative.

Dr. Earl R. Feringa, at a symposium on geriatric medicine at the University of California at San Diego School of Medicine, said that, "More than half of the patients I see have at least one treatable cause for dementia—too many too strong medications."

The pattern of dementia caused by drugs consists of periods of normal intellectual function interspersed with periods of complete impairment. The chemistry of the brain is offset and adversely affected by toxins such as drugs. Often, patients who are drug-toxic experience light-headedness, dizziness, and a fear of falling, accompanied with some loss of vision and an abnormality of the inner-ear affecting balance. The blood pressure tends to drop.

Physicians now follow the rule of halves and the rule of thirds when prescribing drugs for treatment. A patient over age sixty-five should be started on one-half of the usual adult dose, and, if the blood pressure is too high, it should be brought down gradually by one-half of the desired amount for the first week. Too vigorous a treatment for hypertension can also be responsible for brain dementia. In various studies, the known percentage of dementia caused by hypertensive and other medications is in the vicinity of 3 to 10 percent.

Families of patients should question their doctors thoroughly or even look for information in the *Physician's Desk Reference* about the possible side effects of any drug being taken, especially if the patient has begun to show signs of memory failure.

Environmental or Industrial Causes

Chronic Heavy-Metal Poisoning as a Cause of Memory Loss

There are so many synthetic toxins in our environment that it is a wonder that not more calamities occur. The fruits and vegetables which we eat are sprayed with insecticides, chemical poisons are regularly dumped in our rivers, and industrial workers undergo chronic exposure to heavy metals, ranging from arsenic and lead to mercury and cadmium.

Arsenic poisoning has been a fashionable form through the centuries of committing suicide and murder, and, occasionally, was even found in bootleg whiskey. Flaubert's Madame Bovary committed suicide by ingesting arsenic, dying a torturous death. Small dosages of arsenic were also in vogue for the treatment of syphilis.

Heavy-metal poisoning causes bizarre symptoms, including nerve weakness, skin rashes, kidney failure, and gastrointestinal symptoms, such as chronic indigestion, constipation, continual nausea, and loss of appetite.

Chronic heavy-metal poisoning has intrigued epidemiologists and medical detectives in tracking down toxic exposures as, for example, the poisoning caused by mercury salts such as mercuric chloride. Acute poisonings can occur by accidental or deliberate ingestion. As little as 0.1 g. of mercuric chloride may cause poisoning, but fatal doses are usually in excess of 1 g. Traces of metal mercury are found in tuna and swordfish taken from waters contaminated with mercury. Epidemics have occurred in Japan and in several other countries from seed grain treated with mercury as an antifungal agent.

Mercury in a liquid form is highly volatile at room temperature. It is widely used in medical research, clinical pathology laboratories, and in the manufacture of scientific instruments, meters, and vapor lamps. Dentists use it in amalgams along with silver and gold.

Chronic mercury poisoning causes severe mental symptoms, termed "erethism." Behavioral changes are characterized in the behavior of the Mad Hatter in Lewis Carroll's *Alice's Adventures in Wonderland* and *Through the Looking Glass*. (Felt hat makers formerly used mercury salts in the manufacturing process and often became "mad," giving rise to the phrase "mad as a hatter.")

A fascinating case of mercury poisoning was reported in 1965 in Franklin, Kentucky, where electromagnetic relays were manufactured by the Potter and Brunfield Company. A group of employees developed strange symptoms that embraced the nervous system, neuromuscular weakness defined as neuromyasthenia. Dr.

George Miller, now at the Yale University School of Medicine, discovered that the outstanding symptoms were psychiatric: "There was a remarkable inability to concentrate. The people had obvious memory problems. We tried simple tests, recollecting numbers forward and backward. Some people could do only four numbers forward, three backward, and way below what one finds. At one point, it was felt that this was a mass hysteria." It was discovered that the levels of mercury of the employees in the mercury portion of the factory were higher than the levels of those in the remainder of the factory. Investigated in this group were three patients who were under care for mental problems, including "nervous breakdowns." Eventually, a better ventilation system was installed in the factory to eliminate the fumes that were harming these workers.

Dentists use mercury amalgams and are exposed to chronic mercury vapors. Some epidemiologists have noted a high incidence of depression among dentists, along with higher than average suicidal tendencies.

A 58-year-old dentist consulted his physician because he had progressively developed problems of staggering gait, chronic fatigue, inability to concentrate, and memory loss. His wife accompanied him since it was necessary for her to hold him by the arm. His wife stated that he had sudden periods of crying spells followed by fits of laughing. His vision had deteriorated, and he complained of a continuous headache. His movements had become jerky and incoordinated, and his writing had markedly changed. His symptoms reflected numerous neurological illnesses. Several months earlier, the dentist had been a garrulous individual, but now he was shy and withdrawn. He was continually salivating and swallowing hard, his eyes were red as cherries, and his body was limp as a jellyfish. He realized that he had been going downhill progressively over a number of years, and he feared that he was suffering from a brain tumor. He had planned early retirement because of the shaking of his hands and impaired vision. It was only because of his wife's insistence that he sought a doctor.

The dentist looked pale and markedly withdrawn and had difficulty in answering simple questions. He could not retain four words or subtract 7s from 100 in successive order. The general physical examination was entirely unremarkable, except that all his reflexes were overactive, and, when he closed his eyes, he tended to sway to one side, which in neurology, is called a positive Romberg's sign. When his mouth was examined, a faint blue line was seen along the gingival margin, and his gums were markedly thickened and bled easily.

It became evident from further questioning that he had not worn a mask when, for years, he had prepared his amalgam in a small closed, poorly ventilated bathroom. His office was small, with one chair, and there was no assistant other than his wife who came in to help him with the bookkeeping. In his haste in preparing the amalgam, he had often dropped mercury on his carpeted floor and had not bothered to clean it up. The mercury remained on the floor for months, giving off dangerous vapors.

The patient was advised not to immediately return to work, and he was successfully detoxified. His mental abilities completely returned within the next year, as did his abilities to walk normally and to write clearly. Other movements requiring manual dexterity became possible once more. He took a partner, enlarged his office, and now always wears a mask when preparing his amalgam, which he does with great care.

This story illustrates another example of dementia which was discovered by the physician's taking a careful history and suspecting a toxic exposure which was found by a blood test for heavy metals. Unfortunately, some patients with advanced mercury poisoning may not recover but may become progressively demented and eventually die from the effects on the entire nervous system.

Chronic lead poisoning is found primarily in persons in lower socioeconomic groups. Children who eat the lead paint off walls develop a variety of symptoms, including abnormal classroom behavior with poor concentration and performance. After chronic exposure, lead accumulates in the body. Those afflicted with lead poisoning can suffer confusion, walking difficulties, and even coma. Lead poisoning is not generally found in adults but can be obtained from bootleg whiskey which can become contaminated from the lead pipes through which it was distilled. Buckshot containing lead that remains imbedded in the body for long periods of time can also cause chronic lead poisoning.

Historians tell us that during the time of the late Roman empire the wine was distilled in vats contaminated with lead. The water brought into the Roman home was contaminated from newly installed lead pipes. It is further speculated that the "mad" and lewd behavior of the Romans and the wide infertility rate often reported may well have resulted from lead poisoning. Some historians go so far as to theorize that the lead poisoning caused a drop in the birthrate so severe that it contributed to the decline of the Roman empire!

The physician should take a thorough occupational history from the person who has become "demented" and do appropriate tests, especially if he or she is working in an industrial plant or in a laboratory.

Recreational Drugs: Alcohol, Marijuana, and Cocaine

"A Pop or Two": Alcohol as a Cause of Brain Failure

Alcoholism is one of the most serious and prevalent medical problems in the United States. At least 12 to 15 percent of the population may be alcoholics. Alcoholism ranks as the third major health problem in the United States, following cardiovascular disease and cancer.

The earliest known alcoholic beverages—wine and kinds of beer— were low in alcohol content. The Arabs discovered the technique of distilling alcohol and introduced it into Europe in the Middle Ages. Alchemists believed that alcohol was the "elixir of life," a remedy for practically all diseases. (The word "whiskey" comes from the Gaelic term meaning "water of life.") In England in the early 1800s, there was a heavy tax on beer and wine, while gin was cheaper than water. Gin drinking was so widespread that even children of two years of age were often given the calorie-rich beverage to ease their hunger.

Dr. Jacob A. Brody, of the National Institute on Aging in Bethesda, Maryland, estimates that 25 percent of all hospitalizations in patients over age sixty-five are alcohol-related. Alcohol abuse is increasing in older Americans, primarily because of boredom, too much leisure time, and loss of their role in society. Elderly patients often use alcohol to lessen the pain from deaths of family members and friends and of having become third-rate citizens because of the devastating economic burden placed on them. It has been estimated that elderly widows have the highest rate of chronic alcoholism. (Most older people, it should be noted, reside in housing projects and retirement communities, and only 5 percent are confined to nursing homes.)

One elderly woman who sustained a heart attack began to drink cheap wine because of the hopelessness of her financial condition. She refused state aid. She lived in a small apartment, receiving $300 a month from Social Security benefits and $200 a month from her husband's pension. Medicare paid her hospital bills—barely covering the doctors' fees—but *not* the medications, which came to $180 a month!

The diagnosis of chronic alcoholism is difficult. Alcoholics, as a rule, deny their drinking habits; this is especially true in retired elderly patients. Family members will sometimes bring the problem to the attention of the physician, but usually in a light vein: "Pop takes a couple now and then."

The National Institute on Aging has demonstrated that alcohol impairs older subjects (those aged fifty-five to eighty) more than it does younger people. Many middle-aged alcoholics now live on to become older alcoholics. Alcoholism is so prevalent that any patient who is admitted in a semicoma which appears to result from a stroke should have his or her blood tested for alcohol content. Often patients are admitted for an entirely different illness, such as either heart attack or a lung infection, and, while they are in the hospital, will suddenly develop bizarre symptoms such as disorientation and the notorious delirium tremens (d.t.'s) because of the sudden withdrawal of alcohol. Hospital doctors are now well aware that elderly patients, even those in their eighties, can be suffering from chronic alcohol abuse. Cardiologists tell us that any patient with an irregular heartbeat (atrial fibrillation) of unknown cause may have an overactive thyroid—or the patient may be a victim of alcohol abuse. The following clues—unexplained falls, confusional states, impotence, and chronic sleep disturbance—have also been cited relative to the possibility of alcoholism in an elderly patient.

The effects of alcohol on the brain are proportional to the concentration of the alcohol in the blood. It can result in nerve damage and can cause serious neurological and mental disorders, such as memory loss, sleep disturbance, psychosis, and specific illnesses such as Wernicke's encephalopathy and Korsakoff's psychosis.

Alcohol taken by mouth is rapidly absorbed from the stomach, small intestines, and colon, and 90 to 98 percent is completely metabolized. For example, 4 ounces of whiskey or 1.2 liters of beer are metabolized in five to six hours in a person of average size. Different factors can alter the metabolism of alcohol; for example, starvation and insulin increase the metabolism of alcohol. This metabolism, called oxidation, occurs in the liver. Two percent of the alcohol that enters the body escapes the degradation and is released in sweat and tears, bile and juice, and in the urine.

The actual blood alcohol levels are dependent on the total level of water in the body. There are no known chemical ways of increasing the metabolism of alcohol. For the average person, drinking 180 cc. of alcohol on an empty stomach will produce an alcohol level of approximately 100 mg./cc. Elderly patients have less body water and become intoxicated faster.

Social drinking usually results in an alcohol level of 50 to 75 mg. per 100 cc. Actual signs of intoxication occur between 100 to 200 mg. Chronic alcoholics may be perfectly sober at this level. Above 400 mg., alcohol produces stupor and coma and above 500 mg. is generally fatal.

In 1971, the National Council on Alcoholism set criteria for the diagnosis of alcoholism. The major criteria:

1. Alcohol blackouts
2. Withdrawal syndromes (delirium tremens), as described: tremors, convulsions, delirium, and hallucinations
3. Blood alcohol level above 150 mg. without intoxication
4. Continued drinking despite the job problems that it causes
5. Drinking to relieve anger, fatigue, or depression
6. Drinking a fifth of whiskey per day or its equivalent in beer or wine

It still remains to be discovered why alcohol has its effect on the brain. Researchers have found that alcohol affects the cell membranes of neurons and interferes with the neurotransmitters of the brain, affecting memory, emotions, and other functions. Brain cells become dependent on alcohol, and more and more alcohol is needed for continued normal cell functioning in the chronic alcoholic.

As a rule, excessive alcohol has detrimental effects on the heart, liver, and brain. Excessive alcohol ingestion shortens life, and there is an increase in cancer of the mouth, pharynx, larynx, liver, and lung. Alcohol can cause the liver to become progressively destroyed and lead to liver failure, which can cause dementia, delusions, and finally death.

The degree of mental change in alcoholics has been markedly underestimated, especially in older patients. As we saw in Chap. 9, alcohol can interfere with the metabolism of glucose and can cause severe hypoglycemia. It can also result in the opposite effect, causing a marked worsening of diabetes and an increase in mental aberrations. The elderly chronic alcoholic may appear well-nourished—actually overweight with a healthy blossoming color—and seem to be mentally intact, unless specific questions are directed to him or her. Older patients are expected to have some degree of memory loss, and so nobody is shocked if a name is forgotten or an appointment is not kept. Not often is it suspected that the cause of the mental impairment may be too much alcohol.

One hundred years ago, the psychiatrist Dr. Sergei Korsakoff described the mental deficiencies associated with chronic alcoholism. Memory deficiency is especially evident in failure to retain new information or skills. Many times, Korsakoff's syndrome is associated with destruction of the nerves of the arms and legs (peripheral neuropathy), resulting in difficulty in walking and in impaired eye movements. The memory impairment is the result of both temporal lobes of the brain being injured. It is the same kind of brain impairment that is found in infections such as encephalitis, herpes, and a lack of oxygen to the brain.

Patients with this disorder may be disoriented as to time and place, but may be able to name objects and obey commands and accomplish tasks of reasoning and drawing. This is quite different from the patient who has dementia from Alzheimer's disease or the multi-infarction type earlier described.

Short-term memory loss is a classic finding in patients who use excessive alcohol. A mental-status test is very useful to determine the loss of recent memory. Trying to retain three words for five minutes is a difficult task in an alcohol-demented individual. The extreme form of chronic alcohol neurological abnormality is exemplified in Wernicke's encephalopathy. Associated with mental changes are the neurological calamities of paralysis, weakness, and the inability to walk or see. The patient staggers when walking, speech is disturbed, and he or she has episodes of delirium, confusion, agitation, disorientation, and total forgetfulness or amnesia. Wernicke's encephalopathy and Korsakoff's syndrome may occur in the same person, although they are two different illnesses.

The brains of alcoholic patients suffering from the Wernicke-Korsakoff syndrome show destruction of nerve cells and a striking glia reaction, described before, with hemorrhages and other characteristic changes. This syndrome has been observed in complications of patients who have an overactive thyroid and cancer of the stomach, after prolonged intravenous treatment and chronic hemodialysis in the hospital. There is strong evidence that one of the major causes of this syndrome, especially the neurological findings, is a vitamin B_1 (thiamin) deficiency. Thiamin can dramatically reverse some of the signs and symptoms, especially the eye signs and the difficulty in walking. (Those patients who have a thiamin deficiency are generally poorly nourished and have suffered weight loss; they will benefit from supplemental vitamin treatment.)

Elderly patients in particular are prone to Wernicke-Korsakoff syndrome, because, living alone, they may be malnourished. Coupled with alcohol insult, progressive dementia can follow. Some elderly patients who have been found confused and demented on the streets are brought directly into psychiatric hospitals, and a diagnosis of Alzheimer's disease may be mistakenly made. Dr. Brody is quoted as saying: "If an elderly person is found drunk and disoriented, and a rescue squad is called, he is at risk of being permanently institutionalized with a misdiagnosis of 'Alzheimer's disease,' when, in reality, he is suffering from an alcohol dementia."

In an important article that appeared in the *Journal of the American Medical Association* of January 7, 1983, Dr. William R. Deuben et al. stressed the fact that psychiatric symptoms need to be differentiated from illnesses that affect the brain.

A study was performed by Dr. Deuben and his colleagues in

an emergency room of a large metropolitan teaching hospital in Pennsylvania. Nearly 30 percent of the patients who had symptoms of disorientation, belligerence, confusion, impaired memory, hallucinations, depression, and suicidal thoughts had excessive alcohol in their blood. Disorientation was found to be an early symptom of brain failure. The patients lost track of the date, the day of the week, the time, the month, and, finally, the year and the place, in that order. Many of the patients had cloudiness of consciousness, which ranged from being awake and then drifting off to sleep, to being in a stupor, but arousable. For most of the patients, the onset of their disorientation occurred three to six months before they saw a doctor, and it was decided that patients who had visual hallucinations and illusions generally had a medical disorder rather than a psychiatric problem. Visual hallucinations might consist of seeing rabbits walking across the ceiling, and the illusions may involve believing that one is president of IBM.

As I have emphasized, brain cells are undoubtedly lost as we age, and there is some decrease in short-term memory, more pronounced in some than in others and occurring at various ages. Alcohol impairs the ability to retain new information, depending not on the number of ounces taken in per day but on each individual's alcohol tolerance.

In the Veterans Administration hospitals, there is a high proportion of alcoholics among older patients. The picture of the so-called bum applies to only about 5 percent of alcoholics in the United States. Alcoholism is present in nursing homes and in other facilities for the aged. Family members sometimes bring alcohol to the patient, unbeknown to the nursing staff, sometimes carrying it in Listerine bottles. In some nursing homes, older patients bribe staff members to bring the alcohol into their rooms.

I recall a wealthy elderly patient, Lucinda, with a suite of rooms in a nursing home who insisted on having champagne for breakfast, lunch, and supper. No one seemed to be bothered much by this because Lucinda was a lonely, widowed woman who occasionally ordered extra bottles for some of the staff. She showed no signs of dementia and carried her excessive alcohol intake off rather well. Lucinda finally died of a massive cerebral stroke at the age of ninety-four which was caused by atherosclerosis, not necessarily from drinking champagne.

In another illustration, a petite and delightful 80-year-old Italian lady, Amelia, had been suffering from chronic heart disease for a number of years and had been admitted on several occasions into the hospital because of episodes of severe shortness of breath that required intensive treatment to release the water from her body. This treatment is known as "diuresing." She responded well each time, and, during each hospitalization, she was regarded as an affable woman who had difficulties with her memory and invariably became confused, thinking that the doctor was her father, the nurse her sister, and the hospital a resort on the Amalfi Drive. At home, she slept hours on end. Her family attributed her mental condition to her age and to her severe heart failure.

During one of her hospital admissions, when Amelia was more confused than usual, a fourth-year medical student ordered an alcohol level test, and it was found to be 80 mg. which was quite unexpected. Finally, the truth was disclosed. The family did admit that Amelia drank a great deal at home, and that she had been doing so over the past twenty years, ever since her husband died. The family further admitted that she actually hid bottles behind bookshelves and in other ingenious locations. They had accepted her chronic drinking because it was a tidy antidote for her loneliness.

When Amelia was questioned about her alcohol intake, she denied it and was insulted that anybody would suggest such a "horrible thing." She did admit to the memory loss. As she put it, "I have nothing really worthwhile to remember anyway."

Amelia did agree to abstain from alcohol for a period of six weeks, as we also felt that her heart disease was not only due to coronary atherosclerosis but also to the detrimental effects of alcohol. During the six-week period, she felt much better and her shortness of breath improved, along with her rapid heart rate. Her powers of concentration increased, and her chronic fatigue lessened. She still suffered from short-term memory loss, but she was undoubtedly improving. Unfortunately, it didn't take very long for her to return to her drinking habits at home. The family insisted that they took all of the alcohol out of the house, but somehow Amelia was still able to find a source.

In this example, the family knew that the patient was a heavy drinker but were ashamed to admit this to her doctors, and they readily accepted her mental impairment. Finally, they accepted the fact that a heart disease (alcohol cardiomyopathy) was being caused by her chronic drinking habits.

In another case, Sheldon and Gladys, a wealthy couple, had retired to Florida. For most of their adult lives they had been having one or two cocktails prior to dinner. During the next five years after retirement, their lives consisted of going to cocktail parties at least four times a week. At dinner each night, they enjoyed four or five cocktails, wine with dinner, and brandy after dinner. Their lives revolved around eating and drinking (and some golf during the day and a visit to the bank four times a week to manage their investments).

When Sheldon and Gladys went for their annual physical examination and were found to be in generally good health, except that their liver tests were slightly abnormal. They admitted to the hectic social "obligations." It also became evident that both were suffering from impaired memory, which was becoming more severe, and for which they had a ready explanation: "What do you expect? We are in our seventies."

When Sheldon and Gladys underwent a two-month drying-out period combined with an exercise program, they began to realize how chronically intoxicated they had been. Their fatigue lessened, they took up new hobbies, and they decided to spend only six weeks a year in Florida and to return to New England and become involved in more intellectual activities. Both are now in their early eighties and faring extraordinarily well. They have discovered art museums, flower shows, and the theater—excellent substitutes for their hectic social partying.

Drinking becomes such a deeply ingrained social habit that many people are not even aware of the number of drinks they take daily unless they are asked specifically. If, in addition to the daily alcohol drinking, there are medications taken which have a sedative effect, such as antihistamines, mild tranquilizers, sleeping pills, antidepressants, and over-the-counter preparations used for chronic sinus infections, the effects on the brain will be compounded.

In another case, Francine, an obese woman, had been under the care of her physician for hypertension. Every effort was made toward weight reduction, but with no success. She lamented, "I swear I don't eat a thing."

This woman, a champion against drug addiction, child abuse, and other causes, was suddenly struck by tragedy when her husband died of a massive heart attack. A tranquilizer was prescribed to ease the tragedy, and, several weeks later, she visited her physician again, lethargic and somewhat confused, which was attributed to the medication and to severe depression at the loss of her husband. Francine admitted that for many years she had been having memory problems which intensified, and that she had enormous guilt feelings because her relationship with her husband had deteriorated until the time of his death. She said, "Now, Doctor, I have to tell you the truth. I know I should have told you years ago, but I have been drinking a great deal, and I have finally decided to join AA."

Francine's alcohol level was markedly elevated, and, with the combination of antidepressants, she presented as an early demented female. She admitted that for years her brain function had been poor and that she had been making continual mistakes in her checkbook, which had angered her husband. He did not know that she was drinking, since he was not home most of the time. Francine also feared that she was developing Alzheimer's disease because of her memory loss and, in her anxiety, had drunk even more.

It took the death of her husband for Francine to come to the realization that she was a chronic alcoholic and that her brain was becoming impaired. There was a pleasant change in this woman as soon as six weeks after she discontinued her alcohol intake. She went on a diet, lost almost fifty pounds within a period of a little more than a year, remarried, and started a new and fulfilling life.

Marijuana and Memory Loss

Some thirty million Americans use marijuana daily. Little do they know what this is doing to their precious brain cells!

There are some startling nationwide statistics recorded by the National Institute on Drug Abuse on the use of marijuana in the United States. One in five eighth-graders questioned in a 1979 study in Maryland said they were currently smoking marijuana, and one in eleven said they were doing so daily or several times a week. In Maine in 1978, 56 percent of 13- to 15-year-olds had used the drug at least once, and 42 percent were regular users.

Marijuana is a major health hazard in the United States. It causes chronic bronchial and pulmonary irritation in long-term users, leading to chronic lung disease. The smoke is 50 percent hydrocarbonous or more, a condition which is associated with a marked susceptibility to cancer of the lung. Marijuana smokers, in contrast to cigarette smokers, retain the smoke in the lungs for a longer period of time. One marijuana cigarette is equivalent to sixteen tobacco cigarettes. The combination of cigarette and marijuana smoking is lethal to lung tissue. Marijuana has been reported as a cause of diminished fertility, lower testosterone levels in the male, and reduced sperm counts. In the female, long-term marijuana use causes abnormal menstruation, including failure to ovulate, and fetal damage since the chromosome pattern is affected. The susceptibility to infection is well-recorded, as the immune system is markedly impaired.

Marijuana, or cannabis, is a drug known from antiquity which is obtained from the tops of hemp plants. In the Middle East and North Africa, the dried resins of the plant are called hashish, while in the Far East, it is called charas. The active ingredients of marijuana are called cannabinoids, and they have profound effects on the sensorium—the entire brain sensory apparatus—leading to fluctuations in mood, memory, motor coordination, cognitive sensibility, and perception. Often, the user feels an increased sense of well-being, euphoria, relaxation, and an urge toward spontaneous laughter. Balance is markedly affected, even with low dosages. There is a decrease in muscle strength and hand steadiness, and there is an inability to perform relatively simple motor tasks. Perception and attention, such as that needed in driving and piloting are impaired. Tragically, many automobile deaths have occurred as the result of the driver's smoking of marijuana.

Smokers of marijuana often report dry throats and allege a keener sense of hearing and a craving for sweets, among other things. There is an altered perception of time and events. In larger dosages, hallucinations and paranoid feelings can occur, with confused thinking and anxieties that sometimes result in severe panic.

The cardiovascular system responds to marijuana with an increased heart rate and blood pressure—the higher the dosage, the faster the heart rate. The oral temperature tends to drop. Chronic marijuana smoking, as in tobacco smoking, causes bronchitis and may cause asthma.

Although marijuana can indeed make the person feel good or "high," it has profound effects on memory. The French psychiatrist Moreau de Tours in 1845 described the effects of hashish as "a gradual weakening of the power to direct thoughts at will." The most evident impairment of memory occurs between 1½ to 3 hours after smoking. There is clear evidence that marijuana has a direct effect on the memory center, the hippocampus of the brain: it seems to reduce the amount of acetylcholine necessary for neurotransmission. These individuals have been found to have great difficulty in retrieving words from their brain and are unable to recall digits; the ability to store new material is also impaired. The chronic use of marijuana causes the same kinds of memory effects as those experienced in patients suffering from brain infections, Korsakoff's syndrome, and Alzheimer's disease.

The tragedy of marijuana is exemplified in a 1979 national survey of some U.S. Army enlisted men who were known to use hashish on a chronic basis. They exhibited a certain dullness and impairment of judgment and concentration, as well as memory loss. Some, after discontinuing marijuana use, returned to normal within four weeks, while there were others who may deteriorate to the chronic organic brain stage. Marijuana *is* a cause of reversible memory loss, but it remains to be seen if there will be overall long-term chronic brain impairment from its use.

Parents should be made aware that poor performance in school by their teenagers could be due to marijuana usage and alcohol.

At the age of sixteen, Melissa was a devoted, loving daughter of a father who was a surgeon and a mother who was an English professor. Melissa had long brown hair, round bright eyes, and an adorable smile that had magical effects on all who saw her. She was an outstanding student at a private school, excelling especially in chemistry and mathematics, and she had a natural proclivity for writing and literature as well. She was a sports star at the school—she was an excellent tennis player, she was on the lacrosse team, and she loved cross-country running—and she had many friends. Her memory was so extraordinary that, at times, she found it embarrassing to recall the minute details of the football players' scores, and unlike many of us, did not have to spend many hours studying to retain her algebraic formulas or the facts she learned in chemistry.

By all accounts, Melissa was part of a happy family which shared a great deal of love, affection, and respect. In essence, they were the envy of the community.

In the spring of 1982, Melissa fell in love with a senior in school whom we shall call Jim, who was an athlete planning to eventually pursue a political career. Melissa, shortly thereafter, received counseling from Planned Parenthood, and, now, the glow on her face became even brighter. As she was such an excellent student and had fulfilled all the expectations of her parents, her father agreed that she should have driving lessons and also should have her own car.

When summer vacation arrived Melissa went to summer camp as a tennis instructor and Jim worked as a lifeguard on the waterfront. As the camp was only several miles away from home, she often returned on the weekends looking brown, tanned, and healthy.

Several months later, when school started again, Melissa's behavior began to change, although it was not immediately obvious to her parents. Her weight began to increase, and she consumed large amounts of sweets. This was the beginning of her junior year and an important one for college applications and SATs. The pressures were running high. She was Ivy League material, and her father desired her to apply to the best schools in the country. Her teachers noticed that her concentration began to markedly decrease, and the glow on her face changed to a dull appearance. She began to look ill. Formerly, on the spot quizzes, she was the first to finish; now, she barely completed the exam and received grades of C's and even D's. Something was happening to this young woman.

The math teacher called her home and described the changes to her father. "I know there is something wrong," the teacher said. "Have you noticed anything?"

Her father said, "Well, I usually come home late, and I then find her sitting at her desk studying or sleeping, or going to bed earlier than usual."

Melissa's daily habits began to change drastically. She no longer read books, and, when she went out with Jim, she returned in the early hours of the morning. She no longer participated in sports because she had gained so much weight and was "too tired."

Her father, noticing the increased weight gain, suspected a thyroid condition. She went to see a physician who found her to be in excellent physical health except for the weight gain.

At Christmastime, there came an alarming phone call from the police that Melissa was involved in a serious accident and had been brought to the hospital. She had driven her car into a tree, had suffered multiple injuries, and was unconscious.

After two days in the hospital, she was discharged, but her father decided that further studies should be made—perhaps she was harboring a brain tumor, accounting for her changed behavior.

An entire examination was again performed, including a CT scan of the brain, all of which was normal. A neuropsychiatrist conducted brain-testing and found the young woman to have evidence of marked brain impairment, memory loss for immediate recall, and learning abilities that were markedly diminished.

It was only after several weeks of consultations that the family learned that Melissa was smoking marijuana, four to eight cigarettes per day or more, and, in addition, was consuming large amounts of alcohol, both of which she acquired from her boyfriend, Jim. When asked why she did it, she said "to please Jim." This story had a happy ending for Melissa, after months of consultation and therapy, was freed of the effects of marijuana and alcohol, her memory returned, and she became, again, her bright, happy self.

Melissa's case illustrates the tragic circumstance in our society of children who do not perform in school because of the effects of marijuana or excessive alcohol. It behooves parents to investigate and discover if marijuana addiction is present, especially if there is excessive weight gain, chronic fatigue, and poor retention of knowledge.

Cocaine and Mental Deterioration

From the Andes to the city streets of the United States, the coca leaf represents another major health hazard. It can be used in various ways, from being held and sucked inside the cheek, as a fine powder sniffed up the nose, or injected into the arm. The United States is a drug-ridden society. Ten percent or more of the population use cocaine, 10 to 15 percent are alcoholics, and another 10 percent use marijuana, as I have previously described. Some people use all three substances, but these statistics are not available. It is no wonder that brain degeneration is in epidemic form.

Cocaine is a drug used since antiquity; it was quite fashionable and was once easily obtained in many countries in the form of tonics and Coca-Cola. In the 1920s, it was sold as freely as popcorn on the streets of Berlin until the Nazi regime put a halt to this practice.

In 1887, Oregon was the first U.S. state to prohibit the dispensing of cocaine without a prescription. The Pure Food and Drug Act of 1906 was the first piece of federal legislation to regulate distribution of narcotics and cocaine in the United States, and, in 1914, the Harrison Narcotics Act specified the laws regulating the sale and distribution of cocaine. Cocaine had been used in medicine as an analgesic, and is still presently used as a form of local anesthesic by ear, nose, and throat specialists.

The propaganda on cocaine has, unfortunately, motivated its usage by not only young people but also those in other spheres of society, especially the well-to-do.

The injurious actions of cocaine in the body are well known. It increases the heart rate and the blood pressure and causes increased muscle activity. Shaking, convulsions, and vomiting can occur in higher dosages, and the respiratory system may be affected with decreased ability to breathe. It elevates the body temperature and can cause much weight loss in persons who have used it for prolonged periods of time, in contrast to the effect of alcohol. Some cocaine addicts will consume between 5000 to 8000 calories per day and not gain any weight, because the cocaine affects a center of the brain which interferes with weight gain. Cocaine markedly affects sleep patterns and reduces the amount of time that the patient is actually sleeping. As time goes on, depression and exhaustion follow. Excessive amounts lead to hallucinations and paranoid behavior, entitled "cocaine psychosis." Patients may exhibit symptoms of paranoid schizophrenia: they may imagine that there are animals crawling on their bodies or that they are being chased by wild animals.

Those persons who constantly sniff cocaine suffer destruction of the nasal cartilage with actual collapse of the nose. Cocaine users may become prone to infections like AIDS because sometimes the drug causes their natural immune system to fail.

Although there is a temporary increase of intellectual function, scientists report that cocaine is responsible for brain degeneration in due time if used continually and is a cause for reversible dementia.

CHAPTER 12

Head Injuries and Brain Tumors

People grow old only by deserting their ideals. Years may wrinkle the skin, but to give up interests wrinkles the soul.

DOUGLAS MACARTHUR

Subdural Hematomas

Older people, because of visual impairment and decreased muscular coordination with associated diseases such as arthritis of the hip, tend to fall more often than do younger persons. Their medications may cause drops in blood pressure, accompanied by dizzy spells and frequent falls.

In one estimation of a study in the *Journal of the American Medical Association* in May 1984, 30 percent of all pedestrian fatalities occur to people over age sixty-five, and 72 percent of those patients who have fatal falls are also among the elderly.

A minor head injury in an older person, seemingly as "trivial" as striking the head against a branch of a tree or on the fireplace mantel, can cause a condition called chronic subdural hematoma. As a result of such injuries, blood collects between the outer membrane of the brain, called the dura mater, and the skull. Most patients may not even recall that they experienced the head injury, and those elderly patients who are already suffering from some memory loss may not remember the injury at all.

The hematoma, or collection of blood, in older persons tends to be denser than it would be in the younger person because there is more space between the brain and the skull, allowing the blood collection to progressively enlarge—this growth can simulate a brain tumor and progressive dementia.

Several weeks after a head injury, the patient may have mild headaches, lightheadedness, or a change in behavior patterns, with slowing of thought processes, increased drowsiness, and obvious memory loss. Some complain of numbness of their arms and loss of power in their extremities. Visual disturbances with double vision or loss of vision in one part of the visual field may be the signs and symptoms of an early stroke, a brain tumor, or an excessive amount of medication. Depression and early senility can also be the presenting symptoms.

Today, the diagnosis of chronic subdural hematoma is consistently made through the CT scan. Prior to the development of this type of x-ray, it was not uncommon to miss the diagnosis.

In one study of a series of 275 cases of "trivial head injury" in people of all ages, 1 percent of patients died and 1.7 percent had hematomas, according to *International Medical News* in 1979. A "trivial head injury" can occur from a bang on the head from a closet door.

A 63-year-old woman, Stella, who had been suffering from rheumatoid arthritis for thirty years was receiving multiple medications: cortisone for rheumatoid arthritis, Aldomet for blood pressure, Lasix for heart failure, calcium pills, and vitamin D. The patient had been suffering from hypertension and had had a mild heart attack three years previously, as well as two unsuccessful cataract operations which had left her vision partially impaired.

The patient had episodic dizzy spells, due to improper blood circulation to her brain through the basilar artery. She also suffered from cervical arthritis of her neck and had periodic episodes of drops in her blood pressure—all of which her doctors were trying to correct. It was a common occurrence for her to wake up in the morning and feel lightheaded; she needed to hold on to the edge of her bed, lest she fall.

On one particular morning, she was working in the kitchen. She bent over the sink, and, as she did, felt lightheaded and bumped her head against the door of her cabinet. She flinched from the moderately severe pain; it gradually subsided and later in the day she had completely forgotten about the episode.

Several weeks later, her dizzy spells were still continuing in the same fashion, except that by now they were accompanied with some double vision. The patient was advised to see an eye doctor. She hesitated and decided she would wait since she had just gone through cataract surgery.

One week later, double vision and dizzy spells were still evident, but her memory, although somewhat diminished over the past year, was now failing altogether. As previously noted, the combination of her medications, atherosclerosis and hypertension could have been responsible for her memory loss.

Her family began to realize that she could no longer live alone, since her forgetfulness was worsening, and, in addition, she was experiencing episodes of hallucinations with severe paranoid feelings. For example, one day she was certain that somebody was trying to invade her house and that her next-door neighbor had planted electric circuits in her living room. They moved her into her son's house and made certain that she was never left alone. A plan was devised to build her a separate apartment, since the family refused to send her to a nursing home.

Approximately eight weeks after the move, she was found lying in bed paralyzed and unable to speak. It was the consensus that she had probably suffered a stroke; however, when a CT scan was performed of her brain, the doctors discovered that she had a subdural hematoma. An operation was performed to evaluate and remove the clot. She recovered with no residual paralysis, and, after several months, was able to return back to her own home, although her family is somewhat nervous about her remaining alone.

This case is an illustration of the problems which can develop in a patient who forgets about a minor injury to the head. In patients who are receiving corticosteroids, those who have rheumatoid arthritis, or those suffering from softening of the bone (osteoporosis), a minor injury can cause a hemorrhage in the brain. If this had occurred several years ago, before the CT scan had been developed, the diagnosis may very well have been missed.

Younger patients can also suffer minor head injuries and develop subdural hematomas and, months later, may develop bizarre symptoms, including memory loss. It is always possible to forget that "slight bang on the head."

Brain Tumors

Brain tumors can cause disturbances in transient episodes, such as vascular problems of the brain. In 1870, Dr. John Jackson wrote that "The effects of all brain tumors start with an almost imperceptible decline in delicate intellectual processes and a loss of finer emotions. Patients suffered a limitation in their intellectual field. As tumors grow, the behavioral abnormalities may become aberrant."

In one estimate by Beeson and McDermott in *Textbook of Medicine*, dementia was the initial diagnosis in 15 percent of all patients suffering from brain tumors. The dementia may progress slowly and gradually, with difficulty for the patient in reading, writing, and performing simple calculations. Strokes (cerebral infraction) cause more destruction of the brain, but tumors push and infiltrate brain tissue, causing progressive neurological signs.

Slow growing brain tumors are capable of producing symptoms of brain decline similar to those found in Alzheimer's disease. Some statistics have shown that depression is found in about one-half of the patients with brain tumors and schizophrenia is found in 5 to 15 percent of the subjects with paranoia, mania, and other bizarre antisocial behavior. Tumors of the frontal brain lobe are the most frequent type which produce psychiatric symptoms.

Today, the diagnosis of brain tumor is considerably simpler than in previous years because of the availability of the CT scan and the technique of nuclear magnetic resonance (NMR). Any patient who has brain-impairment symptoms should be evaluated with an EEG or a CT scan of the brain. In some cases, a spinal tap may be ordered if a chronic infection is suspected.

Unfortunately, sometimes a cancer, as in the lung or breast, may result in the first symptoms of brain failure. Bizarre behavior, headaches, and memory impairment can result from the spread of the tumor, or metastases, to the brain. Usually, tumors are a later manifestation of a widespread cancer, but it is possible that they may also be the first sign of the cancer's appearance.

A 52-year-old man who was a chronic smoker with a bothersome daily morning cough began to show signs of bellicose behavior at work—he constantly argued and criticized, showed signs of depression, and flew into fits of severe anger over the slightest inconvenience (when, for example, someone by mistake used *his* coffee cup). Some of his fellow employees thought that he was drinking "on the side," and others had the impression that "he was flipping his lid from too much pressure on the job." He was unable to continue a conversation without jumping from one subject to another, and the conversation would often disintegrate into his raving and ranting. Some of his friends noticed that he retold the same story five or six times in one evening. When he became abusive to his wife and children, his wife decided to consult a social worker. The social worker advised her that her husband should be seen by a doctor for a thorough examination.

The company required him to have a physical examination, on the pretext of an annual executive examination. The entire examination was normal, but, because of his strange new behavior and memory loss, the astute physician ordered a CT scan of the brain, which revealed a slow-growing tumor called a meningioma. The executive underwent an operation; the tumor was removed. His memory shortly improved and his bizarre behavior disappeared.

Normal Pressure Hydrocephalus, or Water on the Brain

A 59-year-old executive computer specialist smoked two packs of cigarettes per day, drank one or two martinis with each meal, and, on weekends, drank even more. He never showed signs of drunkenness and conducted his daily business negotiations with skill. One morning, after the July 4th weekend, he complained of general drowsiness, which he attributed to excessive holiday partying. For the next three or four days, he remained irritable, and he became quite forgetful. He decided then and there not to do any further drinking, to give up smoking, and to go on a weight-reduction program to "shape up."

Weeks passed and he did not feel any better. He became quite depressed. In the following months, his memory loss worsened to the extent that he once became confused and lost while driving home. As he became more despondent, he again started to drink heavily and then finally did not return to his home. For weeks, the executive staggered around like a drunkard through the city, unshaven, with his clothing filthy from lying in the gutter. He was finally picked up by the police as he lay on a street corner, and he was brought to a local emergency room. At this point, his family was located and notified.

The initial diagnosis was alcoholism with brain degeneration; however, as part of his examination, a CT scan of his brain was performed, which displayed the classic signs of the condition called normal pressure hydrocephalus (NPH). The CT scan showed that the chambers, or the ventricles, of the brain were enlarged from an excessive amount of fluid on the brain. An operation called a ventricular-atrial shunt was performed to shunt the fluid out of the ventricles and, within weeks, the executive left the hospital with his dementia cured.

Normal pressure hydrocephalus was defined in the early 1960s by Dr. Raymond Adams of the Massachusetts General Hospital. The condition is called normal pressure hydrocephalus because, if a spinal fluid tap is performed, the pressure in the fluid is normal in contrast to the results when there are other causes of water on the brain. It may present with the classic symptoms of Alzheimer's disease dementia, accompanied by the inability to properly walk, frequent episodes of falling, inability to retain urine, and great difficulties in concentration.

Dr. Adams stated that three symptoms must be present for the ventricular-atrial shunt to be considered—forgetfulness, unsteady gait, and urinary incontinence. Fifty percent of the corrective surgeries performed for this condition will be successful. It is sometimes difficult to diagnose normal pressure hydrocephalus, especially if patients have a history of head injuries, since this is not a common condition. In the United States, 4000 to 14,000 cases have been reported since 1965. In some patients, the initial symptoms may be euphoria or antisocial behavior, coupled with episodes of confusion, lethargy, and memory loss.

In a study conducted at Vanderbilt University in Nashville,

Tennessee, by Dr. Frank L. Freemon and reported in the 1982 *Journal of the American Geriatric Society* five patients among 110 patients with dementia were suffering from normal pressure hydrocephalus. The five patients were diagnosed with a CT scan which showed marked enlargement of the brain ventricles. In three patients, significant improvement occurred. Dramatic improvement can occur in the first few days after surgery, but usually the major improvement occurs in the first two postsurgery months.

The reason why excessive cerebrospinal fluid accumulates in the brain and causes it to atrophy is unknown. It seems that there is an interference of the circulation of fluid in the brain. In some patients, brain hemorrhages and inflammation can lead to blocking of the cerebrospinal fluid, and these patients seldom benefit from the shunting operation. This is a procedure which works only in those patients who have the definitive diagnosis of normal pressure hydrocephalus—a difficult diagnosis to make which requires a team of medical specialists including neurologists, neurosurgeons, and radiologists.

Posttraumatic Stress Disorders

Any life-threatening traumatic event which threatens the existence of an individual, whether it be involvement in an automobile accident, house fire, plane crash, or battle (as a soldier), can leave long-lasting scars. Formerly, this condition was called "shell shock," "neurosis precipitated by trauma," "traumatic neurosis," or, most degrading of all, "malingering," and referred to those symptoms suffered following traumatic events. People who were in the midst of a cataclysmal event but emerged unharmed have been noted to suffer the following symptoms: anger, guilt, insomnia, loss of appetite, extreme fatigue, fear of overhead structures, recurrent dreams, nightmares, a hypersensitivity to noises, and, above all, memory loss and difficulty in concentration.

The memory loss may continue for years and sometimes can be permanent. In the wake of the 1981 Hyatt disaster in Kansas City, Missouri, when two skywalks of the Hyatt Regency Hotel collapsed, killing 113 people and injuring 200 others, it was noted that survivors suffered undue fatigue; more than one-half had re-current dreams, often of a nightmarish quality; one-half had sleep difficulties; nearly one-half had problems in concentration; one-fourth experienced a loss of appetite; one-fourth suffered dimin-ished sexual desire; and one-fourth felt isolated and detached from other people.

Dr. Wilkinson, a psychiatrist at the University of Missouri at Kansas City, made these observations. Feelings of guilt were es-pecially common, often expressed as not knowing "why I'm still alive when others who are younger are dead."

Memory loss from a near-death disaster had not been studied to a large extent until recently. Depression and fatigue had been interpreted as "malingering" until the case was settled in court. Some patients with posttraumatic syndrome can develop such se-rious memory loss that they can present as classic cases of senile dementia of the Alzheimer type. (Patients who seek medical at-tention after a trauma as a rule are not asked if they have any memory loss, but unfortunately, are questioned only about their aches and pains.)

Dorothy, a 48-year-old Phi Beta Kappa college graduate and director of an important business organization, was driving a car with her husband as passenger, when she was suddenly struck by a truck which completely demolished the automobile and knocked both the husband and wife temporarily unconscious. Although they sustained relatively minor injuries, they suffered subsequent aches and pains throughout their bodies followed by enormous fatigue. A week later, Dorothy had completely "recovered" and she at-tempted to return to her job. She noticed an inability to concentrate and had difficulty in remembering any recent events, no less to recall some past events. Her husband suffered a similar kind of reaction but experienced more fatigue than memory loss. After she underwent a complete physical examination whose results were normal, she was referred to a psychiatrist. (By 1980, the posttrau-matic psychoneurosis syndrome had become an accepted diagno-sis.)

Extensive psychiatric testing was performed and revealed that Dorothy was unable to retain four words, subtract the number 7 from 100 successively, or retain numbers. When asked to reproduce figures and drawings, she did so with great awkwardness. From these tests, it became evident that she was suffering from brain damage, similar to that seen in elderly patients who are suffering from dementia.

Dorothy was reassured that this was not a malingering psychiatric response, but likely represented a chemical imbalance in her brain which generally is reversible with time and patience, and that the combination of antidepressants and nonstrenuous exertion of her brain would correct the problem. It has now been more than one year since the accident, and the patient has recuperated to some extent, but still has serious short-term memory loss. Sometimes it may be three to five years before full brain function returns. In a small percentage of patients, it never returns.

A 59-year-old insurance salesperson, Edward, was flying from New York to Boston when the plane suddenly caught fire in midair. He recalled, as he later told the Federal Aviation Board investigators, that he was suffocating from the flames and smoke that were moving towards him in the plane. Edward recalled the screaming of passengers around him and then, accepting the inevitability of death, felt a sense of calm and serenity envelop him. He stated that he saw "mountains and valleys covered with snow." The plane crashed in flames into a reservoir, and, when he had regained consciousness, the plane was on fire. He did not recall the impact of the crash. As he crawled out of the plane, he saw that passengers around him were burning and that one person had been killed. He had not suffered any serious injuries, as had the rest of the passengers. The pilots too were scorched.

Edward's examination in the emergency room disclosed merely that his hands were charred and that there were some bruises on his legs and arms.

He had become unconscious from smoke inhalation and perhaps even sustained a cardiac arrest, which could account for the reason he never felt the impact of the crash. It was speculated that the impact of the crash on the ice may have revived him. His descriptions of the calmness and "view of the valley and brightness of the mountains" are often detailed by patients upon resuscitation after sustaining a cardiac arrest.

Month after month of exhaustion, severe depression, and complete inability to concentrate followed. The most catastrophic problems were markedly diminished reasoning power, memory loss, and an almost complete loss of judgment. Edward was unable to continue working. When driving down a street, he often could not recall where he was going and, frequently, he got lost in his own neighborhood. Names of friends and relatives were totally forgotten. Familiar faces were erased from his mind, and he even had difficulty in naming familiar objects. These symptoms, coupled with an enormous fear of driving his car, of flying, or of even looking up at the sky, filled him with terror. Vacations were impossible to take. He was terrified to swim, lest another disaster take place.

During the course of his illness, Edward underwent complete psychological testing which disclosed that his mental impairment was equivalent to that of a patient suffering from Alzheimer's disease. Unfortunately, the examiner told him these results which only made him feel worse. He contemplated suicide but did not have the courage to go through with it. Retesting at intervals showed some improvement in his memory, but no improvement in reproducing figures or in abstract thinking. During this time, he was noted to be extraordinarily irritable; he easily became angry and abusive, and he lost many of his friends.

Finally, when he received antidepressant medications, he began to improve, and, after several years, was able to return to work. Unknown to his employers or the rest of his friends, his memory impairment still remained. He realized his limitations (as do those who lose vision in one eye) and compensated for them by writing everything down on a pad and not relying on his memory to recall new information.

Many posttraumatic syndrome patients make every effort to hide their memory loss and their brain impairment because their employer's knowledge would probably mean the end of their career. However, they should not be ashamed or afraid to disclose these problems to a physician. Patients suffering from these symptoms after an automobile accident, a plane crash, or even surgery should not hesitate to consult their physicians. Memory loss, fatigue, and nightmares can be greatly relieved with antidepressants and psychotherapy.

Amnesic Syndrome

The amnesic syndrome is a condition in which there is a severe deficit in short-term memory. The patient retains long-term memory function and preserves excellent intellectual function. He or she can carry on a normal conversation, but cannot retain any new information. For example, the patient may be told the examiner's name at least ten times in an hour, but then, five minutes after hearing the name, cannot remember it. The person can retain the name and repeat it within a few seconds, but cannot do so after a few minutes.

This condition can follow a severe accident or illness, but patients are unable to remember details that preceded the accident or illness. As the result of memory loss, there is disorientation as to time and place. Many of these patients are so embarrassed by their sudden memory loss that they will confabulate answers to the physician's questions.

The amnesic syndrome can also occur as a result of a circulatory disturbance to the brain—transient global amnesia, or the TGA syndrome. For a day, the person will be confused and cannot remember new information; when he or she recovers, there will be no recollection of the day's events. It is believed to be a transient ischemic attack (TIA), as described before, involving the arteries of the hippocampus. Some patients will not have any recurrences for years, while others will progress into a severely demented state. A state of hysteria is difficult to differentiate from the amnesic syndrome. Typically, in the latter case, the patients will recall what they were doing up to the point of the accident and then will lose track of events for about a full day.

An extraordinarily brilliant World War II Air Force officer had just retired from his job, and, one morning after breakfast, his wife noticed that he acted in a most peculiar manner. She recalled that he did not recognize her, did not know where he was, and that all he did was talk about flying his B26 bomber over Berlin. She took him to the emergency room, and he was admitted into the hospital. The results of a CT scan and an EEG were within normal limits. Twenty-four hours later, he woke up and could not understand what he was doing in the hospital ward. The conclusion reached was that he had undergone a transient global amnesic episode. The man could not recall any events that had occurred during the past twenty-four-hour period, since sitting down to breakfast.

Transient global amnesia is not a common illness, and it disappears within a day or two. Patients with this disorder are generally examined for disease of the carotid arteries, as earlier described.

Repeated Minor Head Traumas, or the Punch-Drunk Syndrome

Multiple repeated head injuries, such as those sustained by boxers, football players, steeplechase riders, and wrestlers, have been reported to often cause long-lasting ill effects. In a recent (May 25, 1984) article in the *Journal of the American Medical Association*, the complete neurological examinations of eighteen former boxers were analyzed. Eighty-seven percent of those studied had evidence of brain damage. The criteria for brain damage were abnormal findings on a series of neuropsychological tests, as well as on the CT scan and EEG. Notably, these former boxers performed poorly on a short-term memory test (the Wechsler-Bellevue intelligence scale). Impairment of short-term memory is a central feature of the condition called the punch-drunk syndrome. The patients who were studied had no history of alcohol or drug abuse or of venereal disease.

This condition was first described by Dr. H. S. Martland in 1928. The brain studied under the microscope showed signs of changes similar to those found to some degree in patients with Alzheimer's disease—widespread neurofibrillary tangles and focal scarring.

The mechanism of brain damage due to repeated trauma has been studied. Hemorrhages, as well as destruction of brain cells, occur due to the sudden accelerated movement of the head. The immobile brain lags behind the skull motion, causing stretching and snapping of vessels. Boxers' brains reveal signs of loss of nerve fibers and nerve degeneration in the hippocampus. All nerve cells may be gone, except for the residual skeletons of the neurofibrillary tangles. This change is more intense than that seen in the brains of patients with Alzheimer's disease and other causes of senile dementia. (Boxing, only too obviously, can induce permanent brain damage, and stricter regulations need to be enforced. Otherwise, this barbaric "sport" needs to be abolished!)

Hypothetically, I can only wonder what effects repeated automobile and motorcycle accidents have on some people's brains. The motorcycle accident is the major cause of epilepsy in young people in the United States.

CHAPTER 13

Infections of the Brain, Slow-Acting Viruses, AIDS, and Collagen Vascular Disease

To me, old age is always fifteen years older than I am.
BERNARD BARUCH

Chronic Infections of the Brain

Chronic infections of the brain, called chronic meningitis, are not rare conditions. Many times, they are superimposed on preexisting conditions, such as leukemia, or they can occur in a healthy person. Tuberculosis is a cause of chronic meningitis, along with other organisms. Acute meningitis and encephalitis can cause symptoms of dementia.

Cryptococcosis

A 68-year-old physician, Mortimer, still active in practice, had been suffering from chronic leukemia for the past five years. He had accepted the diagnosis of chronic leukemia with grace and realized that he would carry this illness for several more years. His leukemia was well-controlled and he had remained totally free of symptoms for the previous two years. Mortimer continued an active practice from morning until night and was devoted to and much loved by his patients for the excellent quality of medicine that he provided.

On one hot July morning, Mortimer awoke with an aching head, accompanied by a nauseated feeling, as if he were drunk. As so many doctors do, he self-diagnosed and decided that he had a summer virus. He medicated himself with an antibiotic and aspirins and felt better by late afternoon.

For weeks, he continued experiencing slight headaches and irritability; the latter was out of character for him. On occasion, his vision became blurred for a second. In the following weeks, he tested his own blood count on two occasions. Satisfied that his leukemic cells had not increased, he felt that there was no reason to call a colleague for help.

Two months later, his irritability was still increasing, and his office nurses noticed that he became quite forgetful. Appointments were missed, telephone calls were not answered unless he was reminded, and he sometimes staggered into the examining room. When Mortimer came home at night, however, he was as jovial as always, due to the analgesics he took for his headaches which left him euphoric sometimes for six hours at a time.

In November he realized that his memory loss was much worse than he had at first ascertained. He began to write everything down. Once he forgot how to get to a restaurant that he frequented at least once a month. There was now no doubt in his mind that he was a victim of senility. Unknown to his wife, he made preparations in the event that he became totally disabled. As his forgetfulness became more serious, he decided to take a leave of absence from his practice—a long vacation, as he told his wife. "It's about time that I take a trip around the world on a slow boat to China."

He found another physician to temporarily take his practice, but, on the day of departure, he suddenly collapsed. When he was admitted into the hospital, he was semicomatose and confused. Blood tests demonstrated that his leukemia had worsened. A neurologist performed a spinal tap, and the fluid was examined for cancer cells and infection. An India ink smear of the fluid revealed circular yeast-type cells under the microscope. The diagnosis reached was cryptococcosis, *not* "senility." (Cryptococcosis is an infection caused by the fungus *Filobasidiella neoformans* which affects the lungs and the central nervous system.) Extensive treatment for the next six weeks entirely cleared all of the doctor's symptoms, and, at the end of two months, he was sailing on a steamship around the world, fully able to enjoy the trip. Although Mortimer died five years later from leukemia, his brain remained sharp to the end.

Syphilis of the Brain

Syphilis was once called "the great pox" to differentiate it from another prevalent virulent destructive infection—smallpox. The great epidemic of syphilis occurred throughout Europe in the late fifteenth century. The epidemic started soon after Columbus returned from the West Indies, and some scientists held that the disease was brought back by the returning sailors. Scholars, however, have found evidence in the Old Testament and in ancient Chinese writings of diseases whose symptoms were similar to those of syphilis. Syphilis rose to its epidemic height in the late fifteenth century as wars prevailed and the disease was rapidly disseminated through the army camps. By the early sixteenth century, it was recognized that syphilis was sexually transmitted. The name was coined by the sixteenth-century poet Girolamo Fracastoro who wrote of the mythical shepherd Syphilus who was afflicted by the illness.

By the eighteenth and nineteenth centuries, effects of syphilis on the brain were also recognized. Many prominent figures of western civilization had syphilis of the central nervous system with the classic symptoms of dementia—hallucinations and paranoia, ending in coma and death. For a long time, syphilis was confused with gonorrhea because of the views of the eighteenth-century British physician, John Hunter (1728–1793). He believed that "the great pox" and gonorrhea were one and the same illness, and, from the pus from the penis of a sufferer of both, he infected himself. The lesion disappeared, and the doctor felt perfectly well. He falsely concluded that both illnesses had left his body. Years later, John Hunter died from the terminal complications of syphilis.

Through the centuries, there has been a long history of research for the treatment of syphilis of the brain, once called dementia praecox. Dr. Wagner-Jauregg of Vienna was a psychiatrist who set out to find the cure of dementia praecox. He noted that in ancient times when cholera swept through an insane asylum and killed hundreds the survivors' brains had returned to normal. He began to reason that perhaps their illnesses had been cured by the inducement of fever. In 1917, he infected insane people with tuberculosis in order to induce high fever, and some subjects did indeed get better. He then injected malaria into the insane, and again there were some who improved. The new technique of "fever curing fever" induced the Swedes to give Wagner-Jauregg the Nobel Prize for the "cure of syphilis" in 1927.

The treatment of syphilis remained unsatisfactory until 1943 when penicillin was introduced and the illness came under general control. Prior to the introduction of penicillin, the "magic bullet" of the German physiologist Paul Ehrlich had introduced arsenic as a cure, a treatment which had to be given for a period of two years.

The natural course of untreated syphilis begins with the appearance of a painless bump on the penis or vagina, called the primary lesion, which may break down to form an ulcer within a 21-day period after exposure. This lesion, called a chancre, occurs 90 percent of the time in the genital region.

Four to eight weeks following the appearance of this primary chancre, other lesions of syphilis develop, accompanied by headache, fever, sore throat, and enlargement of the lymph glands.

The form of syphilis that can masquerade as senile dementia is entitled "general paresis" or "neurosyphilis." Typically, it occurs ten to twenty years after the actual infection. It was formerly thought to be a common cause of insanity. General paresis is rarely seen today in the United States. The recent cases which have been discovered are in elderly demented patients who were never adequately treated, if at all, for syphilis.

There are many behavioral manifestations of syphilis of the brain. The most common ones consist of subtle changes in personality, a lack of attention, poor appearance, poor judgment, aggressiveness, bizarre behavior, peculiarities, mood swings, and concentration difficulties. Delusions of grandeur are present in 20 percent of these patients; however, 50 percent may just have a simple dementia with apathy.

The classic picture is often that of a male with a megalomaniacal Napoleonic complex, who claims to have great financial success, physical strength, and extraordinary powers, as he pathetically parades and struts in ragged clothing. In the earlier stages, there may be depression with moments of delusions of grandeur, personality changes, and evidence of memory loss.

The diagnosis of this illness is made by very carefully taking the history for possible exposure to syphilis. In one study of 200 elderly patients with dementia or psychiatric illness in the November, 1982, issue of *Medical Times*, 1 percent had evidence of untreated syphilis of the brain. The diagnosis is made by syphilis tests of the blood and by the examination of the spinal fluid. Treatment with penicillin can have a favorable prognosis.

Slow-Acting Viruses of the Brain

Syphilis is an example of how an infection can initially attack the brain and then, twenty years later, progress to dementia. In addition, certain viral agents can cause nerve degeneration and the typical pathological findings, called paired helical filaments (PHF), found in patients suffering from Alzheimer's disease and in some patients suffering from Parkinson's disease. These viruses that persist a long time in the nervous system are called slow-acting viruses—the incubation period may be as long as thirty years. Other pathological abnormalities of Alzheimer's disease, called neurofibrillary tangles and amyloid plaques, are also found in certain slow-acting viruses of the brain.

In Papua, New Guinea, tribal people were dying of a bizarre brain illness called kuru in 1963. The natives were cannibals, and a part of their funeral ritual was to feast on brains and other parts of the human body. This strange illness caused the people to shake, slur their speech, and exhibit weird uncoordinated movements, roving eyes, and tantrums. The illness finally ended in death. As the number of deaths mounted, more funeral ceremonies were required and more bone marrow, kidneys, intestines, and brains of males were concomitantly consumed.

A scientist, Dr. D. Carleton Gajdusek, at the U.S. National Institute of Health, came forward to investigate this strange illness. (He later won the Nobel Prize in 1976 for identifying a virus, the slow-acting virus.) He was able in 1965 to produce kuru in chimpanzees by the inoculation of brain tissue, and a year after the inoculation, the chimpanzees were exhibiting the same behavior as that of the cannibals. The disease was reproduced by feeding the kuru agent to chimpanzees. Since cannibalistic practices have markedly diminished in the world, the disease had apparently become almost nonexistent. It was because of Dr. Gajdusek's findings (and those related to a similar disease called scrapie, an infection of sheep) that slow-acting viruses of this type are theorized to be responsible for Alzheimer's disease, although this is not yet proven.

A similar viral illness of the nervous system which is invariably fatal is called Creutzfeldt-Jakob disease, a disease which afflicts individuals primarily between ages forty and eighty. It is a progressive dementia with seizures that have many characteristics similar to those of kuru. The first symptoms of Creutzfeldt-Jakob disease consist of sudden progressive memory disturbance, bizarre behavior, reasoning difficulties, visual distortions of objects and shapes, hallucinations, and confusion. The patient becomes spastic and rigid and may progress rapidly to death within three to twelve months. It is possible to transmit this disease to monkeys, cats, and guinea pigs. An unexpected and confusing finding in patients with Creutzfeldt-Jakob disease is that many of them have had eye operations—a coincidence which no one has been able to explain. The virus which causes this illness has been discovered in the kidney, spleen, lungs, and spinal fluid of patients afflicted with this disorder. It is not transmitted from person to person. Some of these patients may have contracted the illness after previous brain surgery.

Dr. Elias E. Manuelidis, professor of Neuropathology and Neurology at the Yale University School of Medicine, was the first scientist to transmit the Creutzfeld-Jakob virus to small laboratory animals, such as guinea pigs, hamsters, and mice. Dr. Manuelidis is still investigating whether Alzheimer's disease may be caused by a slow-acting virus.

Acquired Immune Deficiency Syndrome (AIDS)

The acquired immune deficiency syndrome, or AIDS, is a serious and dreadful illness; as of November 1984, 6993 cases had been reported in the United States. Of those, 3340 patients have died.

It is considered an epidemic, as each month an average of 165 new cases are reported. The largest number of patients are from New York City, San Francisco, and Los Angeles. Seventeen other countries have reported 122 cases. Approximately 80 percent of the victims in the United States are sexually active homosexual men, 16 percent are intravenous drug users, 5 percent are immigrants from Haiti, and 1 percent are hemophiliacs. More than 90 percent of victims are males between the ages of 20 to 49. This is predominantly a disease of sexual promiscuity, transmitted especially through anal intercourse. The average AIDS victim has had sixty different sexual partners in the previous twelve months. However, heterosexuals and children may also acquire the disease. It is also possible that the virus is transmitted through dirty needles. Many of the AIDS victims are drug users.

The known AIDS epidemic began approximately in 1981 when Dr. Michael Gottlieb, of the University of California at Los Angeles, reported the cases of five patients, all active homosexuals who were suffering from an unusual and deadly form of pneumonia. Their immune systems were markedly impaired, making them prone to serious infections. Simultaneously, Dr. Alvin Freedman-Kine, of New York University, also noted that his homosexual patients had an impaired immune system and were suffering from a rare skin disorder, entitled Kaposi's sarcoma.

The frightening element of this illness is that it has an incubation period of possibly from six months to two years. Every major organ of the body has been found to be involved, predominantly the cardiopulmonary system, gastrointestinal tract, and liver. The endocrine system is also not immune.

The major symptoms of AIDS are a respiratory-tract infection that looks like pneumonia but cultures out a specific organism called *Pneumocystis carinii*, weight loss, fatigue, and lymph-gland enlargement. Other presentations may be swollen glands and high temperature. The gastrointestinal system, when attacked with this illness, may show signs of bloating, belching, burping, constipation, and diarrhea. Skin lesions which have a purplish discoloration may be evident, which, when biopsied will show Kaposi's sarcoma. The patient may have had recent onset of progressive fatigue and memory loss and may actually become demented.

Many of the AIDS victims have suffered memory loss, impaired concentration, and signs of dementia. In the brain cells of those patients who have died and were autopsied, a virus, entitled HTLV–3, was found, to the surprise of many investigators.

In 1985, Dr. George Shaw, from the National Cancer Institute Tumor Cell Biology Laboratory, reported in an article that appeared in the *Journal of Science*, "I think it is safe to say that this is the first time that the HTLV–3 virus had been demonstrated to be present in the brains of humans."

It has also just recently been demonstrated that the AIDS virus is closely related to a group of viruses (which includes the HLTV–3 virus) that infect sheep, cattle, goats, and horses. AIDS represents another example of an infectious process that may incubate for two years and finally cause dementia.

All patients, homosexual or heterosexual, who have different sexual partners and have suffered memory loss, depression, lymphgland enlargement, repeated pulmonary infections, nonspecific gastrointestinal symptoms, and peculiar skin rashes should immediately seek medical attention.

Although AIDS at the present time is incurable and the majority of patients with this illness die, prevention and treatment is surely bound to come. At present, the means of prevention of this illness are to desist from promiscuity, avoid gay bars and bath houses, and eliminate the use of substances such as cocaine and heroin. Condoms should be used whenever possible, although their effectiveness has not yet been established. The homosexual person who is promiscuous should seek psychiatric help to relearn sexual habits.

In conclusion, at the present time, the case report is doubling every five months. Some have predicted there might be a million cases of AIDS in the future, but we can hope that a vaccine will soon be forthcoming and that the eventual fatalities of these sadly afflicted people will be ended.

Collagen Vascular Disease

Collagen vascular disease encompasses a group of diseases classified together because they have overlapping clinical features, as well as some common pathological abnormalities of joints, kidneys, the heart, the lungs, and the brain. Included in this group are rheu-

matoid arthritis, scleroderma, dermatomyositis, polyarteritis no-
dosa, and systemic lupus erythematosus. The word "lupus" means
wolf and has been used since 1230 to describe the inflammatory
red nodules and skin appearance which appear in erythema, similar
to the facial redness of a wolf.

The diseases in this group—in particular, systemic lupus erythematosus—are also associated with dementia, which may be the
predominant neurological presentation. SLE is a chronic inflammation of unknown cause, whose symptoms include the classic rash
on the face, called the butterfly rash, multiple joint involvements,
and disabled heart, lungs, and kidneys. At least 30 percent of SLE
patients have predominant neurological manifestations, such as
psychosis and dementia. Systemic lupus erythematosus may occur
in the absence of any skin disease. It is more common in women
than in men at all ages.

The patient's only symptoms may be purely neurological—
depression, memory loss, difficulty in finding words, periods of
complete delirium, and confusion. The diagnosis is sometimes difficult because the classic finding of lupus cells in the blood may
not be present, but a spinal tap will usually reveal specific abnormalities in the spinal fluid.

Elderly patients who present with dementia and other generalized bizarre symptoms should have a lupus-cell test. This is a
disease that is readily controlled with cortisone treatment. It is,
however, sometimes difficult to differentiate whether the cortisone
itself is causing the neurological symptoms. The writer, Flannery
O'Connor, who suffered from systemic lupus erythematosus, having received her cortisone injections, was quoted as saying that
"The large doses of ACTH send you off in a rocket, and are scarcely
less disagreeable than the disease."

In some patients, certain medications are capable of inducing
a complete neurological picture of systemic lupus erythematosus.
These patients may already have a predisposition to the illness,
and the drug brings it to the forefront.

A 59-year-old man sustained a myocardial infarction with severe
damage to his heart, which required numerous medications to
improve his heart function. A new form of treatment was tried,
involving the use of medications called vasodilators to allow the
heart to pump easier. (One that is currently used is hydralazine,

which is also used in the treatment of hypertension.) The cardiac disease was controlled, but, as the months passed, he became progressively more despondent, followed by increased memory loss and a continual complaint of aching in all his joints.

Other medications were given to relieve him of his joint pains, and his general mental deterioration was attributed to atherosclerosis of the brain, coupled with depression from his cardiac illness. The family accepted the diagnosis that he was deteriorating. He was again admitted into the hospital because of congestive heart failure with fluid in both of his lungs (pleural effusions), mild kidney failure, and anemia. Treatment of his heart failure was successful, but the pleural effusion persisted. The fluid was removed from the lung and examined microscopically but was not found to contain any infections. A lupus-cell test was performed on the blood, and it was markedly positive. Lupus was also found in the pleural fluid. It became evident that the patient was suffering from systemic lupus erythematosus induced by the hydralazine. When the medication was discontinued, the lupus disappeared from his body in several weeks. His joint pains subsided, and his mental state dramatically improved. Other medications can induce systemic lupus erythematosus, including isoniazid, used for the treatment of tuberculosis; phenytoin (Dilantin), used for the treatment of convulsions; and procainamide, a medication in cardiology commonly used to treat irregular heart rhythms. Fifty percent of all patients who are taking procainamide develop actual symptoms.

In a previously mentioned article entitled "Steroid-Sensitive Dementia," published in the *American Journal of Psychiatry* of August 1983, Dr. Paulson tells us that "occasional patients with senile dementia respond favorably to steroid therapy."

He mentions, in particular, that patients may be suffering from an inflammatory disease of the brain, a lupus-type of illness that responds dramatically to steroids. The article also discusses the pros and cons of performing biopsies of brain tissue in order to discover illnesses which may have reversible causes, such as collagen vascular disease, temporal arteritis, and other kinds of steroid-responsive illnesses. Dr. Paulson advocates a brain biopsy in cases of undiagnosed causes of dementia with unusual presentations which raise suspicion that a lupuslike illness is present. At this time, however, the brain biopsy is still primarily a research tool.

CHAPTER 14

Parkinson's Disease, Alzheimer's Disease, and Other Brain Degenerative Diseases

SATCHELL PAIGE (who liked to ask, "How old would you be if you didn't know how old you was?"): *Don't look back; something might be gaining on you.*

Parkinson's Disease

James Parkinson (1755–1824) of London was the first to give an accurate description of Parkinson's disease. He was a pupil of John Hunter, the physician who inoculated himself with syphilis and later died from its consequences. (Dr. Parkinson also reported the first case of appendicitis in 1812.)

Parkinson's disease is a common ailment in the United States. There are approximately 50,000 new cases reported each year with an incidence of close to over one million patients who suffer from this illness. It usually begins between ages fifty and sixty-five, and it affects equally both sexes and all races. This is an illness that results from the decreased activity of the neurotransmitter dopamine.

The classic picture of the Parkinson patient is well known; the patient has a fixed stare and a rhythmic tremor of the limbs. The disease may begin with a slight tremor of a finger, one hand, or a leg, and then proceed to a tremor of both hands. The shaking can involve the legs, lips, tongue, and neck muscles. The Parkinson patient has a classic stooped appearance, a masklike face, and a typical shuffling gait, as if the legs were trying to catch up with the forward movement of the body.

Parkinson's disease was well known after the epidemic of encephalitis of 1917 which followed World War I, when millions of patients suffered from Parkinson's disease as a sequel to encephalitis. Today, the cause of Parkinson's disease remains unknown, except for the few remaining patients who are survivors of the viral encephalitis epidemic.

Patients may simultaneously develop Parkinson's disease and Alzheimer's disease. Mental disturbances are frequently found in those with Parkinson's disease, and some of the brain changes found in Alzheimer's disease are also found in Parkinson's illness. Parkinson victims may have mental changes, such as poor judgment, confusion, memory deterioration, depression, listlessness, poor appetite, and inappropriate crying spells. Dementia has been found in 28 to 32 percent of tested Parkinson patients.

Typically, patients with Parkinson's disease receive levodopa to increase the dopamine levels in the brain. In addition, they may receive anticholinergic agents, such as trihexyphenidyl (Artane) and benztropine (Cogentin); however, patients who exhibit dementia in Parkinson's disease have been shown to have a deficiency in their cholinergic system, which is also found in Alzheimer's disease. The use of anticholinergic agents can worsen the symptoms of dementia.

A 73-year-old Phi Beta Kappa graduate of Yale University had typical signs of Parkinson's disease. He presented with a slow gait, shuffling manner, stooped appearance, blank face, and severe tremor. At the time of his evaluation, he had evidence of mental confusion, memory loss, and depression. He had been receiving anticholinergic agents, which are very useful for diminishing tremors, along with levodopa, which will usually help. The anticholinergic agents were discontinued, and it was noted that his confusion and memory loss lessened.

Anticholinergic agents in elderly patients need to be used with caution, since they can be the cause of confusion and hallucinations.

Levodopa does not ameliorate the progressive cognitive deficiencies that occur in Parkinson's illness, although it can cause some improvement. Depression associated with Parkinson's disease can be improved by tricyclic antidepressant medications. Patients who have Parkinson's disease need to be psychologically tested because, if there is mental impairment not obvious to the examiner, anticholinergic treatment should not be initiated, as memory loss will markedly increase.

Alzheimer's Disease

Twenty-five years ago, when I was a medical student, my colleagues and I would play a game of "medical trivial pursuit" in preparation for the final examinations. One of the questions often asked was, "What is Alzheimer's disease?"

This question *never* appeared on any of the final or medical licensure examinations. Most major American textbooks of the time devoted only one page or two to Alzheimer's disease. In the late 1970s, however, it suddenly surfaced like a bolt of lightning and became a new, fashionable blanket diagnosis for any person exhibiting progressive memory loss. Magazine articles, television talk shows, and newspapers began to inundate the public with news of this "newly discovered illness."

In 1970, Drs. B. E. Tomlinson, G. Blessed, and M. Roth wrote an article entitled "Observations on the Brain of Demented Old People," which appeared in the *Journal of Neurological Sciences* and helped to reintroduce Alzheimer's disease to the medical community. (Yet, as recently as 1982, a standard textbook of medicine devoted only one of its two thousand pages to Alzheimer's disease.) The disease was identified as the major cause of brain degeneration only a *very short time ago*.

During my early medical career, I never made the diagnosis of Alzheimer's disease, but, instead, used the phrase "organic brain syndrome" to describe the mental deterioration that occurs in older people. Occasionally, I learned from friends and colleagues of young patients who developed brain degeneration; usually families inflicted with the "big A" kept it hidden in a closet. This illness has, to a surprising extent, remained in the closet, as have epilepsy and syphilis. Even today, in many families, it is simply not discussed.

Dr. Aaron Lerner, a renowned dermatologist and professor of Dermatology at Yale University, told me that his wife was suffering from Alzheimer's disease. His wife, Margaret, a successful physician and a writer of children's books, had to stop working at the age of fifty-five. During 1980 and 1981, three years after her retirement, her husband recorded some of her comments made between the hours of 3 A.M. and 5 A.M., those hours when she was most lucid. He has given me permission to include, verbatim, the following:

I have a neurological problem. Who needs it? No one.

Nobody likes me. I don't like myself either.

I used to be a physician. I used to drive a car. What do I want? I don't want to be here.

I know that I am not functioning as a mother or a spouse. You have to do all the work.

Am I always going to be sick?

I don't sing anymore. I probably won't sing again.

The worst thing is not having anything to do. Nobody wants you. I can't take it.

I am afraid of everything.

I shouldn't be here. I am just waiting to die.

I don't care about anything anymore.

All I do is nothing.

I don't have anything. I used to be a physician.

Look how nice these boys are—and what a terrible mother. How did I get this way?

I don't want to be here for another birthday.

You need a new wife. This one is no good anymore.

All I am is garbage. I belong in the garbage can.

I think that I am getting better and all the time I am getting worse.

The days go so slow for me.

I would rather be dead than what I am doing here because I am not doing anything.

No one knows my name anymore—because I am nothing.

I don't care whether or not I wake up.

I've lost everything—the health service, typing, and writing. I don't have any skills. All I do is eat. I have to go away. I can't read my own writing.

I am no good anymore. All that I do is to tell lies. I want to be cremated and have the ashes taken to Woods Hole.

I've had a good life—a successful marriage—good children—a good career. Now there is nothing for me. I've lived too long.

I used to be something.

It is hard when one becomes obsolete.

I've lost a kingdom.

When can I be dead? Soon I hope.

I wish I were a little girl again.

Dr. Lewis Thomas, the former dean of the Yale School of Medicine and now chancellor at Memorial Sloane-Kettering Center, has described Alzheimer's disease as the "disease of the century": ". . . the worst of all diseases, not just for what it does to the victim, but for its devastating effects on families and friends. It begins with the loss of learned skills, arithmetic and typing, for instance; it progresses inexorably to a total shutting down of the mind. It is, unmercifully, not lethal. Patients go on and on living, essentially brainless but otherwise healthy, into advanced age, unless lucky enough to be saved by pneumonia."

It has been estimated that Alzheimer's disease afflicts approximately 1 million people, or 50 percent of the 2.5 million Americans who suffer from some sort of dementia. I have taken the liberty of writing about Alzheimer's disease as the last chapter in this book to stress the importance of all the other diagnoses which have to be considered first.

Alois Alzheimer, when he first described in 1906 the brain changes in dementia, probably would never have dreamed that today the very mention of his name brings families despair and a sense of total hopelessness. Dr. Alzheimer, at the research institute in Munich, autopsied a 55-year-old woman who had exhibited mental deterioration for three years. Her brain demonstrated certain distinctive features which he recorded, and the medical profession, to honor Dr. Alzheimer, gave the disease his name. It was at this time that Dr. Emil Kraepelin, also in Munich, set out to prove what Hippocrates more than 2000 years ago had clearly stated—that the mind and brain are linked. Kraepelin wanted to establish that brain changes caused mental problems. With the collapse of the Roman empire and the loss of influence of Greco-Roman culture, the heart replaced the brain as the speculated location of the mind—the very reason that words such as "hearty," "heartstrings," "heartache," and "Valentine's Day" became part of our vocabulary.

In the seventeenth century, the philosopher René Descartes once again linked the mind and the brain. The famous anatomist Francis Gall associated the cerebral cortex with the mind; this association differentiates humans from animals, lower animals having a poorly developed cerebral cortex.

About the same time that Dr. Kraepelin was classifying mental illnesses, Sigmund Freud was linking sexual behavior to the subconscious and to the mind and arguing that the conflicts which occur in the subconscious mind resulted in mental illness.

Dr. Alzheimer was a diligent and meticulous scientist who dissected brain tissue, and he believed that senile dementia was a form of atherosclerosis. He stated that the small arteries become thick and narrow, thus causing strokes because the brain is deprived of blood. This idea has remained intact for almost eighty years. The woman he autopsied had been sick for almost five years and had complained of memory loss, confusion, and erratic behavior. By using a variety of silver stains, Alzheimer displayed peculiar-looking structures scattered over the surface of the brain, which he called senile plaques. He observed abnormal fibers which appear as a tangle of filaments scattered throughout the brain, and he concluded that the plaques and tangles were characteristic of an illness that causes dementia. In the following five years, he demonstrated twelve more cases with similar changes—all found in people younger than age sixty-five, ranging in age from thirty-seven to sixty-four. All of these patients described their illness as having started with memory loss and finally ending in confusion, abnormal behavior, and total brain failure. (Years later, it was discovered that neurofibrillary tangles were found in a variety of conditions other than Alzheimer's disease—for example, in punch-drunk boxers, patients suffering from encephalitis, and even some normal elderly people.)

Cases of Alzheimer's disease are becoming increasingly recognized as additional autopsies are performed. It is impossible to firmly diagnose Alzheimer's disease unless the brain is examined under the microscope, and, even then, it is a difficult task.

During a recent clinical pathology conference at a medical school, a case of Alzheimer's disease was presented. It was preceded by a complete history, which was characteristic of Alzheimer's disease. The slices of the brain were then projected to the students, and the pathologist went on to describe the neurofibrillary tangles, the amyloid plaques, the diminution in the number of neurons in the center (the basal nucleus of Meynert), and the characteristic paired helical filaments (PHF). One of the students asked the pathologist if he would have been able to say with certainty that the patient was suffering from Alzheimer's disease if the history were not available. The pathologist stated that he *would* have had difficulty in making an absolute diagnosis.

Atherosclerosis can affect Alzheimer patients, and the two pathological findings can be found together. To make things even more confusing, persons with Down's syndrome, a genetic abnormality involving an extra chromosome, have the characteristic paired helical filaments, or PHF, in their brain if they survive into adulthood and become demented. PHF has also been found in cases of brain injury, such as in Parkinson's disease. In Alzheimer's disease, these changes of PHF and neuron degeneration occur in the hippocampus.

What, then, is the cause of Alzheimer's disease? These senile plaques are found in Down's syndrome, in Parkinson's disease, and in certain illnesses of the brain caused by transmissible viruses, such as kuru and Creutzfeldt-Jakob disease. The viruses which cause illnesses such as kuru are called slow-acting viruses because of their long incubation period prior to the appearance of symptoms and the progressive course that leads to complete brain failure. Dr. D. Carleton Gajdusek, in 1965, produced kuru in chimpanzees by inoculating infected human tissue, which proved that kuru was a virus. He and his colleague Clarence J. Gibbs then started to do brain experiments in patients suffering from dementia at the National Institute of Neurological and Communicable Disorders and Stroke of the National Institute of Health at Bethesda, Maryland. The brain tissue of a female patient who died from dementia was placed into a spider monkey, and twenty-seven months later, the monkey developed signs of a neurological illness which was indistinguishable from kuru and Creutzfeldt-Jakob disease.

Dr. Elias E. Manuelidis, professor of Neuropathology and Neurology at the Yale University School of Medicine, was the first to transmit the Creutzfeldt-Jakob virus to a small laboratory animal such as a guinea pig. At present, he is trying to transmit Alzheimer's disease as well to discover if Alzheimer's disease is caused by a slow-acting virus. If so, we can soon look forward to a vaccination against the illness. There are significant similarities between Creutzfeldt-Jakob disease and Alzheimer's disease; however, patients with the former generally lapse into coma shortly after the onset and die within a year or two, while Alzheimer's patients can live for some time.

Does heredity play a role in senile dementia? There are rare family pedigrees, some going back as far as six generations, in which 50 percent of the children are affected with Alzheimer's disease. This pattern does suggest the presence of a single abnormal gene.

Dr. Leonard Heston, of the University of Minnesota, has implicated familial factors in cases of Alzheimer's disease. If this is a transmissible virus which may take twenty years to incubate, it might explain how a family might transmit it for decades. Alzheimer's disease is more common among relatives of persons with this illness. Considerably more research will have to be done before this is definitely considered a hereditary disease.

I have previously noted that neurons of the brain cells secrete chemicals called neurotransmitters: acetylcholine is an example. The production of acetylcholine requires another chemical—choline acetyltransferase (CAT). CAT can be measured in autopsied brains and is markedly diminished in patients with Alzheimer's disease. The neurons which secrete acetylcholine are those which are predominantly destroyed by this disease. The number of neurons which produce noradrenaline (earlier described) is also reduced. Scientists have discovered that if you block the cholinergic system's production of acetylcholine with anticholinergic drugs such as curare (which the South American Indians use for poison) and belladonna (the nightshade plant which makes the pupils dilate) some degree of amnesia results. When scopolamine, a belladonna derivative, was given to volunteers, memory loss occurred which was similar to the loss found in Alzheimer's disease. Although neurotransmitters are destroyed in Alzheimer's disease, certain chemicals might be used to increase the acetylcholine content of the brain, such as choline and lecithin, as we saw in Chap. 2.

Not only is there destruction of the neurons and the chemicals of the brain in Alzheimer's disease, but there is also a disturbance of the flow of blood. By techniques which employ radioactive-labeled gas, the precise location of blood that is traveling in the brain can be outlined. These studies have demonstrated a decrease in the flow of blood in the brains of persons with senile dementia—the less the flow of blood, the greater the degree of intellectual impairment. At autopsy, the area where the blood flow was decreased was demonstrated to have the worst decay from Alzheimer's disease. Experiments on brains have demonstrated that when normal persons are asked to do even simple calculations, the flow of blood to the brain increases.

The manufacture of acetylcholine can be delayed by inadequate oxygen to the brain. The lack of oxygen to the brain, or hypoxia, which may occur, for example, in carbon monoxide poisoning or smoke inhalation, can cause deficits in short-term memory such as that seen in patients with Alzheimer's disease. The level of acetylcholine in the hippocampus, the memory center, becomes markedly decreased. This, to be sure, is not the entire story of the cause of Alzheimer's disease. Another chemical whose level is reduced in Alzheimer's disease is somatostatin.

Researchers are finding abnormal infectious protein particles in patients with Alzheimer's disease, Creutzfeldt-Jakob disease, and kuru. These plaques, reported by investigators at the University of California in San Francisco, are smaller than viruses and are called prions. When they aggregate, these prions form the amyloid type of plaques seen in Alzheimer's disease.

The chromosomal abnormality in Down's syndrome has been found in Alzheimer's disease and in chronic leukemia. Chromosome abnormalities have been found in families with Alzheimer's disease.

One of my elderly patients developed Alzheimer's disease at the age of sixty, and, during the course of her illness, she was also found to have leukemia when routine examinations were performed. Because her leukemia was mild, it was decided that she was not to be treated, and, for the next five years, her Alzheimer's disease progressed, but the leukemia did not. It is speculated that the viruses or viruslike particles induce the chromosomal changes, then cause chemical chaos in the brain.

Is there an environmental factor that is responsible for Alzheimer's disease? In 1973, Dr. Donald R. Crapper described in an article entitled "Brain Aluminum in Alzheimer's Disease, An Experimental Neurofibrillary Degeneration" in the *American Neurology Association Journal* his finding of increased aluminum content in brains of individuals with senile dementia. Aluminum was injected into the brains of laboratory rats, and a progressive dementia was induced with the corresponding pathological changes of Alzheimer's disease. The animals experienced a loss of memory and learning ability.

Patients who are receiving hemodialysis may become demented from an excessive aluminum accumulation from the dialysis machine. Autopsied patients with Alzheimer's disease have been found to have increased aluminum concentrations. Concentrations of aluminum are particularly high in the hippocampus, where the memory neurons are located. The aluminum concentrates within the nucleus of the neuron.

Although there has been much professional excitement regarding the possible role aluminum may play in causing dementia as it is absorbed from our cooking utensils, there is a lack of evidence to the effect that aluminum is the primary cause of Alzheimer's disease. Other toxic substances, such as cadmium, for example, have been shown to induce dementia as well. Aluminum, which constitutes 8.4 percent of the earth's crust, is present in normal human nutrition, and a person ingests 30 to 50 mg. per day. It is virtually impossible to avoid the ingestion of aluminum.

One of the hallmarks of Alzheimer's disease is the presence of the amyloid plaque and a type of degeneration called granulovacuolar degeneration in the cells of the hippocampus. Aluminum has not been shown experimentally to induce these changes. Attempts to remove aluminum from the body by chelation have done little, if anything, for the treatment of the memory loss of Alzheimer's disease.

Another illness associated with excessive metal accumulation is called Wilson's disease. This is an extraordinarily rare illness which is genetic in origin and which results from excessive copper storage in the brain, liver, and kidney, causing chronic hepatitis. Some of these patients present with behavioral problems and dementia, and the diagnosis is made by finding an elevation of urinary copper and through a liver biopsy which discloses too large a copper deposit. In these cases, treatment with the chemical D-penicillamine effectively removes copper from the body and causes dramatic clinical results.

The Diagnosis of Alzheimer's Disease

The tragedy of the story below is repeated one million times a year for patients suffering from Alzheimer's disease as well as their families.

I met Alex when he was fourteen years old, in Joan of Arc Junior High School in New York City. Both Alex and I were placed in the third grade, in the front row, because we could speak only German and Polish. The year was 1939, and our families had just narrowly escaped from Nazi Germany. "Greenhorns" had no special place in school.

After several months, we had learned a considerable amount of English, and, at the end of one year, we had become fully Americanized. It was apparent that Alex was a brilliant student, and, years later, we both entered City College of New York as premedical students.

He was a tall, handsome young man with dark blazing and brilliant eyes, and he was a great athlete. We both majored in chemistry; with Alex winning numerous honors and medals. He was an extraordinarily popular young man, especially with women— compulsive, gregarious, boisterous, and enormously likeable.

During the summers, to support ourselves, we worked as waiters at a Catskill Mountains resort. Although college had been free, medical school was another matter. He won a medical scholarship, and, for his part-time enjoyment, became a champion bridge player and won many tournaments. He had an adventurous spirit and lots of chutzpah, as seen in the time he managed to become a contestant on a quiz show by posing as an English professor. He won an Edsel automobile which he sold, and he used the money to travel for an entire year. There was almost no limit to his achievements; he learned how to pilot a plane, became an expert skier, was an electronics whiz, and also wrote poetry. During his medical school training, he was simultaneously getting a Ph.D. in chemistry.

He became a pediatric cardiologist. As would be expected, he developed a large lucrative practice and we met approximately once a year at an annual medical meeting. Each year, it seemed that he had become more successful, embarking on yet another challenge, such as deciding to set up a pediatric cardiac institute.

At the age of forty-eight, he was still athletic-looking but his hair had grayed and he had changed. He had decided to give up his practice of fifteen years and he had also divorced his wife. I noticed that his verbal alacrity, good humor, and good conversation were clearly lacking, which I attributed possibly to depression and midlife crisis. This time, at a medical meeting in Miami, I realized that our usual laugh-a-minute get-togethers had vanished forever.

He said that he was depressed and was not feeling quite himself. He did not want to remain in practice. "I want to practice somewhere I am really needed," he said. "Perhaps in Indonesia or Kenya."

During the following years, we conversed by telephone, and, three years later, at the November meeting of the American Heart Association, we met again. I barely recognized him. He was thinner, and he had a very short haircut. His dress, usually informal, now consisted of a white shirt, tie, and dark suit.

That night we met for dinner, and, as usual, the conversation started with some talk about the most interesting papers presented during the day. I knew Alex had always had a great interest in echocardiography (sonar examination of the heart), since we had both started together in that field. We began to discuss a new technique, called doppler echocardiography, and I realized that Alex was having great difficulties in speaking, which I attributed to a little bit too much wine with dinner.

"What do you think of the new technique?" I asked Alex.

He said, "I think it's new and exciting. It is going to be particularly useful," he continued, "in diagnosing a lesion in . . . you know, that . . . ," and he hesitated. He was trying to say "a congenital lesion of the heart, the tetralogy of Fallot."

"You mean, the tetralogy of Fallot."

He said, "That's right! That's the one I'm talking about."

For a pediatric cardiologist not to remember the tetralogy of Fallot is like a stock broker's forgetting the name of IBM! I dared not ask Alex if he was having memory problems because it was apparent that he was having difficulty not only in remembering medical jargon but also with the names of our former professors and people we both knew well.

We were not staying at the same hotel, and, as we left the restaurant, Alex said to me, "You know, I forgot the name of the hotel I'm staying at. Isn't that ridiculous?" He searched in his pocket and fortunately found a "passport key" with the name of the hotel.

We played tennis the following morning but he was unable to remember the score, and he became angry when I told him that the set was over.

"*But* it was just 40-15!"

"That was the last game, Alex."

After the game, we went to have a drink. He usually ordered Campari and soda, but he was now unable to give the waiter his order.

"You know that drink, that red syrup and soda."

"He means Campari," I told the waiter with great sadness in my heart.

Alex looked at me with his intelligent eyes and said, "I see you understand what's happening."

"When did it start?"

He told me that he had begun to notice his memory loss several years earlier with simple things. His wife had to keep reminding him about appointments and help him with names of people they had known. She interpreted his forgetfulness as just being indifferent, being too preoccupied with his practice, and having too many interests.

"Every single day, I forgot where I had placed my keys and my glasses. I began to have trouble in writing a simple check, but I knew that something was dreadfully wrong when I forgot the dosage of digitalis. Can you imagine a physician's forgetting the dosage of digitalis?"

"One morning, I was more tired than usual and lost my way in the hospital. I was heading for the pediatric heart ward, but I forgot how to get there. I must have wandered around for an hour, ending up in the basement, and I finally found an exit. Once outside the building, I located the emergency room and started out again, and this time ended up in the obstetrics department. I left the hospital in panic and barely found my office. The following week, I took a leave of absence from my practice and pretended having an intestinal ailment. I became more anxious and paranoid and began to distrust my wife. I confused telephone numbers of friends, and the worst thing is that I lost interest in the things that I love—the art collections, the crystal, opera, music, and tennis. I know that I dare not try to fly my plane again."

"Then the horror story really started. Have you ever been a patient?" he asked me. "Have you? Let me tell you. Then you start learning about what doctoring is. The waiting, the testing, the sometimes cold, unsympathetic colleagues, the brusque nurses—and everyone always seems to be too busy. But the most humiliating experience was the psychological testing."

"It was conducted in a small quiet soundproof room, and the examiner kept saying, 'I want you to be as relaxed as possible.' I was being tested as if I were a child. 'What does the proverb "tempest in the teapot" mean?' Here I was, once with an IQ of 180, and I couldn't answer the simplest of questions. The examiner blindfolded me and asked me to identify objects by touch. I couldn't. This particular examiner was so obsequious that I could have vomited. I wanted to scream and run out of the room, but I knew that I had to finish it. 'You're doing just fine, Doctor. Do you want to take a little break?' And then the diagnosis: 'We think, after presenting your case to various physicians, that you are suffering from early Alzheimer's disease. Not to worry. It's not a firm diagnosis.' "

"Can you imagine being told that you have early Alzheimer's disease? A sledgehammer smashing my head would have been less painful. As a doctor I should have been able to handle that diagnosis. I couldn't! I would have committed suicide if I had had the courage. In fact, I began to think of devious ways of doing it that would leave no trace. I could swallow something and leave no trace, or just get into my car, have a few drinks, and crash into a wall."

"So, you're not practicing anymore?" I asked him.

"No, I gave it up."

"What are you doing?"

"What does a person with no brains do? If I lost both arms, both legs, and my eyes, I couldn't be more helpless."

I lost track of Alex for several more years when I received a phone call from his former wife, Amy. She stated that they were together again, but that Alex was now completely confined at home and that they had moved back to New York City.

They were living in a small apartment off Riverside Drive, in the same neighborhood where his family had lived when they had first come to the United States. He was sitting at the table; he seemed just as tall and as thin, and his eyes were remarkably intelligent-looking. A pipe lay next to him; he had been cleaning it for hours.

"Look who's here, Alex. It's your old friend."

He looked up, gave me a smile, and said, "How are you?"

"I'm fine. Do you know who I am?"

"Sure I know who you are. Whatcha doing?"

"Same thing as always."

It was the heart of summer, and I asked him, "Have you been playing tennis?"

"Haven't much of a chance."

"I'll play with you."

He didn't answer.

"How is your crystal collection?"

"As always."

"And the boys?"

"Ask them."

His wife left the room and he asked after her. "Where is Amy?"

"She went to the kitchen."

He continued to clean his pipe, never looking up.

"Where is Amy? Did she go out?"

"No, Alex. Amy is in the kitchen, cooking dinner for us."

And so the conversation continued for the next hour. Each minute he asked where Amy was. Often, he got up from his chair, opened the door, and looked for her. If I hadn't stopped him, he would have walked right out of the house, looking for Amy. It was amazing to me that his wife managed to go on. When our eyes met, I could see the helpless despair the poor woman had to bear.

We sat down to eat, and it became apparent that Alex was not able to use a knife or fork. It was the most pathetic sight I have ever seen. This once brilliant scholar used the fork as a knife and the knife as a fork. Finally frustrated, he dropped both and picked up the small pieces of meat with his hands, eating like an animal. He did not know the name of the food that he was eating, even though it was his very favorite dish, goulash.

"Are you enjoying what you're eating, Alex?" I asked him.

"It's my favorite one. Can't beat it."

"Why don't you use your fork?"

"Too much trouble." Alex was still trying to cover up.

It was evident that Alex had become demented. He did not know who I was, the time of the day, the season, or what he was eating. The only person he seemed able to recognize was his wife.

Amy tried to keep Alex at home as long as she could. He finally was hospitalized because of a respiratory infection and he died of pneumonia. I still miss him.

The following seven stages are adopted from the scale measuring Alzheimer's disease that was developed by Drs. Barry Reisberg, Steven H. Ferris, Mony J. de Leon, and Thomas Crook and described in the 1982 *American Journal of Psychiatry:*

Stage 1: A state of clinical normality.

Stage 2: The forgetfulness stage. Forgetting the names of ones formerly known well is not evidence of memory deficit in a clinical interview and is not a serious handicap in the ability to be employed. There may or may not be an awareness in the patient of what is happening. This phase, which is so common in many people over the age of forty-five, is not always synonymous with the beginning of Alzheimer's disease. Even the mini-memory test at this stage, if it shows a minor deficit, does not always indicate the beginning of brain degeneration.

Stage 3: A mild cognitive decline or early confusional state. This is the stage in which persons will demonstrate decreased ability to remember a name after being introduced to a new person. Things of value may be misplaced or lost and concentration may decline. A person may become lost when traveling to an unfamiliar location. If there is testing at this time, there may be evidence of memory deficiency. Denial symptoms are common during this stage, as well as mild to moderate anxieties. Alzheimer's disease cannot be definitively diagnosed at this stage, especially in someone who is age sixty or older.

Stage 4: Increased cognitive decline. During an interview, abnormalities will definitely be found—for example, inability to continue serial subtractions, inability to travel, inability to handle finances, and markedly decreased knowledge of current and recent events. At this point, there is no disorientation about where one is. Familiar faces and friends are recognized. The ability to travel to known places remains. However, complex tasks which once were performed easily cannot be done at all. There is a denial of the symptoms being present. Mistakes are made on at least three or more items on the type of mental test I have included in the text in Chap. 6.

Stage 5: Moderately severe decline with early dementia, early dementia being defined as the inability to survive without some assistance. The patient now cannot recall his or her address or telephone number, the names of some members of the family, or the name of the high school or college from which he or she graduated. There may be some confusion as to the time of day, week, and season, and the person will find it difficult to count backwards. Major facts are still retained, and the patient will know the name of his or her spouse and children. The patient still has the ability to attend to personal needs, such as going to the bathroom. The patient, however, may have difficulty choosing the proper clothes to wear. Shoes, for example, may be put on the wrong way.

Stage 6: Severe cognitive decline. Now the name of the spouse may be forgotten. There will be complete unawareness of recent events and experiences and there may be only a sketchy knowledge of the past. There is some knowledge of the surroundings, the year, and the seasons. Assistance is now needed for daily activity. The person may become incontinent or require travel assistance. Night and day become confused. The patient does remember his or her own name. There may be delusional behavior; for example, the person may complain that the spouse is really someone else. The patient may talk to people who are not there, even to the reflection in the mirror. Simple cleaning activities may be continued, as was the case with Alex who continued cleaning his pipe night and day, *although* he never smoked it. Sometimes, violent behavior, anxiety symptoms, and agitation may occur and there is the inability to carry on a train of thought.

Stage 7: Very severe cognitive decline, late dementia. There may be a total loss of speech abilities (only grunting remains); incontinence of urine; complete assistance required in feeding; loss of basic skills; and inability to walk. The brain is now totally separated from the body: the patient has become unicellular, like a one-cell organism. At this stage, the patient may continue to survive for a long period, finally succumbing from either respiratory arrest or a superimposed illness.

Any one of the stages may continue on for years, especially stages 3 through 6. The hardship on the family is inconceivable unless one is personally struck by this calamity. Not for one second can the victim be left alone. He or she may wander off, become hopelessly lost, and possibly die of exposure. Or patients may seriously injure themselves at home. There is total loss of recognition of potential dangers, such as fire, hot stoves, or poisons.

The normal length of time in each stage before progression to the next occurs is not known. One may remain in stage 3 for decades, with only moderate cognitive decline, and then suddenly deteriorate to later stages. It is difficult to know when a person passes from one stage to the next. It is imperative during stages 3 and 4 that the patient be thoroughly investigated to determine if there is a cause for mild forgetfulness. (This book has been devoted to describing reversible causes at all stages described.)

After talking to many patients through the years, I have come to the conclusion that stages 2 and 3 are extraordinarily common in people who are over the age of fifty. My own father lived to the age of eighty and complained continuously to me about how forgetful he had been since he was sixty, but he never declined further. Many younger people also have the symptoms that I have described in stages 2 and 3, which can be attributed to many causes, including alcohol, depression, medications, and plain inattentiveness. Unfortunately, we do not have any blood tests, skin tests, or even x-rays that can make the firm diagnosis of Alzheimer's disease. There are some indications that the white blood cells and the chromosome patterns may be abnormal, but these indications cannot be used at the present time as a screening device.

X-ray examinations of the brain are not very helpful. The CT scan very frequently shows some minor brain atrophy in normal aging persons which is not diagnostic of Alzheimer's disease. Perhaps, in the future, we will be able to do histological examinations of the brain tissue while the person is in the early stages of the illness and make neurochemical determinations of the cholinergic system by taking tissue samples from the hippocampus and the temporal lobe, where the illness is predominantly present.

The electroencephalogram has consistently shown diffuse slowing of the brain-wave test in Alzheimer's disease patients. This finding remains to be proven and is still controversial.

Cerebral blood flow can be measured in Alzheimer's disease and is consistently found to be reduced; however, this flow is also reduced as a result of many other diseases which cause mental impairment.

The positron emission tomography (PET) test may become extraordinarily useful in differentiating Alzheimer's disease from other dementia illnesses, based on the pattern of the regions of the brain that are most impaired. The PET test can show changes in the metabolism of glucose in the brain. In the PET test, a subject is given a radioactive form of glucose, and the PET machine picks up the activity of the isotope in the brain. It has been shown that in Alzheimer's disease there is a reduced cerebral metabolism, but similar changes have also been found in multi-infarction dementia. For the present, the test is limited to research centers such as the one at the UCLA School of Medicine but can assist us in learning more about the pathophysiology of Alzheimer's disease.

Of all the techniques so far described, nuclear magnetic resonance (NMR) imaging will probably be the most significant diagnostic tool for differentiating Alzheimer's disease from multi-infarction dementia. The technique of NMR does not use x-rays, but, rather, a series of magnets which cause the movement of protons by magnetic force, thus creating an image. NMR will routinely be used in the very near future by physicians for diagnosing not only Alzheimer's disease and multi-infarction dementia but also strokes and tumors. NMR can analyze the water-fat ratio in specific areas of the brain in order to spot degeneration. Brain atrophy is described by the Scot Dr. John O. Besson as similar in appearance to "white fjords" around the margins of the brain. According to Dr. Besson an accurate differentiation between Alzheimer's disease and multi-infarction dementia can be made by the water-fat content ratio.

Other Brain Degenerative Diseases

Pick's Disease

Pick's disease is a rare degenerative disease of the brain which is, in the beginning, often indistinguishable from Alzheimer's disease. Both diseases cause severe brain impairment. Pick's disease, however, tends to present with a change in personality and social behavior. Loss of social inhibition followed by lewd, totally inappropriate, and perverse acts cause the person, on occasion, to be arrested for his or her actions. The cognitive functions during the early stages are preserved, as are memory and language. Patients with Pick's disease do not use substitutions for words, calling a "knife" a "horse" and so forth, as is the case in Alzheimer's disease. There is not in Pick's disease the same marked disruption of language, although the patient with Pick's disease will have scant speech. Pick's disease patients develop a ravenous appetite as their illness progresses. The age of onset in Pick's disease is generally in the middle fifties. The life expectancy is usually not beyond seven years after the diagnosis. Some 20 percent of patients will live longer than ten years.

Huntington's Chorea

There are many other rare degenerative diseases which will not be mentioned, but something should be written about Huntington's chorea, which presents with marked mental deterioration and bizarre movements, or chorea. As in Pick's disease, there is a change in emotional and social behavior. Patients with Huntington's disease are moody, quick-tempered, and aggressive, and sometimes become physically abusive. The intelligence quotient tends to remain normal longer than in the other illnesses. Eventually, severe mental deterioration develops. Chorea movements—Sydenham's chorea—are uncoordinated movements with muscle weakness, clumsiness of limbs, and an abnormal gait. A patient sometimes has the appearance of being suspended by strings, like a puppet. These involuntary movements also consist of tics and spasms of the neck, grimacing, and difficulty in speech, chewing, and swallowing.

Violence can occur, even as it can in Alzheimer's disease, as the temporal lobes of the brain are destroyed by the neurofibrillary tangles and necrotic plaques; fits occur because the temporal portion of the brain is part of the limbic system which deals with emotions.

Unproven Methods of Treatment of "Senility," or Alzheimer's Disease and Aging

The Nobel Prize winner, Alie Metchnikoff, a Russian biologist who won the prize in 1908 for the discovery of phagocytosis (the destruction of bacteria by white blood cells), entertained the theory that the accumulation of toxins was responsible for the degeneration of cells. He, therefore, advocated yogurt as a solution for warding off the process of aging, since the bacteria found in yogurt produces lactic acids and the aged people of the Caucasus mountains in the Soviet Union consume a great deal of yogurt and allegedly often live to the age of 130. The numerous different types of treatments and suggestions which have been used throughout the centuries to ward off the aging process could fill another entire book.

It is not always easy to separate worthwhile experimentation from quackery, especially when the stakes are so high and when relatively little has been clearly substantiated.

The neurologist Dr. Charles Brown-Sequard believed that "the weakness of old men was partly due to diminution of the function of their sexual glands." He attributed physical and mental decline to decreased sexual abilities. In 1889, he smashed the testicles of a young dog, passed it through filter paper, and "injected the liquid into his own leg." The powerful placebo response made him feel stronger and physically improved.

Other scientists have tried similar experiments. Recently, Dr. Paul Niehans, who retired in Vevey, Switzerland, organized a European health clinic, La Prairie. He allegedly rejuvenated people based on his theory of cellular therapy. This theory holds that if an organ malfunctions, the extract of an organ derived from a normal healthy animal should be injected. The injection must be done within seconds after the new organ is found. Famous patients who used his injections include Bernard Baruch, Gloria Swanson, Somerset Maugham, and Konrad Adenauer. Pope Pius XII was also one of his patients in 1954. Niehans saw the pope when he was apparently quite ill, and through his treatment, Niehans allegedly cured him. Physicians to this day have not been able to ascertain why the pope did recover. The cure consisted of three days of total rest and one month of abstinence from alcohol, tobacco, and strenuous exercise. No one has yet been able to prove this cellular therapy invalid—it has simply not been evaluated by physicians.

Another physician who is currently involved in treating brain degeneration to offset the aging process is the Romanian Dr. Anna Aslan. She has established a renowned rejuvenation center, the Bucharest Institute of Geriatrics, where she uses a chemical known as procaine with a buffering agent. The procaine, buffering agent, plus novocain (a local anesthetic), is now called Gerovital-H3. It has been claimed that Gerovital-H3 can turn white hair dark again and restore memory. Famous patients include Charles de Gaulle, Ho Chi Minh, Marlene Dietrich, John F. Kennedy, and Nikita Krushchev. It has been discovered that Gerovital-H3 does inhibit the formation of MAO (monoamine-oxidase), which increases in older people. Depression and memory loss are associated with high MAO levels. Physicians prescribe MAO inhibitors for the treatment of depression.

The theory of aging is linked to what scientists call cross-linkages. The cross-linkages are a means of collagen buildup and reduction of the elasticity of tissue which is necessary for organ function.

Older people have an abundance of "free radicals" (nonionic compounds whose central element is linked to an abnormal number of atoms) which are generated by ultraviolet lights and the breakdown of body chemicals. Free radicals are molecules that link up to other molecules causing cross-linkage, making the connective tissue more rigid, less flexible, and less elastic. They interfere with molecular work. Twenty-five percent of all body tissue has collagen tissue. Increased rigidity of tissue retards passage of nutrients and hormones, and it reduces the elimination of waste products which can lead to hypertension, reduced kidney function, and hardening of the arteries. Cross-linkage is very likely the cause of aging. Cross-linkage has been associated with slowing down the elimination of lipofuscins. Vitamin E may prolong the life of cultured cells but has not been shown to be of any benefit in brain degeneration.

Chelation therapy (EDTA) is at present being used for the treatment of coronary artery disease, but there is no scientific evidence that it is effective. In the same way, it is being used for Alzheimer's disease on the presumption that it binds with the excessive aluminum which is found in the brains of patients with Alzheimer's disease and removes it.

The glutamic acid L-glutamine serves an important function in brain metabolism. Unfortunately, reports that L-glutamine has improved the IQs of mentally deficient children have been unsubstantiated. It *has* been recommended to fight fatigue, depression, impotence, and memory loss.

Acceptable Management of Alzheimer's Disease

The hopelessness of Alzheimer's disease is shared by the medical profession and the public. Once the patient has reached stages 6 and 7, or advanced dementia, there is little left to do but provide minute-to-minute custodial care. This will surely change in the near future. For the present, the goal of treatment of this perfidious illness is to attempt to arrest its progress in the early stages and alleviate the symptoms of dementia in the later stages. I cannot discuss means of prevention because we do not know the cause. The basic chemical catalyst appears to be a deficit in the acetylcholine-synthesizing enzyme, choline-acetyltransferase (CAT), in the cerebral cortex and hippocampus. The strategy, at the present time, is to use substances that will increase the CAT activity in the brain to enhance learning and memory, and to carefully manage the associated depression, agitation, and sleeplessness. To this end, an expert psychiatrist should be consulted.

Choline

Choline, found in many foods such as eggs and liver and a component of lecithin, has been tested in a series of studies. Choline is necessary for the synthesis of CAT, and, since CAT is reduced to 70 percent in patients with Alzheimer's disease, it was concluded that administration of choline, in the form of lecithin, would raise the CAT level and diminish memory loss. Repeated studies showed conflicting evidence. The majority, however, disclosed that lecithin was not helpful. Some studies have revealed that lecithin might slow the mental deterioration, and it is possible that lecithin may be more useful in the beginning stages of the illness. Scientists such as Dr. Richard Wurtman are trying to discover if the ingestion of foods which contain lecithin will improve memory. The use of natural dietary substances to treat Alzheimer's disease may play an important role in curing the early stages of the illness.

At the Yale–New Haven Medical Center, Dr. David Samuel, of the Center of Neurosciences and Behavior Research at the Weitzman Institute of Science in Israel, found that egg yolk may be useful to patients suffering from memory deficits. Egg-yolk extract seems to improve impaired memories in alcoholics and drug addicts. At present, I would not advocate the use of egg yolk to improve memory. Egg yolk is harmful since it is one of the richest sources of cholesterol; we should await further studies before this is considered an effective form of treatment.

Piracetam

Piracetam is a relatively new drug which has improved the learning ability of animal subjects and protected them from memory loss when they were deprived of oxygen. This medication increases the firing rate of transmission between neurons. (Not only is it desirable to increase acetylcholine synthesis in early stages of dementia, but it is also desirable to increase transmission.) In a study cited in *Aging* in 1982, a group of students who were given Piracetam performed better on writing examinations than did those who received a placebo. It is clearly not of any benefit in the later stages 6 and 7 of dementia. Piracetam belongs to a group of drugs called nootropics. It is still under investigation in the United States and has not been approved for general use. Nootropics are a group of medications discovered by the Belgian pharmacologist C. Giurgea in 1972. They are widely used in Europe and have no sedative or tranquilizing effects.

Hydergine

The most effective medication available today is called Hydergine. It has been approved by the U.S. Food and Drug Administration for the treatment of Alzheimer's disease and is used in most institutions. This drug is called a vasodilator because it belongs to a group of drugs which increase the flow of blood through the brain. It is derived from the fungus grown on rye bread and other cereal grains. There have been approximately sixty clinical trials which have demonstrated that the use of Hydergine results in some improvement of memory loss, decreased confusion, and increased alertness 80 percent of the time. The medication works by increasing the metabolism of glucose and cerebral oxygen, which is diminished in Alzheimer's disease. This medication has few or hardly any side effects and can be given either by mouth as a pill or sublingually, under the tongue (the latter method is not as effective). The medication is available in one-half- and one-mg. tablets, and the total dosage which has been used in various studies in early stages of the disease has been approximately 4.5 mg. Hydergine combined with lecithin may possibly be useful in stages 3 to 5 of Alzheimer's disease. Families who are involved with patients taking this medication report more moments of lucidity than without the medication.

Hydergine should not be used in patients with documented multi-infarction dementia since it may worsen their symptoms. Since it causes the blood flow of the brain to decrease, most researchers have found that it can make atherosclerosis dementia worse because it may divert blood from areas of the brain which most need it. In patients who have a combination of multi-infarction dementia and Alzheimer's disease, it is worth a trial. Hydergine should be given for at least six months or longer before it is considered ineffective.

Physostigmine

If scopolamine is given to normal subjects, there is a severe memory loss which is reversed by the administration of a medication called physostigmine. Physostigmine increases the levels of acetylcholine by inhibiting the CAT enzyme. Dr. Kenneth L. Davis, professor of Psychiatry and Pharmacology at Mt. Sinai School of Medicine, has demonstrated that there may be a mild improvement in memory loss secondary from Alzheimer's disease. In one of his studies, 20 percent of patients showed improvement on their test scores. Clinical trials of physostigmine are in progress.

Synaptic Medications

This form of treatment is still at the research level. It consists of medications which increase the available acetylcholine by slowing its breakdown, providing the nerve cells are intact. One of these medications is at present being evaluated.

Postsynaptic Medications

These are a group of medications that work directly on the receptor sites. One, called arecoline, is being tested at present and is available only in the intravenous form.

Neuropeptides

These are substances made of amino acids which are the building blocks of proteins. Normally, neuropeptides are produced by the pituitary gland and function as neurotransmitters. Hormones produced by the pituitary are, for example, adrenocorticotrophic hormone (ACTH), melanocyte-stimulating hormone (MSH), and vasopressin. One study by Dr. Ferris, cited in 1980 in the American Psychology Association report, has found that a single dose of ACTH seems to improve sustained attention and diminish depression in demented persons. Neuropeptides are still under experimentation. Vasopressin is another neuropeptide that improves memory and is under study. Vasopressin nasal spray was given to people with memory disturbances; there seemed to be some improvement in attention, recall, and concentration. These findings were described in 1978 by Dr. J. Legros and his research colleagues in the medical journal *Lancet*.

A recently discovered neuropeptide, called enkephalins, a natural substance found in the brain, may someday be used to improve thinking and memory.

Naloxone

The brain has natural morphine compounds, called opiates, which play a role in memory storage. When the opiate naloxone was given intravenously, the memory of patients suffering from Alzheimer's disease improved. In the March 24, 1983 issue of the *New England Journal of Medicine*, a study described how naloxone indirectly helps to make acetylcholine available.

In conclusion, at the present time, the medications available on a routine clinical basis for the possible amelioration of the symptoms of Alzheimer's disease are (1) natural food nutrients which contain lecithin and choline and (2) Hydergine which may be especially effective in the early stages of Alzheimer's disease.

Unfortunately, there is not yet available a proven and effective treatment for Alzheimer's disease, but this is surely no reason to despair. Different avenues are being approached with great skill and determination. Research and experimentation efforts continue to accelerate. For those only too personally familiar with this horror, it may be both unkind and unrealistic to advise patience, but time is precisely what is needed. Although we still know far too little about this disease, we should yet be aware that we know much more about it now than we did only a few years ago. Almost helpless to treat the sufferers, we yet offer hope that the near future will finally spell the end of Alzheimer's disease.

EPILOGUE:

Prolonging Middle Age to Old Age

The creed of the street is, old age is not disgraceful, but immensely disadvantageous.

RALPH WALDO EMERSON

Life in the United States has never been better than it is today in spite of the views of the skeptics. Never before have men and women been as preoccupied with living as long as possible, providing their bodies are healthy and their brains remain intact.

Everyone laments the cost of medical care, yet we are usually the cause of our own illnesses and the culprits who shorten our own lives. At least half of our hospital population have been hospitalized due to automobile accidents or other traumas, drugs, hypertension, smoking, obesity, diabetes, and improper dieting. We could cut our medical expenditures in half if we follow some of the simple rules that I have outlined. We cannot hope to live as long as either the mythical biblical Methuselah, who allegedly died at the age of 969, or Lark, the god-king, who lived to the age of 28,000. We *can* look forward to living well into our nineties and certainly even to 100 years, provided we do not accelerate the aging process with illnesses which we can prevent. Unfortunately, there are some that we cannot prevent as yet, such as cancer of the breast and Alzheimer's disease.

Strokes in this country have been decreased by 40 percent in the past ten years because of improved control of hypertension, a low-salt diet, and perhaps less fat. Cardiovascular deaths have decreased by 25 to 30 percent for the reasons cited, yet, cancer of the lung is increasing in women because of cigarette smoking. The epidemic of Alzheimer's disease, which is killing 100,000 people per year, is going to be stopped.

In 1974, the U.S. Congress established the National Institute of Aging as part of the National Institute of Health "to conduct and support biochemical, social, and behavioral research and training related to the aging process, and to disease and other special problems in the needs of the aged."

Today, we can look forward to a brilliant future, with the best years of our lives still ahead. The "fountain of youth" lies within ourselves as long as we can keep our juices flowing. We can take hope from Dr. Linus Pauling, twice winner of the Nobel Prize, who claims that the proper intake of vitamins and nutrients, the elimination of tobacco, and the decrease of sugar in the diet can lengthen the average life span by 16 to 24 years.

A myriad of scientifically unproven but popular rejuvenants have been used throughout history to avert or slow the aging process, including the jelly of bees, hyperbaric oxygen, and injection of dogs' testicular tissue. At present, thousands of people have taken injections of procaine at the Bucharest Institute of Geriatrics to improve memory, muscle strength, and skin texture, and darken their gray hair. None of the gimmicks have been proven to be of any worth in prolonging life or preventing memory loss.

Citizens of those regions of the world which have been linked with longevity, such as the small kingdom of Hunza in northwestern Kashmir, the Andes region of Ecuador, and the Abkhazia republic of the Soviet Union, lying between the Black Sea and the Caucasus, adhere to daily diets of approximately 1500 calories, compared to the average 3500 calories of the American. Intake of animal fats and proteins is low in these communities, and vegetables, rough grains, and fruit are the staples.

Normal aging can occur gracefully, provided we are not beseiged with the condition of poverty or an illness that accelerates the aging process. There is no denying that overweight persons age faster, as well as those people who smoke and drink in excess.

There are certain rules that we should all begin and follow in early age because so many illnesses can be prevented. The habits of smoking cigarettes, cigars, and pipes have to be eliminated, as these are injurious to lungs and accelerate arteriosclerosis. Our diets should be high in fiber and fresh vegetables but low in fats, cholesterol, and sweets. Alcohol should be taken moderately. Salty foods are to be avoided, and calcium intake should be kept adequate with foods such as yogurt, cottage cheese, and macaroni.

The control of hypertension is essential for the prevention of heart attacks, strokes, and the acceleration of the aging process. Strict weight reduction, a low-salt diet, and moderate exercise can help to control blood pressure.

Medications not prescribed by a physician should be avoided. On the other hand, medications prescribed by the physician should be scrupulously taken as prescribed and not skipped, or, for that matter, taken excessively.

Periodic examinations by a physician are important, including blood pressure examination and blood tests.

Beware of automobile accidents (drive intelligently!) and avoid careless accidents at home, such as falling off a stool or ladder, or otherwise bumping a head.

Undue physical exertion should be avoided, such as shoveling snow in the winter when you are not accustomed to that type of physical activity. Walking is an excellent form of exercise and should be practiced regularly.

Avoid sleeping pills if possible and consult with your family physician if you must regulate your sleep.

Adequate fluids need to be taken daily to keep the urine flowing, and the bowels should be kept as regular as possible with ample bran and, if necessary, the addition of bulk in the form of Metamucil.

The addition of supplementary vitamins is recommended, but *not* megavitamins. One therapeutic vitamin pill that contains the recommended daily allowance of vitamins A, C, and B_6, thiamin, riboflavin, niacin, calcium, iron, phosphorus, magnesium, zinc, and copper is useful.

A much neglected everyday addition to prolonging middle age and avoiding early brain failure is the retaining of a sense of beauty, enjoying every bit of your surroundings, and making note of all that occurs in the 24-hour day. An interested, curious person will remain alert much longer than one who is glued to a television set.

Laughter is excellent therapy, as the noted writer Norman Cousins has shown us so beautifully. Sexual activity should be extended as long as possible and should not be set aside because "I'm too old to think of those things."

These simple rules I have given can probably prevent many of the problems for which the majority of patients are hospitalized. Certainly, more than 50 percent of patients are hospitalized as a result of something that they did to themselves—too much alcohol, smoking, drugs, or food.

It is true, for the present time, that Alzheimer's disease and Pick's disease cannot be prevented, but this will surely change in the future.

Much memory loss may have a reversible cause, as I have tried to point out through this entire book. Any person, either yourself or someone you know, who is beginning to show signs of losing his or her memory should *not* accept the diagnosis of senility as the result of aging because that it is a myth. Today, in 1985 in the United States, we have the greatest medical advances and techniques in the world. Researchers are working at a furious pace to discover the cause of brain diseases. An entire new field of neurochemistry is emerging, mobilizing biochemists, engineers, geneticists, infectious disease experts, and a new breed of doctors called gerontologists, who specialize in the problems of the aging. Never has such a national effort been launched since the campaign to wipe out polio, smallpox, and tuberculosis. The physicians and scientists are as much concerned about this problem as the lay person, for they, too, are not immune to the ugly affliction of brain loss. Scientists realize that we are in the midst of an epidemic which will worsen since the population is living longer. Some call it a "silent epidemic" because in many families the affliction has not come out of the closet. As I am writing this text, a medication called clonidine is being tested for patients who have memory loss.

The following are some suggestions for family members on what should be done when a member is suffering memory loss:

1. A thorough examination of the person has to be performed preferably in consultation with a neurologist.
2. A battery of blood tests needs to be done to detect the presence of diabetes, thyroid illness, and the metabolic and

endocrine abnormalities which I have discussed throughout the book.

3. A cardiovascular examination should be performed, and should include blood pressure readings, examination of the arteries to the head with new diagnostic tests, electrocardiograms, echocardiograms, and chest x-rays.

4. A thorough neurological examination which should include a CT scan of the brain and an electroencephalogram.

5. A thorough review of the patient's alcohol intake, nutritional status, and the medications being taken.

These are just a minimal number of basic tests which every patient who is beginning to show chronic memory loss deserves.

Robert Browning quoted these famous words of Rabbi Ben Ezra: "Grow old along with me, the best is yet to be. The last of life for which the first was made."

Appendix

Organizations for the Elderly

American Aging Association
University of Nebraska Medical Center
Omaha, Nebraska 68105

American Association for Geriatric Psychiatry
230 N. Michigan Avenue, Suite 2400
Chicago, Illinois 60601

American Association of Homes for the Aging
1050 17th Street, N.W., Suite 770
Washington, D.C. 20036

The American Geriatrics Society
10 Columbus Circle
New York, New York 10019

American Psychological Association
1200 17th Street, N.W.
Washington, D.C. 20036

Association for Gerontology in Higher Education
600 Maryland Avenue, S.W.
Washington, D.C. 20024

Commission on Legal Problems of the Elderly
American Bar Association
1800 M Street, N.W.
Washington, D.C. 20036

The Gerontological Society of America
1835 K Street, N.W., Suite 305
Washington, D.C. 20006

The Institute of Retired Professionals
The New School of Social Research
60 W. 12th Street
New York, NY 10011

National Association of State Units on Aging
600 Maryland Avenue, S.W.
Washington, D.C. 20024

National Council of Senior Citizens
925 15th Street, N.W.
Washington, D.C. 20005

Chapters of the Alzheimer's Disease and Related Disorders Associations

National headquarters
360 North Michigan Avenue
Suite 601
Chicago, Illinois 60601
(312) 853-3060

Arizona
5821 East Bloomfield Road
Scottsdale 85254
(602) 948-6418

2751 South Sarnoff Drive
Tucson 85730
(602) 885-2766

California
11321 Iowa Avenue
Suite 9
Los Angeles 90025
(213) 473-1442

210 Via Cordova
Newport Beach 92663
(714) 675-0257

6009 Beech Avenue
Orangevale 95662
(916) 988-9319

1305 Diamond Street
San Diego 92109
(714) 272-6030

918 Isleta Avenue
Santa Barbara 93109
(805) 965-6944

Colorado
1330 Knox Drive
Boulder 80303
(303) 494-2398

4545 East 9th Avenue
Suite 020
Denver 80220
(303) 393-7675

Connecticut
95 Anita Street
New Haven 06511
(203) 865-4779

Florida
6303 Sun Eagle Lane
Brandenton 33507
(813) 755-4331

1028 72nd Street, N.W.
Brandenton 33529
(813) 792-4226

9301 Sunrise Lake Boulevard
Suite 109
Sunrise Lake 33322
(305) 741-3984

Georgia
Wesley Woods Campus
1817 Clifton Road, N.E.
Atlanta 30029
(404) 955-5268

Hawaii
3627 Kilauea Avenue
Suite 411
Honolulu 96816
(808) 531-0441

Illinois
1603 Orrington Avenue
Suite 1200
Evanston 60201
(312) 864-0045

Iowa
Iowa Methodist Medical
   Center
1200 Pleasant Street
Des Moines 50308
(515) 283-6212

Kansas
4550 West 90th Terrace
Shawnee Mission 66202
(913) 262-4191

Maryland
P.O. Box 9751
Baltimore 21204
(301) 792-7800, ext. 7224

819 Aster Boulevard
Rockville 20850
(301) 424-9420

Massachusetts
Edith N. Rogers Memorial
   VA Medical Center
GRECC
200 Springs Road
Bedford 01730
(617) 275-7500, ext. 642

Boston University
School of Medicine
80 East Concord Street
Boston, 02118
(617) 247-6087

Michigan
1225 Astor Drive, Suite 222
Ann Arbor 48104
(313) 662-6638

P.O. Box 643
Bloomfield Hills 48013
(313) 540-2373 (Lombardo)
       332-4110 (Glover)

816 Northwood, NE
Grand Rapids 49505
(616) 243-0231 (Hale)
       456-5664 (Lenihan)

9370 Rosebush Road
Mt. Pleasant 48858
(517) 465-6602

Minnesota
2501 West 84th Street
Bloomington 55431
(612) 888-7653

Missouri
Washington University
Department of Neurology
660 South Euclid Avenue
St. Louis 63110
(314) 454-2384

Nebraska
Education Therapy Clinic
3925 Dewey Avenue
Omaha 68105
(402) 559-5137
       559-5106

New Jersey
1435 Tenth Street
Fort Lee 07024
(201) 224-0388
(212) 736-3670

New Mexico

8303 Indian School Road, NE
Albuquerque 87110
(505) 299-8223

New York

87 Brookline Avenue
Albany 12203
(518) 438-4929

Dent Neurological Institute
Millard Fillmore Hospital
3 Gate Circle
Buffalo 14209
(716) 875-2977

125 West 76th Street
New York 10023
(212) 873-0216

103 Round Creek Drive
Rochester 14626
(716) 225-0271

785 Mamaroneck Avenue
White Plains 10605
(914) 428-1919 (Pollack)
664-1587 (Perry)

North Carolina

Duke University
    Medical Center
Civitan Building, Room 153
Durham 27710
(919) 684-2328

Ohio

1104 Portage Lakes Drive
Akron 44319
(216) 644-1229

Cline Building, Suite 11
15 South Court Street
Athens 45701
(614) 592-1913

1801 Chestnut Drive
Cleveland 44106
(216) 721-8457

Martin Janis Senior Center
600 East 11th Avenue
Columbus 43211
(614) 422-9414

9830 West Road
Harrison 45030
(513) 367-4831

Oregon

252 NE 61st Street
Portland 97213
(503) 232-0306

Pennsylvania

57 Indian Park Turnpike
Levittown 19057
(215) 945-0993 (Shapiro)
    485-4528 (Bates)

1501 Arrott Building
401 Wood Street
Pittsburgh 15222
(412) 355-5248
    469-1567

Rhode Island

600 Mt. Pleasant Avenue
Gerontology Center
Rhode Island College
Providence 02908
(401) 456-8276

Texas

Route 6
Box 760
Amarillo 79106
(806) 381-1010

11216 Dumbarton Drive
Dallas 75228
(214) 270-9604

6545 Fiesta Drive
El Paso 79912
(915) 581-4926

8101 Amelia
Apartment 304
Houston 77055
(713) 869-5546 (bus. hrs.)
465-9505 (other hrs.)

Virginia

VA Medical Center
Salem 24153
(703) 982-2463, ext. 2477

Comprehensive Mental
Health Service
Pembroke 3, Suite 109
Virginia Beach 23462
(804) 490-0583

P.O. Box 2715
West Springfield 22152
(703) 273-5453 (Dingle)
569-3367 (Janson)

Wisconsin

1306 Windsor Drive
Waukesha 53186
(414) 547-6406

The Hypertensive's Guide for a Balanced Diet

Sodium Potassium Calories*

BREADS, ROLLS, ETC.	Amount	Mg Sodium	Mg Potassium	Calories
White	1 slice	142	29	76
Rye	1 slice	139	36	61
Whole wheat	1 slice	132	68	61
Biscuit	1 (2″ diameter)	185	18	104
Cornbread	2½″ square	263	61	178
Frankfurter roll	both halves	202	38	119
Hamburger roll	both halves	202	38	119
Pancake	1 (6″ diameter)	412	112	164
Waffle	1 (7″ diameter)	515	146	206
Graham crackers	2 (2½″ squares)	95	55	55
Brown rice	1 cup (cooked with salt)	550	137	232
White rice	1 cup (cooked with salt)	767	57	223
Bran flakes	1 cup	207	137	106
Corn flakes	1 cup	251	30	97
Oatmeal	1 cup (cooked)	523	146	132
Puffed rice	1 cup	148	33	140
Wheat flakes	1 cup	310	81	106
Flour, wheat	1 cup (all purpose)	130	0	499
Egg noodles	1 cup	3	70	200
Macaroni	1 cup	1	103	192
Spaghetti	1 cup	1	103	192

*Source: *Nutritive Value of American Foods in Common Units.* Agricultural Handbook No. 456. Agricultural Research Service, 1975.

FRUITS	Amount	Mg Sodium	Mg Potassium	Calories
Apple	1 (2½" diameter)	1	116	61
Apricots, fresh	3 medium	1	301	55
Apricots, dried	5 large halves	6	235	62
Banana	1 medium	1	440	101
Blackberries	1 cup	1	245	84
Cantaloupe	½ (5" diameter)	33	682	82
Cherries, sweet	10	1	129	47
Dates	10	1	518	219
Fig	1 large	1	126	52
Grapefruit	½ small	1	132	40
Grapes	1 cup	3	160	70
Honeydew	½ (6½" diameter)	90	1,881	247
Orange	1 medium	1	290	66
Peach	1 (2¾" diameter)	2	308	58
Pear	1 (2½" diameter)	3	213	100
Pineapple	1 cup	2	226	81
Plum	1 (1" diameter)	Trace	30	7
Prunes, dried	10 medium	5	448	164
Raisins	1 tablespoon	2	69	26
Raspberries, black	1 cup	1	267	98
Strawberries	1 cup	1	244	55
Tangerine	1 (2⅜" diameter)	2	108	39
Watermelon	1 cup	2	160	42

DAIRY PRODUCTS	Amount	Mg Sodium	Mg Potassium	Calories
American cheese	1 slice	322	23	105
Blue cheese dressing	1 tablespoon	164	6	76
Cheddar cheese	1 slice	147	17	84
Cottage cheese, low-fat	1 cup	580	144	172
Cream cheese	1 cup	580	172	868
Parmesan cheese	1 oz	208	42	111
Swiss cheese	1 oz	201	29	105
Butter (salted)	1 stick	1,119	26	812
Butter (unsalted)	1 stick	<1	<1	812
Buttermilk	1 cup	319	343	88
Skim milk	1 cup	127	355	88
Whole milk	1 cup	122	351	159
Evaporated milk	1 cup	297	764	345

DAIRY PRODUCTS	Amount	Mg Sodium	Mg Potassium	Calories
Heavy cream	1 tablespoon	5	13	53
Ice cream (no salt)	1 cup	84	241	257
Hot chocolate	1 cup	120	370	238
Hot cocoa	1 cup	128	363	243
Egg yolk	1 medium	8	15	52
Egg white	1 medium	42	40	15
Egg, fried	1 medium	135	56	86
Egg, boiled	1 medium	54	57	72
Egg, scrambled	1 medium	144	82	97
Yogurt, plain	1 cup	115	323	152

MEAT AND POULTRY	Amount	Mg Sodium	Mg Potassium	Calories
BEEF				
Corned beef hash	1 cup, canned	1,188	440	398
Frankfurter	1 medium	627	125	176
Heart	1 oz	29	65	53
Hamburger	2.9 oz, lean	49	221	235
Kidney	1 cup	354	454	353
Liver, beef	3 oz	156	323	195
Rib roast	10 ¾ oz	149	680	1,342
Flank steak	3 oz	45	207	167
Porterhouse steak	10.6 oz	145	664	1,400
Sirloin steak	10.9 oz	173	793	1,192
T-Bone steak	10.4 oz	141	644	1,395
LAMB				
Chop	1 medium	51	234	341
Roast	3 oz	60	273	158
PORK				
Bacon	1 slice	123	29	72
Chops, shoulder cut	3 oz	47	214	300
Ham, baked	3 oz	770	241	159
Roast	3 oz	698	218	281
Spareribs	6.3 oz	65	299	792
VEAL				
Cutlets	3 oz	56	258	184
Calves' liver	3 oz	100	385	222
Loin cut	9.5 oz	174	795	629
Roast	3 oz	57	259	229
Sweetbreads	3 oz	†	†	143

CHICKEN	Amount	Mg Sodium	Mg Potassium	Calories
A La King	1 cup	760	404	468
Broiled	7.1 oz	133	551	273
Liver, chopped	1 cup	85	211	231
Light meat	1 piece, 2½″ × 1⅛″ × ¼″	16	103	42
Dark meat	1 piece, 1⅞″ × 1″ × ¼″	9	32	18
TURKEY				
White meat	2 pieces 4″ × 2″ × ¼″	70	349	150
Dark meat	2 pieces 2½″ × 1⅝″ × ½″	42	169	87

†Adequate data not available.

FRESH VEGETABLES	Amount	Mg Sodium	Mg Potassium	Calories
Asparagus	1 cup	3	375	35
Beans, lima	1 cup	3	1,008	191
Beets	1 cup	81	452	58
Broccoli	1 lb	68	1,733	145
Carrot	1 medium	34	246	30
Celery	1 stalk	50	136	7
Corn, sweet	1 ear (no butter or salt)	Trace	151	70
Cucumber	1 large, 8¼″ long	18	481	45
Eggplant	1 cup, cooked	2	300	38
Lettuce, iceberg	1 head (6″ diameter)	48	943	70
Onion	1 cup, chopped	17	267	65
Peas	1 cup	3	458	122
Potato, baked	1 medium	6	782	145
Potato, boiled	1 medium	4	556	104
Radishes	10 large	15	261	14
Spinach	1 cup	39	259	14
Sweet potato	1 medium, boiled	15	367	172
Tomato	1 medium	4	300	27
Watercress	1 cup	18	99	7

FRESH FISH AND SEAFOOD	Amount	Mg Sodium	Mg Potassium	Calories
Bass, striped	3 oz	†	†	168
Clams, cherrystone	4 clams	144	218	56
Cod	3 oz	93	345	144
Crab	1 cup	†	†	144
Flounder	3 oz	201	498	171
Haddock	3 oz	150	297	141
Halibut	3 oz	114	447	144
Lobster	1 cup	305	261	138
Mackerel	3 oz	†	†	201
Oysters	3 small	21	34	19
Salmon	3 oz	99	378	156
Shrimp	3 oz	159	195	192

†Adequate data not available.

CANNED VEGETABLES	Amount	Mg Sodium	Mg Potassium	Calories
Asparagus	14½ oz can	970	682	74
Beans, green	8 oz can	536	216	41
Beans, lima	8½ oz can	1,070	1,007	322
Beets	8 oz can	535	379	77
Carrots	8 oz can	535	272	64
Corn, creamed	8¾ oz can	585	241	203
Peas	8½ oz can	569	231	159
Spinach	7¾ oz can	519	550	42
Tomatoes	16 oz can	590	984	95

SWEETS	Amount	Mg Sodium	Mg Potassium	Calories
Angel food cake	¹⁄₁₂ cake	170	53	161
Brownie	1¾" × 1¾" × ⅛"	50	38	97
Chocolate, bittersweet	1 oz	1	174	135
Chocolate cupcake	1 (2½" diameter)	74	35	92
Chocolate chip cookies	10 (2¼" diameter)	421	141	495
Chocolate syrup	1 oz	20	106	92
Gelatin, sweet	3 oz	270	†	315
Honey	1 tablespoon	1	11	64
Jelly	1 tablespoon	3	14	49
Sherbet, orange	1 cup	19	42	259
Sponge cake	¹⁄₁₂ cake	110	57	196
Sugar, brown	1 cup	44	499	541
Sugar, granulated	1 cup	2	6	770
Sugar, powdered	1 cup	1	4	462

†Adequate data not available

BEVERAGES	Amount	Mg Sodium	Mg Potassium	Calories
Coffee, instant	1 teaspoon	1	29	1
Coffee, regular	1 cup	2	65	2
Beer	8 oz	17	60	101
Gin, rye, rum,	1 oz 80 proof	Trace	1	65
scotch, vodka	1 oz 86 proof	Trace	1	70
	1 oz 90 proof	Trace	1	74
	1 oz 94 proof	Trace	1	77
	1 oz 100 proof	Trace	1	83
Sherry	2 oz	2	44	81

FRUIT JUICES (Canned or bottled)	Amount	Mg Sodium	Mg Potassium	Calories
Apple	1 cup	2	250	117
Apricot nectar	1 cup	Trace	379	143
Cranberry	1 cup	3	25	164
Grape	1 cup	5	293	167
Grapefruit (unsweetened)	1 cup	2	400	101
Lemon	1 tablespoon	Trace	43	7
Orange (fresh)	1 cup	2	496	112
Pineapple (unsweetened)	1 cup	3	373	138
Prune	1 cup	5	602	197
Tomato	1 cup	486	552	46

HERBS AND SPICES

The following herbs and spices contain minimal amounts of sodium.

Allspice	Cumin	Mace	Pepper, black, red, and
Anise seed	Curry	Marjoram	white
Basil	Fennel	Mint	Poultry seasoning
Bay leaf	Garlic bud	Mushrooms, powdered	Rosemary
Caraway seed	Garlic chips	Mustard, dry	Saffron
Cardamom	Garlic powder	Nutmeg	Sage
Chives	Ginger	Onion, instant	Savory
Cinnamon	Horseradish	Orange peel	Sesame seeds
Cloves	Juniper	Oregano	Tarragon
Coriander	Lemon peel	Paprika	Thyme
			Turmeric

HIGH SODIUM FOODS

FLAVORS, BLENDS, AND SEASONINGS

Bouillon cubes
Candies
Catsup
Celery salt
Celery flakes
Chili sauce
French dressing
Garlic salt

Gelatin, flavored
Horseradish with salt
Mayonnaise
Meat extracts
Meat sauces
Meat tenderizers
Molasses
Mustard
Olives

Onion salt
Pickles
Pudding mixes
Relish
Rennet tablets
Salt
Salted nuts
Salt or sugar substitutes
Soy sauce
Worcestershire sauce

BEVERAGES

All canned soups
Cocoa instant mixes

Chocolate milk
Malted milk

Milk shakes
Salted buttermilk

MEATS

All canned meats, soups, and stews
Bacon
Bologna
Brains
Chipped beef
Corned beef

Frankfurters
Ham
Kidneys
Liverwurst
Pickled meat
Salami

Salted meat
Salt pork
Sausage
Smoked meat
Spiced meat

MISCELLANEOUS

All canned fish
All canned vegetables
All salted fish
All shellfish
All smoked fish

Anchovies
Caviar

Salted cheeses
Salted ice cream and sherbet
Salted butter
Salted buttermilk
Salted popcorn, potato chips, and pretzels

FOOD ADDITIVES HIGH IN SODIUM

Baking powder
Brine
Di-sodium phosphate

Monosodium glutamate
Sodium (Na)
Sodium alginate

Sodium bicarbonate
Sodium benzoate
Sodium chloride
(salt)

Sodium hydroxide
Sodium propionate
Sodium sulfite

LIQUID
MEASURES   WEIGHTS

LIQUID MEASURES		WEIGHTS	
3 teaspoons	= 1 tablespoon	1,000 mg	= 1 gram
16 tablespoons	= 1 cup	5 grams	= 1 teaspoon
2 cups	= 1 pint	15 grams	= 3 teaspoons or 1 tablespoon
2 pints	= 1 quart	30 grams	= 1 oz
4 quarts	= 1 gallon	240 grams	= 8 oz or 1 cup
		960 grams	= 1 quart or 2.2 lbs

NOTE:
Salt is approximately 40% sodium, 60% chloride. One level teaspoon of salt equals 1,965 mg of sodium.

All figures on this chart are approximate and may vary depending on brand name, manufacturer, food processor, or actual size of item.

This chart is provided as a service to the medical profession by Ayerst Laboratories.

Reprinted with permission from Ayerst Laboratories.

Index